D1616658

Praise for Anonymous Is a Woman

"Dr. Nina Ansary has written a powerful book on a critical subject. Gender discrimination continues to pose a challenge to women's equality and inclusion everywhere. The author makes a strong case for accelerated collective action by all of us to advance women's progress. This is an indispensable, brilliantly written call to action. Read the book and heed her call."

—*Melanne Verveer, Former US Ambassador for Global Women's Issues and Executive Director of the Georgetown Institute for Women, Peace and Security at Georgetown University*

"Inspiring and insightful: An expert journey and an elegant authoritative exploration of gender and society in this jewel of a book. Fifty shades of genius—exquisite portraits, splendid sketches and a gorgeous tribute to women long forgotten by history and an expert guide to help ensure it won't happen again."

—*Lyse Doucet, OBE award-winning journalist and BBC's Chief International Correspondent*

"*Anonymous Is a Woman* makes an essential contribution to illuminating the current social, economic, and political trends that are squashing the potential of at least 50 percent of the human population. This timely book highlights forgotten pioneering women in history and the repercussions of obstructing the full depth of human potential."

—*Scott Barry Kaufman, Author, Professor of Psychology, Barnard College, Columbia University*

"Dr. Nina Ansary has written a must-read book for everyone who wants to understand the roots and manifestations of systemic gender discrimination in everyday life. This insightful book makes the invisible visible, shedding light on how gender inequality permeates everyday life. Read this book—and learn from one of the best."

—*Michelle King, Director of Inclusion, Netflix*

"*Anonymous Is a Woman* is an eye-opening wake-up call and an essential reading that impacted my views of the world, as a man and a father, as much as *Half The Sky: Turning Oppression into Opportunity for Women Worldwide*. Any man who doubts the overwhelming benefits of diversity and gender equality in life, business, and politics needs to read this book. If Ansary's compellingly succinct and common-sense approach doesn't leave you banging your head against your desk about all the opportunities you're missing, you're simply beyond saving."

—*Gregory Hogben, author of* **My Daughter's Army,** *Advocate for Women's Rights and LGBT Equality*

"To ensure an equitable and thriving global future, Nina Ansary has written one of this new decade's most significant books that will inspire every culture to understand the power of historical gender bias, recognize, and even seek out their female innovators."

—*Claudia Chan, Founder of S.H.E. Summit & Author of* **This Is How We Rise**

"This beautifully written and elegantly illustrated book deserves wide readership. Dr. Nina Ansary has added to the historical record while striking an important blow on behalf of all humankind."

—*Jerrold D. Green, President and CEO, Pacific Council on International Policy*

"Full of fascinating stories and clearly a labour of love, an inspiring addition to the work of rediscovering the remarkable women of the past—would make the perfect present for any woman or girl finding her way into our shared history."

—*Rosalind Miles, Award winning Journalist, Critic, BBC Broadcaster, and Author of*
Who Cooked the Last Supper? The Women's History of the World

"*Anonymous Is a Woman* is a testament to the true resilience of women. Women whose voices were silenced by societal norms, whose achievements went unrecognized or were attributed to others, whose potential was squashed by systemic discrimination and bias. Dr. Ansary is changing history—and challenging today's world where women continue to be marginalized —through the impact of her work which powerfully screams the names and stories of those for too long ignored."

—*Kristy Wallace, CEO, Ellevate Network*

"In *Anonymous Is a Woman,* Dr. Nina Ansary analyzes the historic eclipsing of female achievement and explains why that period is coming to an end. She also reclaims the stories of fifty phenomenal trailblazers (many international women of color) adding shining new faces to our growing catalogue of women to be remembered and celebrated."

—*Julie Hébert, Peabody Award winning television writer, director, producer, and Founder of* **Look What She Did!**

"Nina Ansary's portraits of fifty "forgotten" female innovators bring them out of obscurity to underscore the costs of holding back half the Earth's population. Her impassioned appeal to accelerate the global movement for gender equality challenges each of us to spread the carpet of justice to unlock the potential of women everywhere."

—*Bill Clifford, President and CEO, World Affairs Councils of America*

"Too often in history, the voices of women have gone unheard. This lovely, important and much-needed compendium puts that right."

—*Dr. Peter Frankopan, Professor of Global History at Oxford University*
and Director of the Oxford Centre for Byzantine Research

Anonymous Is a Woman

Also by Nina Ansary

Jewels of Allah: The Untold Story of Women in Iran

Anonymous Is a Woman

A GLOBAL CHRONICLE OF GENDER INEQUALITY

Nina Ansary, PhD

Revela Press
Los Angeles, California

978-0-9864064-4-7 (hardcover)
978-0-9864064-5-4 (paperback)
978-0-9864064-3-0 (eBook)
Library of Congress Control Number: 2019918549

Publisher's Cataloging-In-Publication Data

Names: Ansary, Nina, author. | Dufkova, Petra, illustrator.

Title: Anonymous is a woman : a global chronicle of gender inequality / Nina Ansary ; [interior illustration artist: Petra Dufkova].

Description: Los Angeles, California : Revela Press, [2020] | Includes bibliographical references and index.

Identifiers: ISBN 9780986406447 (hardcover) | ISBN 9780986406454 (paperback) | ISBN 9780986406430 (ebook)

Subjects: LCSH: Sex discrimination against women--History. | Women--Social conditions--History. | Women--Biography. | Sex role--History. | Patriarchy--History. | Anonymous persons--History. | LCGFT: Biographies.

Classification: LCC HQ1237 .A57 2020 (print) | LCC HQ1237 (ebook) | DDC 305.42--dc23

To my father and my daughter—always in my heart.

One hundred percent of the proceeds from the sale of this book will be donated.

The primary recipients will be The Center for Human Rights in Iran, a New York-based 501(c)(3) registered nonprofit, nonpartisan organization dedicated to the protection and promotion of human rights in Iran, and The London School of Economics Centre for Women, Peace, and Security, an academic space for scholars, practitioners, activists, policymakers, and students to develop strategies that promote justice, human rights, and participation of women in conflict-affected situations around the world.

66

. . . the struggle we engage in
on behalf of all humanity
is fundamental to life itself.

— *Nina Ansary*

The sketches of the fifty forgotten innovators profiled in this book are artist renderings.

In several cases, no known images or artifacts of their likeness exist. In cases where they do exist, images often reflected cultural, social, and historical restrictions as to appearance, dress code, posture, and facial expression, as well as the social mores and historic perspective of the respective artists at the time of the rendering.

It is the author's intent that their accomplishments be accompanied by portraits that capture the spirit, courage, and true self of each woman.

Contents

Forgotten Innovators

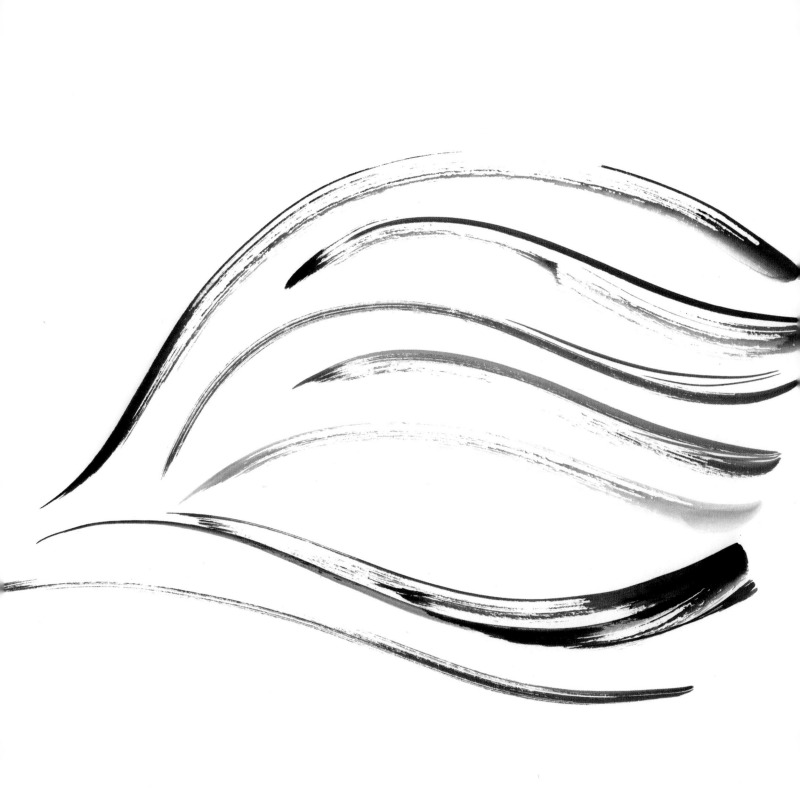

FEMALE ANONYMITY

In 1929, British novelist Virginia Woolf (1882–1941) ran her fingers along the spines of the books in her library wondering why no woman during Shakespeare's era had written "a word of that extraordinary literature, when every other man, it seemed, was capable of song or sonnet."[1] She concluded, "Indeed, I would venture to guess that Anon, who wrote so many poems without signing them was often a woman."[2]

Nearly a century after Woolf penned those incisive words—frequently modified as "For most of history, Anonymous was a woman"—the phenomenon of female anonymity persists, as women worldwide continue to be restricted by society's formal and unspoken barriers.

Throughout history women have had to contend with overwhelming obstacles preventing them from realizing their full potential. Although there has been incremental progress and advancement, women still have a long road to travel before they are equally represented within the global community.

Why have women been consistently denied opportunities that are automatically given to men? And why does Virginia Woolf's statement still echo in the twenty-first century?

As a woman born in pre-revolutionary Iran during a relatively progressive period, I witnessed my homeland radically shift with the Islamic Revolution (1979–) and with it the lives of its women, whose burgeoning freedoms were extinguished in the immediate aftermath by the plethora of gender-discriminatory decrees embedded in policy and law.

My first book, *Jewels of Allah: The Untold Story of Women in Iran* (2015), based on my doctoral thesis for Columbia University (2013), shattered the stereotypical assumptions about the often misunderstood story of women in Iran. Highlighting many courageous female leaders and advocates throughout Iran's history, the book illuminated the unanticipated factors contributing to the development of a women's rights movement in post-revolutionary Iran.[3]

Anonymous Is a Woman: A Global Chronicle of Gender Inequality expands the lens beyond my birth country of Iran and takes readers on a 4,000-year historic journey to expose the roots and manifestations of institutionalized gender discrimination and the myriad ways it permeates nearly every aspect of modern life.

The primary focus of the book is to challenge discriminatory policies, laws, and ingrained stereotypical assumptions that create barriers for women and girls to succeed at a level commensurate with their aptitude and skills. This includes the failure to acknowledge and give proper recognition to notable women for their significant contributions throughout history.

Part One (Shakespeare's Sister: Are We Anonymous?) explores Virginia Woolf's contention through the fervent calls for women's rights—from Western countries to the Middle East, the Far East, Africa, to South America. Voices that contest traditional patriarchal ideology, challenge and argue against a worldview that consigns women to an inferior status—a global resistance demanding change, expanded opportunities, and equality for women.

Part Two (Women by the Numbers) examines the state of the current gender gap and global statistics that underscore the repercussions of gender inequality and discriminatory practices for the global community at large.

Part Three (Yinyang and the Economics of Gender Balance) advances an unconventional argument for equality and inclusivity combining economic and philosophical analyses that reveal the benefits of gender balance.

Part Four (Forgotten Innovators) dismantles centuries of historical bias to reveal a formidable array of women who achieved distinction despite a tradition of oppression. The biographical profiles of fifty extraordinary, yet forgotten innovators refute gender-based assumptions which continue to limit opportunities for women and girls in the twenty-first century. To varying degrees, despite their significant contributions, individuals profiled have not received the accolades and the breadth of recognition bestowed on their male counterparts.

Distinguished by their innovative spirit and creative brilliance, all of these women were born before 1900—from 2300 BCE to 1892—when opportunities were even more limited for women than they are today. They represent a mere fraction of those deserving acclaim in every sector of achievement yet have been relegated to the back pages of history.

The motivation and inspiration for writing *Anonymous Is a Woman* stems from my unwavering commitment to women's rights and gender equality, as well as my work both as a Visiting Fellow at the London School of Economics Centre for Women, Peace and Security, and as a UN Women Global Champion for Innovation.

The academic and advocacy journey leading into this project culminated in research exploring centuries of gender inequality, including the present imbalance whereby women are underrepresented and undervalued in practically every sector. The global community faces interconnected challenges, and the advancement of women's social, economic, and political rights is of critical importance.

A crucial ingredient to providing support and raising awareness of the ongoing gender apartheid in countries like Iran requires building bridges with the international community, as the multitude of issues related to women in conflict cannot be divorced from wider gender discrimination around the world. The opportunity to collaborate in a manner that not only values global partnerships, but also provides substantive influence and expertise to accelerate gender equality and women's rights, is of vital importance. In this respect, I am immensely grateful to be part of two extraordinary communities whose respective platforms resonate and align with my overall objective.[4,5]

Building a sustainable and lasting infrastructure enabling women's equal participation and contribution entails not only bringing about changes in policy and law, but also challenging antiquated myths and pervasive gender inequalities. *Anonymous Is a Woman* engages in that challenge by combining traditional and contemporary theoretical frameworks—a paradigm disclosing how systemic discrimination and bias obstructs human potential.

According to Dr. Bettany Hughes: "Women have always been 50% of the population, but only occupy around 0.5% of recorded history. . . These are brilliantly feisty women that should be household names but just aren't."[6] And in her 1981 foreword to Virginia Woolf's essay *A Room of One's Own*, American author Mary Gordon (1949–) writes, "the challenge Woolf gives to women writers is to capture these [women's] lives in all their variety: 'All these infinitely obscure lives to be recorded.'"[7]

In capturing the "obscure lives" of these accomplished, yet forgotten female innovators, my hope is that this book inspires women and girls to move beyond gender-based barriers and assumptions by not viewing obstacles as roadblocks, but as challenges that can be overcome. If this book contributes, even in a small way, to creating a more equitable path for future generations, including my own daughter, then it will have succeeded.

ONE

Shakespeare's Sister

ARE WE ANONYMOUS?

In *A Room of One's Own* published in 1929,[1] Virginia Woolf considers why there was no female Shakespeare and why the shelves in her library that ought to house the titles of plays by Shakespearean-era women are completely empty. With wit and historical perspective, she speculates that a sixteenth-century woman, even one born into a privileged family, would have had to contend with overwhelming barriers in order to freely practice the art and craft of writing, much less get her book published or have her play performed:

> *Let me imagine ... what would have happened had Shakespeare had a wonderfully gifted sister, called Judith, let us say ... She was as adventurous, as imaginative, as agog to see the world as he was. But she was not sent to school. She had no chance of learning grammar and logic, let alone of reading Horace and Virgil. She picked up a book now and then, one of her brother's perhaps, and read a few pages. But then her parents came in and told her to mend the stockings or mind the stew and not moon about with books and papers. They would have spoken sharply but kindly, for they were substantial people who knew the conditions of life for a woman.*
>
> *Before she was out of her teens, she was to be betrothed to the son of a neighbouring wool-stapler. She cried out that marriage was hateful to her, and for that she was severely beaten by her father. Then he ceased to scold her. He begged her instead not to hurt him, not to shame him in this matter of her marriage ... How could she disobey him? How could*

she break his heart? The force of her own gift alone drove her to it.

> *She ... let herself down by a rope one summer's night and took the road to London. She was not seventeen ... She had the quickest fancy, a gift like her brother's, for the tune of words. Like him, she had a taste for the theatre. She stood at the stage door; she wanted to act, she said. Men laughed in her face ... She could get no training in her craft. Could she even seek her dinner in a tavern or roam the streets at midnight? Yet her genius was for fiction and lusted to feed abundantly upon the lives of men and women and the study of their ways.*

> *[Judith] killed herself one winter's night and lies buried at some crossroads.*

> *That, more or less is how the story would run, I think, if a woman in Shakespeare's day had had Shakespeare's genius.*

After imagining this darkly realistic scenario, Woolf goes on to assert that [in Shakespeare's day]:

> *Genius of a sort must have existed among women ...*
> *But certainly it never got itself on to paper.*[2]

Or did it? Perhaps there were those female writers who somehow managed to overcome societal impediments and to successfully engage in their creative work. But rather than suffer the condemnation, disregard, or ridicule of attaching their names to their work, they became **anonymous**. Again, Virginia Woolf speculates:

> *Indeed, I would venture to guess that Anon, who wrote so many poems without signing them, was often a woman ... And undoubtedly, I thought, looking at the shelf where there are no plays by women, her work would have gone unsigned.*[3]

It is an unfortunate reality that throughout much of our history women writers have felt compelled to hide their female identity in order to publish and/or gain acceptance of their work. It may surprise some readers to learn that a number of highly regarded literary works of the last several centuries were either "unsigned" or unacknowledged as written by a woman.

For instance, during her lifetime, English novelist Jane Austen's (1775–1817) books were all published anonymously. The byline of her first published novel, *Sense and Sensibility* (published in 1811), read simply "By a Lady." Her next published novel, *Pride and Prejudice* (published in 1813), read "By the Author of *Sense and Sensibility*." While she identified herself as female, perhaps one reason she preferred to be anonymous was to preserve her modesty and protect her reputation, a priority in nineteenth-century English society.[4]

More recently, female authors have taken on male or gender-ambiguous pseudonyms in order to assure that their work would be regarded more seriously or to avoid the assumption that their books were "for women readers only." Such prominent examples include:

- French author Amantine Lucile Aurore Dupin (1804–1876) (George Sand)
- English author Emily Brontë (1818–1848) (Ellis Bell)
- English author Charlotte Brontë (1816–1855) (Currer Bell)
- English author Anne Brontë (1820–1849) (Acton Bell)

- English author Mary Ann Evans (1819–1880) (George Eliot)
- American author Louisa May Alcott (1832–1888) (A. M. Barnard, prior to the publication of *Little Women* in 1868)
- American author Nelle Harper Lee (1926–2016) (Harper Lee)
- Canadian author Lucy Maud Montgomery (1874–1942) (L. M. Montgomery, author of *Anne of Green Gables*, published in 1908)
- Danish author Karen Blixen (1885–1962) (Isak Dinesen, author of *Out of Africa*, published in 1937)
- English author Joanne Rowling (1965–) (J. K. Rowling[5])
- American author Nora Roberts (1950–) (J. D. Robb)
- American author Amy M. Homes (1961–) (A. M. Homes)

It is an interesting phenomenon that Woolf's actual quote is very often misquoted as: "For most of history, Anonymous was a woman." Why is the quote so often altered and yet repeatedly referenced in numerous contexts? (Including its appearance on consumer items from coffee mugs and water bottles to bracelets, T-shirts, tote bags, pillows, and bath mats!) I believe the revised quote reveals that women continue to relate to its essential truth—women are too often unacknowledged and unknown.

Why do such discrepancies persist in the twenty-first century? Why have women been consistently denied opportunities that are freely and automatically given to men? And why has the historical record failed to adequately recognize notable women?

According to French writer Simone de Beauvoir (1908–1986):

> *This world has always belonged to males, and none of the reasons given for this have ever seemed sufficient.*[6]

RESISTING MISOGYNY

Despite de Beauvoir's pronouncement that women have always lived in a man's world, there have been progressive thinkers throughout history who have contested traditional patriarchal ideology. While in the minority, these outspoken individuals have challenged and argued against a worldview that consigns women to an inferior status.

Italian-French writer Christine de Pizan (1364–ca. 1430), author of *The Book of the City of Ladies* (published in 1405) and *Epistle to the God of Love* (published in 1399), was one of the first women to denounce misogyny and write about the relationship of the sexes. In *The Book of the City of Ladies*, de Pizan envisions a city populated by intelligent, courageous women from the past who embody admirable traits that boldly contradict negative female stereotypes. Among the numerous often-quoted passages:

> *Therefore, it is not all men, especially not the most intelligent, who agree with the view that it is a bad idea to educate women. However, it's true that those who are not very clever come out with this opinion because they don't want women to know more than they do.*[7]

Several centuries after de Pizan, the writings of Mexican poet and scholar Sor Juana Inés de la Cruz (1651–1695) "celebrated woman as the seat of reason and knowledge rather than passion."[8] Having joined a convent in order to have "the freedom to study, write, and conduct scientific experiments—pursuits that women were not allowed to engage in at the time,"[9] de la Cruz wrote thousands of poems, including one of her most celebrated, entitled "Hombres Necios" ("Foolish Men"). The poem "highlights the double standard that women lived with in New Spain" and is "a scathing criticism of Spanish colonial patriarchy."[10]

> *You foolish men, who accuse*
>
> *Women without good reason,*
>
> *You are the cause of what you blame,*
>
> *Yours the guilt you deny.*[11]

Also challenging the conventional mindset that denigrated the intelligence and status of women was French philosopher François Poullain de la Barre (1647–1723) who employed Cartesian principles in his *Three Cartesian Feminist Treatises*, originally published separately in the 1670s. He used these principles to demonstrate "by rational deduction that the supposedly 'self-evident' inequality of the sexes was nothing more than unfounded prejudice."[12] In one of the three treatises, *On the Equality of the Two Sexes*, Poullain de la Barre states:

> *We have to recognize that those who drew up the laws, being men, favored their own sex, as women might well have done if they had been in the same position; and since, from the very beginning of societies, laws were made as they are now with respect to women,*

the lawmakers, who had their own biases, attributed to nature a distinction that derives mainly from custom.[13]

In *A Vindication of the Rights of Woman* published in 1792, British novelist Mary Wollstonecraft (1759–1797) called for a revolution committed to educating and respecting women as the equally intelligent half of the human race. Wollstonecraft discloses the manner in which "religion," and "the language of men," have devalued women and deprived them of their "natural prerogatives" in life.[14] She makes the compelling argument that "the nature of reason must be the same in all, if it be an emanation of divinity":

> *Reason is, consequently, the simple power of improvement; or more properly speaking, of discerning truth. Each individual is in this respect a world in itself. More or less may be conspicuous in one being than another, but the nature of reason must be the same in all, if it be an emanation of divinity, the tie that connects the creature with the Creator; for can that soul be stamped with the heavenly image that is not perfected by the exercise of its own reason? . . . This understanding, strictly speaking, has been denied to woman; and instinct, sublimated into wit and cunning, for the purposes of life, has been substituted in its stead.*[15]

In nineteenth-century Europe and the United States, which were traditional patriarchal societies, a movement advocating the advancement of women was under way. The first women's right's convention in the United States, known as the Seneca Falls Convention, took place in New York State in 1848. American suffragist

Elizabeth Cady Stanton (1851–1902) took the stage to address the necessity "for women's wrongs to be laid out before the public." She believed that:

A woman herself must do this work, for woman alone can understand the height, the depth, the length and the breadth of her own degradation.[16]

At the core of Stanton's address was a declaration that women have the right "to be free as a man is free":

But we are assembled to protest against a form of government existing without the consent of the governed—to declare our right to be free as man is free, to be represented in the government which we are taxed to support, to have such disgraceful laws as give man the power to chastise and imprison his wife, to take the wages which she earns, the property which she inherits, and, in case of separation, the children of her love; laws which make her the mere dependent on his bounty. It is to protest against such unjust laws as these that we are assembled today, and to have them, if possible, forever erased from our statute books, deeming them a shame and a disgrace to a Christian republic in the nineteenth century. We have met to uplift woman's fallen divinity upon an even pedestal with man's. And, strange as it may seem to many, we now demand our right to vote according to the declaration of the government under which we live.[17]

In her book *The Woman's Bible* (published in two parts in 1895 and 1898), Stanton and twenty-six other women boldly challenged the Judeo-Christian tradition by concluding that "the Bible in its teachings degrades women from Genesis to Revelation."[18]

There was, however, a chasm between Stanton's movement advocating equality for women and that of African American suffragists. While mainstream accounts of the early women's suffrage movement tend to ignore this rift, increasingly historians are focusing on it, including Lori Ginzberg, professor of history and women's studies at Penn State University and author of *Elizabeth Cady Stanton: An American Life* (published in 2010):

In the post-Civil War period, when there was a battle among abolitionists—of which Stanton counted herself —between having a 15th Amendment that gave black men the vote or holding out for a suffrage amendment that granted the vote to all adult Americans, Stanton and her friend Susan B. Anthony stood on what they claimed was the highest moral ground by demanding universal human rights for all and — historians have argued about this ever since.

[Stanton] didn't just stand on the moral high ground. She also descended to some rather ugly racist rhetoric along the lines of, 'We educated, virtuous white women are more worthy of the vote.'[19]

While it is important to rightfully acknowledge feminist trailblazers like Stanton, it is equally important to acknowledge the unfavorable facts as they relate to the exclusion of women of color in nineteenth- and twentieth-century women's movements. For example, in 1913, organizers of a parade in Washington D.C., sponsored by the National American Woman Suffrage Association, demanded that Black participants march in an all-Black assembly at the back of the parade.[20] African American feminist, journalist, anti-lynching advocate, and abolitionist Ida B. Wells (1862–1931) refused, stating:

Either I go with you or not at all. I am not taking this stand because I personally wish for recognition. I am doing it for the future benefit of my whole race.[21]

Initially, Wells left the parade, suggesting that she was obeying the organizers' request. But she soon returned, marching with her Illinois delegation with the support of her white co-suffragists Belle Squires and Virginia Brooks. This event, and specifically Wells' actions, was met with significant newspaper coverage that illuminated the harsh reality for African American involvement in politics.[22]

Despite clashes between African American and white suffragists, in the aftermath of Elizabeth Stanton's declarations, major figures established a number of initiatives to eradicate patriarchal norms, attacking the institutions that reduced women to a life of confinement and obedience.

Among them was American feminist Charlotte Perkins Gilman (1860–1935), an author whose works include her short story "The Yellow Wallpaper" (1892) about a depressed woman under the control of her husband, and the novel *Herland* (1915), a response to the male-centered ideology of divine scriptures. Gilman declared that there is "no female mind, as the brain is not an organ of sex."[23] She advanced the notion that:

A normal feminine influence in recasting religious assumptions will do more than any other thing to improve the world.[24]

A core issue in the quest to achieve gender equality is the challenge of freeing oneself from the domestic shackles that prevent women from working and achieving fulfillment outside the home. Although poor and working-class women don't always have the choice *not* to work outside the domestic sphere, it is still the case that throughout history women have had to deal with their fathers' and husbands' ingrained notions of female inferiority, which result in household confinement.

In her emotionally charged speech "Professions for Women," delivered to the Women's Service League in 1931, Virginia Woolf mocks a narrative poem by British poet Coventry Patmore (1823–1896)[25] entitled "The Angel in the House." Patmore's description of his proper Victorian wife reveals her to be, above all, pure, in addition to passive, submissive, pious, charming, and graceful, among other qualities. Satirical in tone, Woolf's clever parody ridicules the image of Patmore's "angel" by professing the need to "kill" this selfless, obedient, devoted creature, whose sole purpose is to accommodate the needs of her husband and children. Woolf conveys that the metaphorical annihilation of this submissive being is essential if women are to reveal their true selves and develop minds of their own. She asserts that if she is to engage in a profession, in her case as a writer, she will need to "kill the angel" in the house:

I should need to do battle with a certain phantom. And the phantom was a woman, and when I came to know her better, I called her after the heroine of a famous poem, The Angel in the House. . . . It was she who bothered me and wasted my time and so tormented me. . . . I will describe her as shortly as I can. She was intensely sympathetic. She was immensely charming. She was utterly unselfish. If there was chicken, she took the leg, if there was a draught she sat in it——in short, she was so constituted that she never had a mind or a wish of her own, but preferred to sympathize always with the minds and wishes of others.[26]

For Woolf, the only way for women to gain their freedom was to destroy this "phantom" no matter how difficult the struggle. In an exhilarating finale, she describes the outcome:

I killed her . . . The Angel was dead—She died hard. Had I not killed her, she would have killed me![27]

In a forceful feminist tone, she calls on all women to summon the courage and strength to consciously release their minds as part of a continuous struggle to disentangle the imprisoned soul:

Those aims cannot be taken for granted; they must be perpetually questioned and examined. You have won a room of your own in the house hitherto exclusively owned by men. But this freedom is only the beginning. The room is your own but it is still bare. It has to be furnished; it has to be decorated; it has to be shared.[28]

Female advocates in the twentieth-century women's movement continued to echo the theme of killing/relinquishing the traditional female roles promulgated by patriarchal values in order to achieve personal fulfillment and gender equality. One of the most notable writers who illuminated this theme was American Betty Friedan (1921–2006), author of the bestselling *The Feminine Mystique*, published in 1963. She skillfully articulated "The problem that has no name"—the dissatisfaction of white, middle-class housewives who felt stultified by the post-World War II fiction that women ought to be utterly fulfilled in their appropriately "feminine" role as wife, mother, and household maven:

Just what was this problem that has no name? What were the words women used when they tried to express it? Sometimes a woman would say, "I feel empty somehow . . . incomplete." Or she would say, "I feel as if I don't exist."

We can no longer ignore that voice within women that says: "I want something more than my husband and my children and my home."[29]

According to historian Lindsay Blake Churchill, "feminists of color, including bell hooks, found Friedan's manifesto both racist and classist, not at all applicable to African Americans and other working-class women who joined the labor force from necessity."[30] Nonetheless, *The Feminine Mystique* awakened many middle-class women to their heretofore unspoken need to seek fulfillment beyond the role of homemaker.

GLOBAL RESISTANCE

The fervent call for women's rights arose not only in Western countries. From the Middle East to the Far East, Africa to South America, voices demanding change, expanded opportunities, and equality for women refused to be silenced.

Qurrat al-'Ayn, known as Tahirah (c.1817–1852), considered the first suffrage martyr in Iran, was a Persian theologian and spiritual advocate of women's emancipation.[31] She was a follower of Sayyid 'Ali Muhammad of Shiraz who claimed to be the Messiah, or Bab, and wanted a break from established Sharia or Islamic law. Tahirah gave lectures espousing her views, which were widely attended by both women and men, but which also drew the attention of critics. At a gathering in 1848 in support of a new Babi religion that supported the equality of women, Tahirah appeared without a veil, shocking many attendees. It was not long afterward that the government crushed the Babi movement and executed the Bab. Tahirah was placed under house arrest and put to death in 1852.[32]

Revered by members of the Baha'i faith, the religion that succeeded the Babi movement after her death, Tahirah is remembered as an important spiritual figure, a martyr for the Babi cause and for women's emancipation. In her poem translated as "The Morn of Guidance," Tahirah expresses her disdain for religious hypocrisy, superstition, and "false commands"—and proclaims her reverence for "the carpet of justice" and "the seeds of friendship and unity":

> **The Morn of Guidance** (Translated by Susan
> Stiles Maneck and Farzad Nakhai)
> Truly the morn of Guidance commands the breeze
>   to begin
> All the world has been illuminated; every horizon;
>   every people,
> No more sits the Shaykh in the seat of hypocrisy
> No more becomes the mosque a shop dispensing
>   holiness
> The tie of the turban will be cut at its source
> No Shaykh will remain, neither glitter nor secrecy
> The world will be free from superstition and vain
>   imaginings
> The people free from deception and temptation
> Tyranny is destined for the arm of justice

> Ignorance will be defeated by perception
> The carpet of justice will be outspread to everywhere
> And the seeds of friendship and unity will be spread
>   throughout
> The false commands eradicated from the earth
> The principle of opposition changed to that of
>   unity.[33]

Articulating grievances similar to those expressed in *The Feminine Mystique* in 1963, Indian feminist and essayist, Tarabai Shinde (ca. 1850–1910) published an essay in 1882 contesting "the patriarchal foundations of social customs that confined women to prescribed roles of wife and mother and made great demands on them to live up to models of *pativrata* (ideal womanhood)."[34] Addressing the male establishment on behalf of women in nineteenth-century India, Shinde's outrage was profound, as evidenced in this excerpt from her essay:

> You label women with all sorts of insulting names, calling them utterly feeble, stupid, bold, thoughtless— you beat out the sound of their names in shame. You shut them up endlessly in the prison of the home, while you go about building up your own importance.... Starting from your childhood you collect all rights in your own hands and womankind you just push in a dark corner far from the real world ... dominated as if she was a female slave.[35]

Another important women's advocate in the late nineteenth century was Japanese feminist Kishida Toshiko (1863–1901).[36] Toshiko spoke out against the inequality of Japanese women, and in her celebrated 1883 speech "Daughters in Boxes," she referred to her contention that Japanese daughters were unjustly locked into the commonly referred to "boxes" that were symbolic of particular requirements they were obligated to fulfill. The first box required that daughters were not to leave their rooms and that they were not to have access to anything that belonged to the outside world. The second box referred to a daughter's obligation to obey her parents without complaint. And the third box required that daughters be taught ancient knowledge, of which Kishida strongly approved due to her conviction that authentic education always serves to empower women. But her unique contribution to this conceptual value system was the belief that a girl's freedom should be the crucial element in the "box" that defines her life, meaning that her envisioned "box" would have no walls and would be completely open for her to explore the world:

> The expression "daughters in boxes" is a popular one, heard with frequency in the regions of Kyoto and Osaka. It is the daughters of middle-class families and above who are often referred to as such.
>
> A box without walls is one that allows its occupants to tread wherever their feet might lead and stretch their arms as wide as they wish. Some may object and say: is your box not one that encourages dissipation and willfulness? No, it is not so at all. My box without walls is made of heaven and earth—its lid I would fashion out of the transparent blue of the sky and at its bottom would be the fathomless depths of the earth upon which we stand.[37]

A number of significant women's rights leaders in Africa have also spoken out and instigated change, including Nigerian activist, anti-colonialist, and political leader Funmilayo Ransome-Kuti (1900–1978), who vigorously promoted the cause of Nigerian women's right to vote. She also headed the successful campaign to abolish separate tax rates for women and founded the Federation of Nigerian Women Societies. Her argument for women's equality and the right to vote was founded in large part on economic justice. In advocating for women who were being taxed unfairly, she spoke out with an impassioned sense of righteousness:

> Inasmuch as Egba women pay taxes, we too desire to have a voice in the spending of the taxes.[38]

Feminist ideas and movements were also taking root in South America, often advocating for poor and working-class women. With the initial publication in 1873 of her groundbreaking journal O Sexo Feminino (The Female Sex), Brazilian educator Francisca Diniz (dates of birth and death unknown) introduced an inspiring new voice that resonated profoundly. In this excerpt from 1890, Diniz elucidates the empowering potential of education for women, at a time when "even the few Brazilian women who were literate had no access to higher education."[39]

> Women's emancipation through education is the bright torch which can dispel the darkness and bring us to the august temple of science and to a proper life in a civilized society.[40]

She goes on to give an impassioned rationale for women's political representation and the right to vote:

> By right we should not be denied expression in Parliament. We should not continue to be mutilated in our moral and mental personality. The right to vote is an attribute of humanity because it stems from the power of speech. Women are human beings, too.[41]

THE FREE AND THE UNFREE

One of the most revolutionary treatises advocating for women's freedom and equality is Simone de Beauvoir's *The Second Sex*, published in 1949. A leading existential intellectual, de Beauvoir made a significant contribution to feminist rhetoric by philosophically challenging women's assigned role as "the second sex":

> *The situation of woman is that she—a free and autonomous being like all human creatures—nevertheless discovers and chooses herself in a world where men compel her to assume status of the Other.*[42]
>
> *History has shown that men have always held all the concrete powers; from patriarchy's earliest times they have deemed it useful to keep woman in a state of dependence; their codes were set up against her; she was thus concretely established as the Other.*[43]

The author's repeated use of the word "Other" has an almost subliminal effect, conveying the message that, in relegating "woman" to the position of the "other," man has effectively designated himself as the "one." From this perspective he is free to profit from her existence in any way that is to his benefit. This gender-role construction explains the enduring legacy of a "master" and "slave" relationship—one in which a woman's "natural" place in life is specified and structured according to man's wishes:

> *This world has always belonged to men and still retains the form they have imprinted on it.*[44]

"One is not born, but rather becomes, woman,"[45] de Beauvoir's powerful statement, rejects the notion that women are biologically sanctioned to a "state of subjection" and to a life of servitude. In order to disengage from this destructive assignment, the author implores women to seek an intellectual awakening, to free themselves from patriarchal domination by destroying false social distinctions between the sexes.

The struggle for freedom to which de Beauvoir refers is not precisely the same as that which women of color must confront. While white women have to endure servitude of one sort, women of color have had to endure the added degradation of racism. The multiple burdens of racial and gender discrimination are referenced in African American poet and civil rights activist Audre Lorde's (1934–1992) keynote presentation in June 1981 at the National Women's Studies Association Conference in Storrs, Connecticut. She addressed the issue of white women's attitudes toward women of color and vice versa, the righteous anger felt by women of color and how that anger can be used for meaningful growth. She poignantly alludes to women's differences and similarities with a potent reference to "shackles ... different from my own":

> *My anger is a response to racist attitudes and to the actions and presumptions that arise out of those attitudes. If your dealings with other women reflect those attitudes, then my anger and your attendant fears are spotlights that can be used for growth in the same way I have used learning to express anger for my growth. But for corrective surgery, not guilt. Guilt and defensiveness are bricks in a wall against which we all flounder; they serve none of our futures.*
>
> *I am not free while any woman is unfree, even when her shackles are very different from my own. And I am not free as long as one person of Color remains chained. Nor is anyone of you.*[46]

Contributing to the conversation about African American women's unique sense of identity and challenges, Pulitzer Prize-winning author Alice Walker (1944–), in her book *In Search of Our Mother's Gardens: Womanist Prose* (1983), speaks of Phillis Wheatley, a slave in the 1700s who had a gift for poetry. Walker took what Virginia Woolf had written about in *A Room of One's Own* one step further in order to articulate that the burden of a white woman writer was, in fact, different from that of a black woman writer. She asserted that an enslaved woman writer, like poet Phillis Wheatley, not only did not have money or a room of her own but did not even own herself:

> Virginia Woolf, in her book, *A Room of One's Own*, wrote that in order for a woman to write fiction she must have two things, certainly: a room of her own (with key and lock) and enough money to support herself.
>
> What then are we to make of Phillis Wheatley, a slave, who owned not even herself? This sickly, frail, Black girl . . . had she been white, would have been easily considered the intellectual superior of all the women and most of the men in the society of her day.[47]
>
> . . .A woman who still struggled to sing the song that was your gift, although in a land of barbarians who praised you for your bewildered tongue. It is not so much what you sang, as that you kept alive, in so many of our ancestors, the notion of song.[49]

I am not free while any woman is unfree, even when her shackles are very different from my own.

—*Audre Lorde* [48]

When asked in a 2006 interview how she came up with the term "womanist," Walker had this to say:

> *Well, first of all it's feminist, but it's feminist from a culture of color. So there's no attempt to evade the name "feminism," which is honorable. It actually means womanism—I mean, it's French in its essence—la femme, so feminism would be womanism, actually. Womanism comes though from southern African American culture because when you did something really bold and outrageous and audacious as a little girl, our parents would say, "You're acting 'womanish.'" It wasn't like in white culture where that was weak—it was just the opposite. And so, womanism affirms that whole spectrum of being which includes being outrageous and angry and standing up for yourself, and speaking your word and all of that.[50]*

RESISTING TOGETHER

With its uncompromising commitment to egalitarianism, the global movement for women's equality is, by its nature, expansive, and we engage in the struggle on behalf of all women.

Our diversity is powerful, as it enables our movement to grow. And today especially we can feel that the momentum fueling our quest for women's rights is steadily building—across ethnic, ideological, and national boundaries.

I believe that our movement's ever-expanding scope and composition is its greatest strength. History has proven that social movements tend to achieve tangible results when they reach a critical mass—as those who are demanding action become an ever-widening group of like-minded people.

In 1930, Indian activist Mahatma Gandhi (1869–1948) set out with seventy-eight followers on a 241-mile march to the sea, protesting British rule in India. By the time he reached the coast three weeks later, tens of thousands had joined his procession. Among the marchers were Brahmans and "untouchables," Hindus and Muslims, Christians and Sikhs. In the fight against colonialism, all were welcomed.

Similarly, in 1955 in Alabama, American seamstress Rosa Parks (1913–2005) refused to give up her seat on the bus for a white man. Soon millions of Americans were staging sit-ins, boycotts, demonstrations, and freedom walks throughout the United States. The civil rights movement included whites as well as African Americans, women as well as men, old people as well as young.

On two different continents, under different sets of circumstances, each of these movements achieved the unthinkable. What began as a protest over salt led to independence in India. What began as a refusal to vacate a seat on the bus led to the end of legalized segregation in the United States.

History has proven that social movements tend to achieve tangible results when they reach a critical mass...

Social movements must build in size and scope over time, expanding their agendas as changing circumstances dictate. In the case of the women's movement, we are an increasing mass of people who believe that half of the Earth's population should, at long last, be on equal footing with the other half. An estimated five million people around the world joined forces in the 2017 Global Women's March. In the United States alone, more than 400 separate marches across the nation combined to create the largest single-day demonstration in American history. The March included women of virtually all ethnicities, classes, ages, political affiliations, and gender identifications. It also drew a sizeable group of men.

Why was the turnout so high? Why did the Global Women's March exceed even the wildest expectations? Because at its core, the struggle for women's rights is not just about women's rights—it's about human rights—the right for all people, regardless of gender, to achieve and contribute, to exercise free will, to feel safe, and to thrive.

History shows us that the most successful social movements are not only large but also unified. If the movement for women's equality is to continue to flourish, it must be a rising tide that lifts all ships. A river carries more force than a stream, and an ocean more than a river. An ocean of women from all corners of the globe, united in determination, can raise the tide for all.

TWO

Women by the Numbers

Nearly a century after Virginia Woolf decried the sexist barriers that "Shakespeare's sister" confronted in the sixteenth century and that her contemporaries faced in the early twentieth, women continue to come up against similar hurdles. Although there has been some progress, and in some cases cause to celebrate, women are still in the midst of an arduous journey toward full gender equality[1] throughout the world.

Yet, it would be remiss not to acknowledge the milestones women have achieved. In the United States, the number of women in Congress in 2019 was at an all-time high, with a record-breaking twenty-five women holding seats in the Senate and 102 serving in the House of Representatives, with four female nonvoting delegates representing American Samoa, Puerto Rico, the District of Columbia, and the Virgin Islands.[2] Out of those serving in both the Senate and House, forty-seven are women of color.[3]

In other parts of the world: Spain for the first time in its history has more women than men in its Prime Minister's cabinet. (Thirty years ago they had no female cabinet members.[4]) A week after Ethiopia's Prime Minister appointed women to half of the country's cabinet, its Parliament elected its first female president, another milestone in the journey toward gender parity.[5,6] Women in Saudi Arabia are finally legally allowed to drive. The courageous women of Iran continue to fight for gender equality, refusing to surrender to discriminatory practices and an inferior status embedded in policy and law.

In addition, eighteen years after the Taliban's overthrow in Afghanistan, the country's women initiated a remarkable conference: a delegation of more than 700 Afghani women from thirty-seven provinces met in Kabul on February 28, 2019. Refusing to remain silent, they demanded that the men negotiating with the Taliban not sacrifice women's hard-earned rights and freedom in the name of peace.[7]

Despite such strides, much work still needs to be done. Progress, as evidenced by the statistics, facts, and figures[8] that follow, has been incremental at best. Part Two examines the numbers that both underscore the challenges posed by gender gaps and provide optimistic indicators of positive change.

UNDERSTANDING THE GLOBAL GENDER GAP

Understanding the gender gap is key when discussing gender inequality and discrimination. The gender gap is the difference between women and men, particularly in relation to political, social, or economic opportunities.

Studied annually by the World Economic Forum, *The Global Gender Gap Report* includes statistics and country rankings to illustrate worldwide trends. The report explores four distinct criteria to evaluate a country's ranking and determine global change:

1. Economic participation and opportunity
2. Educational attainment
3. Health and survival
4. Political empowerment

Countries are ranked from zero (disparity) to one (full parity), resulting in a percentage score that indicates a country's success across the four evaluated criteria. The 2018 report asserts that although advances have been made globally "no country had achieved parity."[9]

The Global Gender Gap score, the average score of all assessed countries, stands at 68 percent of parity.[10] Only the ranking's top seven countries earned a score

At the G20 summit in Argentina in November 2018, there were fewer female heads of government than in any other previous meeting of the group.

above 80 percent. Iceland tops the list at 85 percent, followed by Norway, Sweden, Finland, Nicaragua, Rwanda, and New Zealand.[11] The United Kingdom ranks fifteenth, just above Canada.[12] With a score of 72 percent, the United States seems to be a global leader in closing the gender gap, but it trails behind in fifty-first place, below Mexico.[13] Even more alarming is how the US has fallen twenty-three places since 2015, when it ranked twenty-eighth.[14] The US isn't alone; out of the 144 countries covered in both the 2018 and 2017 reports, fifty-five countries have regressed, while eighty-nine have at least marginally closed their gender gap.[15]

The 2018 report also gives us insight into future change, estimating that, if current trends continue, it will take another 108 years to close the global gender gap.[16] The US is even further away from closing its gender gap, at 208 years.[17]

WOMEN IN POLITICS

The gender gap is the most difficult to close in the political field. As of 2018, less than a quarter of this gap has been closed; Iceland, while the category's leader, has closed only 33 percent of its political gap.[18] For comparison, the United States has closed just 13 percent of its political gap. The four worst-performing countries—Kuwait, Lebanon, Oman, and Yemen—have each closed less than 3 percent of their gaps.[19]

The political gender gap is most obvious when examining the women's presence (or lack thereof) in top political positions. Only seventeen countries have women as heads of state, while, on average, just 18 percent of ministers and 24 percent of parliamentarians globally are women.[20] While fifty-nine countries have had a female leader in the past century, the United States has yet to elect a female president or vice president.[21]

At the G20[22] summit in Argentina in November 2018, there were fewer female heads of government than in any other previous meeting of the group (which began holding leader summits in 2008). With only German Chancellor Angela Merkel, British Prime Minister Theresa May, and the International Monetary Fund's Chairman Christine Lagarde,[23] the meeting registered the lowest number of females participating since 2010.[24] When Merkel missed the event's group photo, the lack of participating women was especially evident, further underscoring the lower number of female leaders among the industrialized nations of the G20.

There has undoubtedly been progress in political representation. The 2018 elections in the United States saw a record number of women elected to Congress.[25] In Iran's 2016 parliamentary election, female candidates claimed seventeen seats, and though women comprised only 6 percent of the 290-member parliament, they outnumbered clerics for the first time since the 1979 Islamic Revolution.[26] At 61 percent, Rwanda's share of female parliamentarians is the highest in the world, and also boasts near-parity in ministerial positions.[27] These cases, among others, are optimistic in a field otherwise dominated by gender inequality. If nothing else, they set an important precedent, but remind us that there is plenty of progress to be done.

WOMEN IN THE WORKPLACE

The workplace has been a notorious battleground for gender equality. Equal pay, equal employment opportunities, and paid maternity leave are among the top issues faced by women in today's workforce. While significant strides have been made in the past century, there are many cases where equality is not legally ensured.[28] For example, two countries—Bahrain and Uzbekistan—made reforms negatively impacting gender equality. Bahrain legally designated the husband as having authority within a family, and having control over if and when his wife is permitted to leave the house or work.[29] Uzbekistan now has mandatory retirement ages that are unequal for men and women.[30]

A 2019 report published by the World Bank Group entitled *Women, Business and the Law* studied 187 economies to determine women's equality and opportunities in employment and entrepreneurship. The report determined that, on average, there is legal gender inequality in approximately one quarter of surveyed economies.[31] Women are on equal legal standing with men in just six countries (Belgium, Denmark, France, Latvia, Luxembourg, and Sweden).[32] Although this list is short, it represents a recent spike in gender reform, as a decade ago saw no countries with equal legal equality.[33] This increase in gender equality is due to recent legal milestones like, for example, France's introduction of a domestic violence law, criminal penalties for workplace sexual harassment, and paid parental leave.[34]

"Change is happening, but not fast enough," says World Bank Group Interim President Kristalina Georgieva, "and 2.7 billion women are still legally barred from having the same choice of jobs as men."[35] Georgieva also notes, "Around the world, women are given only [three-quarters] of the legal rights that men enjoy, constraining their ability to get jobs, start businesses, [and] make economic decisions that are best for them [and] their families."[36]

A longtime marker of workplace equality, equal pay statistics continue to highlight that women are paid significantly less than their male counterparts. In 2018, American women earned just 49 cents to the typical man's dollar, a statistic conspicuously lower than the 80 cents typically cited.[37] According to the Institute for Women's Policy Research, it will take until 2049 for women in the United States to reach pay parity.[38] For women of color, the rate of change is appallingly slower: Black and Hispanic women will have to wait until 2119 and 2224, respectively, for equal pay.[39]

Women are struggling to even find employment. In 2018, less than half of women worldwide were employed, and women were 26 percent less likely to be employed than men.[40] Furthermore, women are vastly underrepresented in senior positions, representing just 27 percent of managers and leaders, despite being more likely to have a higher level of education than their male counterparts.[41] In fact, women with a university degree are two and a half times more likely as similarly educated men to be either unemployed or outside the labor force.[42]

Mothers face a unique set of workplace obstacles, particularly those in the United States. The US is the only advanced economy where mothers are entitled to zero weeks of paid maternity leave under federal law.[43] As of 2019, only six states have passed paid family leave laws, while the others are not legally obligated to guarantee more than the Family Medical Leave Act (FMLA) of 1993's unpaid leave requirement.[44] For comparison, new mothers in Finland get up to three years of paid leave, Norway ninety-one weeks, UK thirty-nine weeks, and Canada, a year.[45] Research shows that policies like paid family and medical leave and affordable childcare are important to a healthy economy as they can increase participation in the labor force.[46]

WOMEN AND GIRLS AT RISK

Legal loopholes and insufficient legislation cause women and girls to be left vulnerable in the face of sexual harassment, domestic violence, and child marriage. In the workplace, for example, women are often vulnerable: fifty-nine countries have no legislation protecting women from sexual harassment in the workplace.[47] In the classroom, safety is also not guaranteed, as 65 percent of economies lack legislation protecting women and girls from sexual harassment in education.[48]

Both girls and women are also susceptible to household abuse. As of 2018, forty-five countries have no laws prohibiting domestic violence, and seventy-two countries lack criminal penalties for domestic violence offenders.[49] Marital rape is not explicitly criminalized in 111 countries.[50]

Globally, child marriage is rampant: an estimated 12 million girls are married before the age of eighteen. According to Girls Not Brides, a global partnership spanning over ninety-five countries committed to supporting girls and ending the practice of child marriage, married girls are robbed of their essential rights to education, safety, and health.[51] The impact of child marriage is substantial: not only are child brides physically and emotionally unprepared for marriage and motherhood, they risk complications from pregnancy and childbirth, sexually transmitted diseases, domestic violence, and limited access to education and economic opportunities.[68] On a larger scale, married girls' lack of economic participation further inhibits their countries' growth.[69]

QUICK FACTS: GENDER INEQUALITY WORLDWIDE

- One hundred four countries have legislation that prevents women from working in certain jobs.[52] Gender-based discrimination is most common in industries like mining, manufacturing, construction, and agriculture.[53]
- In eighteen countries, women can be legally prevented from working by their husbands.[54]
- In forty-four countries, at least 20 percent of women are illiterate.[55]
- Fifty-nine countries have no laws preventing workplace sexual harassment.[56]
- Forty-five countries do not legally prohibit domestic violence, and in seventy-two countries, there are no determined criminal penalties for domestic violence offenders.[57]
- Over 2.7 billion women worldwide are legally prevented from having the same job choices as men.[58]
- Between 1992 and 2018, women accounted for 13 percent of negotiators, 3 percent of mediators, and 4 percent of signatories, despite evidence that peace agreements with female signatories are connected with longer-lasting peace.[59]
- In 2017, just 2.2 percent of venture capital in the United States was awarded to companies founded by women.[60]
- As of 2019, just seven of the CEOs leading Financial Times Stock Exchange (FTSE) 100 companies in the UK were women.[61]
- A 2019 study of eighteen major American museums' collections revealed that women artists are desperately underrepresented, finding that 87 percent of the collections' artists are men.[62]
- Women make up just 22 percent of artificial intelligence (AI) professionals worldwide.[63]
- In the United States, women comprise less than a quarter of the STEM (science, technology, engineering, and mathematics) workplace.[64]
- As of 2019, women led just 17 percent of the world's top 200 universities, unchanged from the previous year.[65]
- In 2016, the percentage of women presidents at colleges and universities stood at 30 percent, up just four percentage points from 2011.[66]
- Out of the 904 individuals awarded the Nobel Prize between 1901 and 2018, just fifty-one have been women.[67]

Girls in Iran can be legally married at thirteen years of age and boys at fifteen.[70] But with a father's and judge's consent, girls can marry even as young as nine.[71] The UN Special Rapporteur on the situation of human rights in Iran reports that between 2012 and 2013, over 40,000 marriages of girls under fifteen years of age were registered, of which more than 8,000 involved men who were at least a decade older than their brides.[72] South Asia is consistently home to the largest number of child brides, followed by sub-Saharan Africa, where population growth threatens to put more girls at risk.[73] West and Central Africa, the region with the highest pervasiveness of child marriage, has some of the slowest progress in the world.[74]

Child marriages are not limited to developing countries; in the United States there are no federal laws banning child marriages. Every state except Delaware and New Jersey allows people under the age of eighteen to marry as long as they have some combination of a judge's order, parental permission, premarital counseling, or proof of pregnancy.[75] Until as recently as 2018, Missouri had the reputation for the easiest state in the union where a fifteen year old could marry. It's now the ripe age of sixteen.[76]

In November 2018 in the UK, government ministers refused to back a bill fighting forced marriage that would have increased the legal age of marriage to eighteen. They cited a lack of evidence that it would help reduce child marriage, despite testimony from campaign groups and forced marriage survivors.[77]

THE COST OF GENDER INEQUALITY

Institutionalized gender discrimination continues to create social, economic, and political impediments for women throughout the global community. Worldwide statistics reveal the economic toll of this ongoing inequity.

According to the World Bank's May 2018 report *The Cost of Gender Inequality*, which studied 141 countries and measured the economic toll of gender inequality both globally and regionally, a "lack of opportunities for girls and women entails large economic costs not only for them, but also for their household and countries."[78] Although a country's wealth is derived from multiple types of capital such as factories, infrastructure, and agriculture, its biggest asset is its people: human capital, which is measured as the value of a person's earnings over their lifetime, is the most significant component of global wealth.[79] It is for this reason that gender equality is essential at an economic level. The report estimates that, if gender equality in earnings is achieved, human capital wealth could increase by over 20 percent, and total global wealth could increase by 14 percent.[80]

Simply put: "Ending gender inequality by investing in girls and women is essential to increase the changing wealth of nations and enable countries to develop in sustainable ways."[81]

In a March 2019 speech for International Women's Day, Christine Lagarde noted that some countries could increase the size of their economies by 35 percent if they discard discriminatory legislation and fully take advantage of their female population.[82] In her words, "Empowering women can be an economic game changer for any country … If you discourage half the population from fully participating in the labor market, you are essentially behaving like an airline pilot who shuts down half his engines in mid-flight. Sure, your plane will likely continue to fly, but it would be such a crazy thing to do."[83]

CHANGING MINDS, CHANGING LIVES

Overturning society's stereotypical gender-based assumptions is not easy, even in developed countries that are thought to be more progressive. Often it takes an accumulation of role models—real-life examples of what girls and women are able to do if given the opportunity—in order to change entrenched attitudes.

A case in point: in a study often referred to as the draw-a-scientist test (DAST), originally conducted between 1966 and 1977 by social scientist David Chambers, 4,807 elementary-school children, primarily from the US and Canada, were asked to draw a scientist.[84] Published in 1983, the study revealed that of the approximately 5,000 drawings, only twenty-eight (or a measly 0.6 percent) depicted a female scientist—and all were drawn by girls![85] In studies from the 1980s onward, this number has risen to 28 percent.[86] David Miller, PhD,[87] attributed the shift to changes in the actual number of women scientists, saying: "It's optimistic that children's stereotypes change as gender roles change in society too."[88] For instance, in the United States women earned 48 percent of chemistry degrees in 2015 compared to just 19 percent in 1966. Despite the steep increase in drawings depicting female scientists, the number still falls well below the halfway mark, demonstrating that there remains a strong perception of scientists as being male.

More recently, in January 2017, the DAST was given to 445 first-year students across different faculties at a South African university, and their results were similar to that of the international research literature: "A typical scientist—as depicted in this study—is a man of uncertain age, who wears eyeglasses and a lab coat, and is surrounded by laboratory equipment."[89]

In 2018, at a summer STEM camp in the United States, students in grades three to five were asked to draw a scientist for their science notebook's cover. The results again resembled those of the DAST studies from decades ago: "Twenty-four percent of the class drew female scientists. Once again, all of the female scientists were drawn by girls."[90] Here are some of the reasons the students gave for drawing a male or female scientist:[91]

- Usually men are scientists, not women, so I drew a man for my scientist. (male student)
- Because I just see more men than women. It's just that I've never seen a girl one. And the boys find more things than the girl ones, I think. Like, they figure out more things to fix up. (female student)
- Because most [scientists] are [men]. (female student)
- When I usually think scientist, I think man. (male student)
- I don't really see girl scientists a lot, like on TV. I know they are there. That's just the first thing that came to my mind. (female student)
- I never saw a scientist on the movies that was a girl. (male student)

If there is anything we can conclude from the DAST, it is this: no one is born with a limited perspective on women; it is ingrained in our patriarchal cultures and learned early on. But such embedded attitudes are also subject to positive change. Given that women continue to be underrepresented in various professions even in the twenty-first century, if we want to experience meaningful change, we desperately need women and men to advocate for that change and for women to embody it.

How can we work toward more gender equality successes? In an article for the World Economic Forum, Magnea Marinósdóttir and Rósa Erlingsdóttir, both from the Equality Unit at the Ministry of Welfare in Iceland, explain how their country has topped the *Global Gender Gap Index* for nine years in a row:

What is the secret to Iceland's success? What are the lessons learned? In short, it is that gender equality does not come about of its own accord. It requires the collective action and solidarity of women human rights defenders, political will, and tools such as legislation, gender budgeting and quotas.... As is the case worldwide, our incremental progress can firstly be attributed to the solidarity of women human rights defenders challenging and protesting the monopoly of power in the hands of men and the power of men over women.[92]

Progressive steps toward gender equality have been taken in developing countries as well.[93] In 1993, for example, the Indian government passed a constitutional amendment requiring states to reserve a certain proportion of

UNDERREPRESENTATION IN OBITUARIES

Women are not only underrepresented when they are alive but also when they have passed on. With their ongoing series "Overlooked," *The New York Times* acknowledges its grave mistake of ignoring the names and personal histories of notable women, instead publishing obituaries of primarily white men. Some of the women whose belated obituaries have been published recently in the *Times* include:

- Julia de Burgos (1914–1953), Poet Who Helped Shape Puerto Rico's Identity
- Leticia Ramos Shahani (1929–2017), Philippine Women's Rights Pioneer
- Emma Gatewood (1887–1973), First Woman to Conquer the Appalachian Trail Alone
- Beatrice Tinsley (1941–1981), Astronomer Who Saw the Course of the Universe
- Clara Lemlich Shavelson (1888–1982), Crusading Leader of Labor Rights
- Edmonia Lewis (ca. 1844–1907), Sculptor of Worldwide Acclaim

The fact that these women failed to be recognized in *The New York Times* obituaries contributes to a conscious and systemic overlook of their accomplishments. This issue is emblematic of the many arenas in which women continue to be kept "anonymous" despite their significant contributions.

all council chief—or "pradhan"—seats in its villages for women.[94] The objective was described as follows:

> *Aside from the obvious outcome of greater gender balance in male-dominated arenas, one possible and expected effect of quotas is that the first women to fill these quotas will act as role models, opening up previously male-saturated environments for other women and lowering gender barriers.*[95]

Over time, this exposure to female leaders in India has been shown to directly impact young girls in terms of leadership, aspiration, and education. The results of this initiative suggest that the villages' gender gap was narrowed not by female pradhans' female-friendly legislation, but rather by the visibility of the female leaders as role models for young girls and women.[96]

A shift in ideology and a changing of attitudes are key to changing policy. As is evident by the statistics presented in "Women by the Numbers," it is overwhelmingly clear that the gender gap remains a concern for countries worldwide. Not only are women suffering inequality in many areas, including the political fields and in the workplace, but economies are overlooking the benefits of fully allowing their female population to participate. The gender gap will not close without targeted action. Meaningful, tangible, and economically beneficial change can only be achieved through the inclusion of women. We cannot afford to exclude or ignore half of the world's population.

THREE

Yinyang and the Economics of Gender Balance

When considering the latest global statistics regarding gender equality—especially in the health, education, political, and economic sectors—it is clear that we have a long way to go before women and men are equally represented. It is disheartening to note that although women make up 49.4 percent of the global population, no nation in the world has full gender parity.[1] According to the United Nations, as of 2014 fifty-two countries have yet to guarantee equality between men and women in their constitutions.[2] (This includes the United States, forty years after Congress approved the Equal Rights Amendment.[3])

If we don't strive for a balanced male/female presence in the world how will it accurately reflect the values and thinking of an entire population, rather than just half of it? And if we fail to bring about gender balance, what valuable economic, cultural, and social benefits will we squander? In order to move toward full gender equality, we must understand the benefits of creating a balanced society, benefits that include economic profit and social symmetry.

THE BENEFITS OF GENDER BALANCE

It is evident in "Women by the Numbers" that women have been prevented from reaching their full potential. The findings of the *Global Gender Gap Report 2018* demonstrate that the overall global gender gap is closing at a glacial pace; for North America alone, it will take 165 years to reach gender parity.[4] The World Economic Forum has urged legislators and other stakeholders to work toward faster progress, citing a need for both social equality and economic profit derived from a stronger, broader, and more diverse population.[5] Why? Because diversity is not just a political, social and moral issue but an economic one. Many may be surprised to learn that when women are held back from achieving a level of success commensurate with their aptitude, families, communities, society, and the global economy suffers. From a strictly economic standpoint, gender equality is crucial.

Scott Page, social scientist and professor of complex systems, political science and economics at the University of Michigan, makes an excellent case for this position in his 2017 book, *The Diversity Bonus*.[6] He asserts that in today's fast-changing, multifaceted world, the best teams to deal with complex problems are those that are diverse.[7] Teams that are deliberately composed of diverse individuals and different thinkers are more likely to find success.[8] In a 2019 interview for the podcast *The Knowledge Project*, Page elaborated on the differences between individual and group thinking:

> You yourself are not going to solve the obesity epidemic . . . create world peace . . . [or] solve climate issues. Your brain just isn't going to be big enough. But collections of people by having different ensembles of models, creating a larger ensemble of models actually have a hope of addressing these problems . . . . The reason you want diverse people in the room is because different people bring different basic assumptions about how the world works, they construct different mental models of how the world works, and they're going to see different parts of a problem.[9]

When faced with making difficult decisions, it has been proven that groups, rather than individuals, make better decisions, and diverse groups make better decisions than homogenous ones. In our information-driven society, diversity has proven to be an asset. In fact, when solving complex tasks, diverse teams achieve far more than the average of the individual answers, outperforming even their best member.[11] But as Page emphasizes, talent must be diverse. If individuals all have the same ideas, there is no diversity bonus.

This sentiment is echoed by Laurence Douglas Fink, chairman and CEO of BlackRock, an American multinational investment management corporation and the largest money-management firm in the world. In his 2018 annual letter to chief executive officers, Fink stated that the investment company would "continue to emphasize the importance of a diverse board" at companies BlackRock invests in.[12] Companies with diverse boards

When you hold back half of our population, [we cannot realize] 100 percent of our potential.

—*Ban Ki-moon, former secretary-general of the United Nations. International Women's Day, United Nations, 2015* [10]

are, Fink wrote, "less likely to succumb to groupthink or miss threats to a company's business model [and] they are better able to identify opportunities that provide long-term growth."[13] The same year, in a letter to clients, he emphasized the importance of "building a culture where all voices—not just the loudest or the most familiar—can contribute ... [to nurture] diverse, cohesive, complementary leadership teams."[14]

Meeting a diversity quota is just part of the solution. Another significant step toward experiencing the diversity bonus is building a company culture that not only embraces diversity but views it as a necessary asset. A recent Harvard Business School study of over 1,000 firms across thirty-five countries and twenty-four industries concluded that a company-wide belief in the importance of gender diversity is vital to success:

> Gender diversity relates to more productive companies, as measured by market value and revenue, only in contexts where gender diversity is viewed as "normatively" accepted ... [meaning] a widespread cultural belief that gender diversity is important. In other words, beliefs about gender diversity create a self-fulfilling cycle. Countries and industries that view gender diversity as important capture benefits from it. Those that don't, don't.[15]

Clearly, cultural bias can impede growth and success. A more specific example of ingrained bias relates to women's low representation in science, technology, engineering, and math (STEM) fields, which stands at a paltry 24 percent in the United States.[16] Research suggests that one of the reasons behind this low percentage is a lack of encouragement and faith in women's innate ability.[17] This mindset starts young—American girls as young as age six have been socialized to believe they are less capable of intellectual brilliance than boys.[19] The negative effects of this mentality follows women as they join the STEM workforce: women in these industries are 45 percent more likely to leave their job than men, citing male-dominated work environments, bias, and a lack of female role models as motivating factors to quit.[20]

These statistics signify the importance of diversity in creating healthy, balanced work cultures where differences are valued and embraced. Identities are complex tapestries of components like gender, race, age, religion, ethnicity, and sexual orientation. An individual's unique identity shapes and influences what they know, how they

> 66
>
> The extreme yin brings cold wind, the extreme yang brings bright light. They are in intercourse and connection, which completes the stage of harmony and then myriad things are generated. If there are so many males but no females, how can anything be transformed and be able to produce? This is the argument without words and the way without saying.
>
> —*The Huainanzi, an ancient Chinese text of Western Han philosophy, second century BCE*[18]

see the world, and how they think.[21] Scott Page asserts that if we are to reap the benefits of diversity, team members "cannot check their identities at the door. They must bring their whole selves—their identities, their experiences, their education and training—to achieve [diversity] bonuses."[22] In other words, success requires unity *and* difference.

YINYANG: A PARADIGM FOR GENDER BALANCE DISCOURSE

The belief that harmony is contingent on the dynamic balance between male and female is certainly not a new one. It dates back thousands of years to the ancient Chinese philosophical theory of *yinyang*,[23] typically defined in relation to gender: *yin* as female, and *yang* as male. Philosophy scholar Robin R. Wang elaborates, "Yinyang bring all things into oneness … This harmony, however, is not pursued for its own sake, but rather a way of becoming successful and prosperous. Yinyang is a strategy for success in the world."[24] Yinyang theory offers us a conceptual resource for gender balance discourse, underscoring the premise that the world does not benefit from an uneven playing field as well as providing us with a deeper understanding of what it means to live in a balanced world.

The ancient Chinese worldview considers all things as shaped by yinyang; they are the energetic life forces of the universe, serving as "the binary language of the universe defining all phenomena in opposing paired sets."[25] In yin and yang order, these sets include: female and male, night and day, cold and hot, and soft and hard.[26] The iconic symbol of yinyang exemplifies these dualities: a circle formed by the combination of two equal teardrop shapes, one white (yang), the other dark (yin), each containing an element of the other, shown as a dot or small circle, depicting the opposing yin within yang, and the opposing yang within yin. Yin and yang at once oppose and complement each other, creating conflict and tension alongside harmony and stability.[28] Yang is always transforming to yin, and yin to yang. They are relative to one another, each containing a part of the other. Their bonding and interaction "are absolutely essential for existence and the sustenance of all life and universal activity."[29] One cannot exist without the other. Out of their interplay comes transformation and growth.

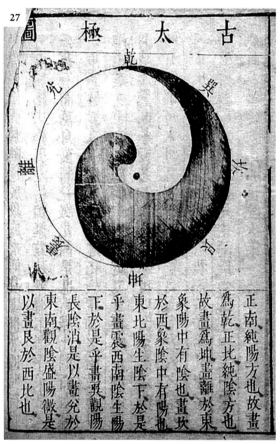

The complementary interconnectedness of yin and yang make it an ideal model for the benefits of gender diversity. Balance, according to Chinese thought, doesn't occur as a result of avoiding disagreements and dissimilarities but "arises from handling conflict and tension, difference and diversity, thereby creating harmony."[30] Scott Page argues for balance in a similar way: if people share ideas, a team can be as good as its best member, but when ideas are "challenged and combined, they can be better than those of its best member. Those challenges and deep engagements with ideas are a necessary component of the type of inclusive culture that maximizes bonuses."[31]

In fact, in 2018 McKinsey & Company found that businesses excel when there is gender and ethnic diversity.[32] Their report asserts: "Companies in the top-quartile for gender diversity on executive teams were 21% more likely to outperform on profitability and 27% more likely to have superior value creation. The highest-performing companies on both profitability and diversity had more women in line (i.e., typically revenue-generating) roles than in staff roles on their executive teams."[33] Another study done by the Peterson Institute of International Economics found that going from no women in corporate leadership to a 30 percent share improves a company's profitability by 15 percent.[34] These findings reinforce that there is a clear correlation between diversity and profitability.

When male and female combine, all things achieve harmony.

— *Lao-Tzu, Chinese philosopher credited with founding Taoism.*[36]

It is important to note that there have been differences in the interpretation of the yinyang theory during the various Chinese dynasties. Some historical interpretations contradict original yinyang concepts and were biased toward yang (the male energy), and a hierarchy of yang (male) over yin (feminine) developed. Dr. Wang assesses the interpretation of yinyang by Dong Zhongshu (179–104 BCE), the first prominent Confucian philosopher, in her essay, "Dong Zhongshu's Transformation of *Yin-Yang* Theory and Contesting of Gender Identity."[35] Wang writes: "As the result of Dong's work, *yin-yang* theory lost many of its earlier meanings, and the construction of the gender identities grounded in it was impoverished. Yin-yang concepts served to validate the subordination of women … Scholars have agreed that Dong clearly favors yang over yin."[37] This interpretation had detrimental consequences for women at the time, who were "trained to conform and be ordered" rather than embrace their capacities and virtues.[38] Thankfully, this imbalanced understanding of yinyang was not the original nor the sole interpretation.[39] Early Chinese thinkers did not denigrate the female when drawing yinyang comparisons, such as inferring that men are good/yang and women are evil/yin, as some later texts did.[40]

Yinyang is a complex and diverse theory with a myriad of interpretations. This book prioritizes the early Chinese associations of yinyang to serve as a paradigm for gender balance. What we can say with certainty is that yinyang theory is rooted in balanced change and harmony and provides a lens through which to view the world. This lens complements and magnifies arguments for gender equality, offering spiritual support for equality alongside economic benefits.

According to the Yellow Emperor's Classic of Medicine, an ancient Chinese treatise on health and disease:

The law of yin and yang is the natural order of the universe, the foundations of all things, mother of all changes, the root of life and death ... In the universe, the pure yang qi ascends to converge and form heaven,

while the turbid yin qi descends and condenses to form the earth ... Yang is the energy, the vital force, the potential, while yin is the substance, the foundation, the mother that gives rise to all this potential.[41]

YINYANG INTERACTION AND DYNAMIC HARMONY

If the optimal functioning of the world is contingent on the balance of yin (female) and yang (male), and if that yinyang interaction and dynamic harmony has a myriad of benefits, why does gender imbalance persist? Perhaps

━━━ YINYANG BALANCE IN OTHER WORDS ━━━

The concept of equilibrium between masculine and feminine is not unique to yinyang theory. Other philosophers and intellectuals, such as Carl Jung and Simone de Beauvoir, have explored similar ideas, providing alternative ways to understand the complexities of gender balance.

The ideas of German philosopher Georg Wilhelm Friedrich Hegel (1770–1831), particularly his concept of the "unity of opposites," can be compared to yinyang theory: "The 'unity of opposites' in Hegelian philosophy shares some similarities with the concept of the 'unity of Yin and Yang' (阴阳合一) in Chinese traditional philosophy in that they are both 'opposite and complementary to each other' (相反相成) ... In fact, Hegel's 'unity of opposites' is entirely based on the 'subject—object dichotomy.' It asserts that the 'positive' inherently contains the 'negative' within it (内在的)."[42]

The thoughts of Ednah Dow Littlehale Cheney (1824–1904), an American writer, philanthropist, and reformer, also parallel yinyang theory. Influenced by transcendentalists like Margaret Fuller and Bronson Alcott, Cheney was a celebrated champion for African American and women's rights, supporting post-Civil War schools for freedmen and campaigning for women's suffrage.[43] Her philosophies on the relations between men and women are articulated in her 1902 book, *Reminiscences of Ednah Dow Cheney (Born Littelhale),* in which she writes: "The whole meaning of sex is a mutual relation and the one sex must be fit to mate the other. 'All are needed by each one; nothing is fair or good alone.'"[44] This statement emphasizes the necessity of balance between the sexes. **CONTINUED ❯**

humanity's lack of vision and insight to imagine what could be generated by dynamic harmony holds us back. When we view the world through a yinyang lens, we can "appreciate the intricacies and delicate balance that is the human race without judgment or prejudice, because it reminds us that our differences exist so that we may exist."[45] In other words, yinyang aids us in embracing balanced diversity so that we may understand our need for gender equality and thrive, both socially and economically.

Gender equality is not merely a women's issue. When we classify it as such, we unwittingly endorse the male/female divide. The rewards of inclusiveness benefit us all—our communities become stronger, our workforce more dynamic, and our economies more profitable. This success can only be experienced when we work together to reap the rewards of a more equitable world.

Swiss psychiatrist and psychologist Carl Jung's (1875–1961) notion of anima and animus can also be seen as reflective of the yinyang concept. As part of his theory of the collective unconscious, "the anima [feminine side of men] and animus [masculine side of women] are the contra-sexual archetypes of the psyche, with the anima being in a man and animus in a woman." Both male and female contain aspects of each gender. Jung did not see either masculinity or femininity as superior but rather "as two halves of a whole, such as light and shadow, halves which ought to serve to balance one another out."[46]

Physicist and Nobel Prize winner Albert Einstein (1879–1955) understood the interdependence and transformation in nature, and evidence of the yinyang theory can be found in his theory of relativity. Energy (yang) and matter (yin) are interchangeable; energy converts to matter, and matter to energy. "[Yin and yang] are different forms of the same thing and can transform into one another."[47]

French intellectual Simone de Beauvoir (1908–1986), best known for her writings on feminist theory and existentialism, also has thoughts mirroring the concept of yinyang. In her 1949 book *The Second Sex*, de Beauvoir writes: "It is when the slavery of half of humanity is abolished and with it the whole hypocritical system it implies, that the 'division' of humanity will reveal its authentic meaning and the human couple will discover its true form."[48] Her words echo yinyang theory: once women (yin) are released from subjugation and are equal with men (yang), balance harmony between the two sexes (yinyang) can be achieved.

FOUR

Forgotten Innovators

While global statistics reveal an ongoing gender gap, evidence challenging discriminatory laws and policies reflects the benefits of a balanced, equitable world. The biographical profiles of fifty extraordinary, yet forgotten women innovators presented in this section dismantle centuries of historical bias and refute ingrained stereotypical assumptions, which continue to limit opportunities for women and girls in the twenty-first century.

Their stories represent a mere fraction of the thousands of accomplished women who have been inadequately acknowledged in world history and relegated to obscurity and anonymity despite their achievements. Illuminating these exemplary women not only expands the historical record, but also provides young girls with role models to inspire their pursuit of goals and aspirations.[I]

The objective was to highlight women from a range of countries, cultures, ethnicities, and fields of endeavor. All of these women were born before 1900—from 2300 BCE to 1892. A significant piece of each woman's story is her determination to overcome gender-based barriers and obstacles. To varying degrees, these fifty individuals were born when opportunities were not readily available to women, when females were often barred from edu-

cational institutions and from holding certain positions in society, or when their achievements were underplayed and undervalued. Many of their successes were alleged to have been attained by the men with whom they worked.

It was a challenge to select *only* fifty women. Inclusion was based on several factors: the individual had not been widely written about, she is virtually unknown beyond her country of origin, and/or her life story was particularly illuminating with respect to the quest for gender equality.

A number of women were selected because their relative lack of recognition is in stark contrast to their male counterparts. For instance: Spanish cubist painter María Blanchard is virtually unknown, especially in comparison to her fellow Spaniard, Pablo Picasso; South African

Charlotte Maxeke was born forty-three years before the revered Nelson Mandela, but her accomplishments paved the way for her country's momentous political changes as well as its first women's movement; and English biologist Marianne North documented and painted more than 800 plant species, a similar endeavor to that of John Audubon (whose specialty was birds), yet she has scant name recognition.

From the beginning of world history, despite formidable cultural barriers, women have developed their skills and talents, employed their intellect and creativity, and achieved distinction in diverse endeavors. Their life stories point toward a gender-balanced society beyond anonymity.

En Hedu-Anna

EN HEDU-ANNA
CA. 2300 BCE, AKKADIAN
WORLD'S FIRST KNOWN FEMALE ASTRONOMER

A mere 4,000-and-some-odd years had passed before the world's first known female astronomer received an honor befitting her historic accomplishments: a crater on Mercury was named after her.[1]

She was revered in her lifetime. In the twenty-fourth century BCE, **En Hedu-Anna** was an Akkadian priestess[2] —*en* is a title of leadership and *Hedu'anna* means "ornament of heaven," the name given to her when she was installed as en-priestess.[3] As astronomer Sethanne Howard[4] writes, the tradition of women in science and technology begins with En Hedu-Anna: "She was the chief astronomer-priestess and as such managed the great temple complex of her city of Ur. She controlled the extensive agricultural enterprise surrounding the temple as well those activities scheduled around the liturgical year." The responsibilities associated with her honored position "required her to make detailed astronomical calculations and observations."[5]

En Hedu-Anna's scientific calculations are known to us through her distinguished poetry, which was recorded on cuneiform tablets[6]—the literary medium of the day, typically small enough to fit into one's pocket. According to Howard, poetry had a more wide-ranging function in ancient times; it was used for "stories, religious works, laws, regulations" and more.[7]

En Hedu-Anna has not only been referred to as the "Shakespeare of ancient Sumerian literature," she also "used her creative talents in the written word [to spread] her ideas and beliefs."[8] One of her poems contains a clue as to her astrological endeavors:[9]

> in the gipar[10] the priestesses' rooms
> that princely shrine of cosmic order
> they track the passage of the moon.[11]

Howard goes on to explain that "there must have been some sort of calendar keeping (astronomy) intrinsic to her position. As we know, it is from the work of these early trackers of the moon that modern liturgical calendars developed. We date Easter, Passover, and Ramadan using the work derived from the ancient Sumerians." In another poem, En Hedu-Anna describes her work:

> The true woman who possesses exceeding wisdom,
> She consults a tablet of lapis lazuli
> She gives advice to all lands . . .
> She measures off the heavens,
> She places the measuring-cords on the earth.[12]

Howard goes on to further assess this ancient poem and pay tribute to En Hedu-Anna as follows: "This is the work of a scientist ... to measure off the heavens is to engage in astronomy. To measure the Earth is surveying as well as astronomy. These are all technical subjects requiring great skill to accomplish ... En'Hedu'anna is our first woman of power and scholarship whose name we know, and the last in a long line of unknown powerful women of the past who followed the stars and the cycles of the Moon."

In a journal article entitled "Science Has No Gender: The History of Women in Science," Howard poignantly states, "Science is a traditional role for women. For over 4,000 years of written history women have participated in this great human adventure. Science and technology are neither new nor difficult for women any more than they are for men."[13]

In "measuring off" the heavens and placing the "measuring-cords on the earth," En Hedu-Anna was one of the first to partake in that boundless adventure.

Tapputi-Belatekallim

TAPPUTI-BELATEKALLIM
CA. 1200 BCE, BABYLONIAN
WORLD'S FIRST CHEMIST

The world's first recorded chemist was a woman—and she lived over 3,000 years ago. The chemist's identity was discovered in a cuneiform tablet dated around 1200 BCE in Babylonian Mesopotamia. Her name was Tapputi, but she was also known as **Tapputi-Belatekallim**.[1] (*Belatekallim* is her title—"mistress of the palace.")

As the overseer/mistress (manager) of the Mesopotamian Royal Palace, Tapputi was a powerful figure in the Mesopotamian government. Her legacy, however, is not her impressive position as a manager; it is the scientific breakthroughs she made that resulted in a product that women (and men) throughout the centuries have consistently used in their personal grooming regimen—perfume. But in ancient Babylon, perfume was not solely used for personal enhancement. Scented substances were used for medicinal purposes and were also an integral part of religious rituals.[2]

According to the Getty Villa's education specialist Erin Branham, using perfume in various public and private spaces was a near-necessity in the ancient world, especially among those of the privileged classes.

To us the ancient world would perhaps be most overpowering in terms of smell. Sweating men and animals and their waste filled a city's streets, making it vital to set off sacred spaces as well as those of luxury by making them smell sweet. Fragrance was everywhere in the ancient world, from scented oils used to adorn the body to incense burnt in homes and temples.

Perfumes had many uses and meanings: they could be holy, used in the worship of the gods or the burial of the dead; they could be a symbol of status and superiority, used by athletes, aristocrats, politicians, and royalty; they could be medicinal, used to relieve ailments of the lungs or skin.[3]

As the royal perfume maker, Tapputi developed a unique process for scent extraction that provided the basis for creating modern-era perfume. Working alongside another female chemist, whose name survives only partially as "[−]ninu," Tapputi recorded her methodology to create what may be the first treatise on perfume making.[4] Secondary sources attest to the fact that her techniques were centuries ahead of her time. Although she didn't invent the perfuming still, she modified its design to get better results. Experimenting with distillation and cold *enfleurage*,[5] her scent-extraction techniques became the foundation of natural perfume making. By preparing the fragrant oils in a concrete of fat and wax, similar to a modern enfleurage pomade, Tapputi was able to preserve delicate floral fragrance in transit across the Babylonian Empire.[6]

Tapputi's most innovative breakthrough involved the use of solvents. Specifically, she distilled the essences of flowers and other aromatic ingredients—such as calamus, cyperus, myrrh, and balsam—filtered them, and then added solvents like water and grain alcohol before returning them to the still.[7] She then distilled and filtered the remaining substance to produce a vastly improved perfume, which was lighter and longer lasting.[8] This technique is the first recorded use of the still, making Tapputi one of the oldest known chemical engineers.[9]

Indeed, Tapputi's innovative brilliance as a chemist bequeathed a sweeter-smelling world to women and men for centuries to come.

Kentake Amanerinas

KENTAKE AMANERINAS
60s–50s BCE–CA. 10 BCE, ETHIOPIAN
QUEEN AND DEFENDER OF THE KINGDOM OF KUSH AGAINST ROMAN AGGRESSION

How many of us are familiar with an ancient kingdom in northern Africa that was ruled for a time by women? And how could contemporary women and girls *not* be inspired by the history of this time and place?

For 500 years (from the third century BCE until the second century CE) there were female rulers in the ancient Kingdom of Kush (present-day northern Sudan), "a kingdom known for strong female leaders," a unique characteristic in the ancient world.[1] Also a "rich and vibrant trading culture," the Kush Kingdom lived at peace with its neighbors for centuries, "almost certainly due to its role in commerce and in the transportation of goods." And its succession of female rulers "represents an innovation not seen in any other major civilization."[2]

These ancient female leaders used the title *Kentake* or *Candace*, meaning "queen." Among them was Kentake Amanerinas (also spelled Amanirenas and Amanerenas), who reigned from about 40 BCE to 10 BCE. Amanerinas was called upon to defend her kingdom against an invasion by the Romans.

Following their conquest of Egypt in 30 BCE, the Romans hurried to secure the rest of their southern border. Included in these plans was a plan to also conquer the Kingdom of Kush. Amanerinas ordered her Kushite army to attack the Roman Empire's southern towns of Syene, Elephantine, and Philae, destroying their statues of Caesar.[3] In response, the Romans destroyed the Kushite city of Napata. Amanerinas was undaunted, masterminding an attack on the Roman military fortress Qasr Ibrim (then Primis) in 22 BCE.[4]

Amanerinas's aggressive militarism was matched equally by her negotiation skills. Following these years of conflict, now referred to as the Meroitic War (27–22 BCE),[5] Amanerinas ended hostile relations between the Kushites and the Romans by negotiating a peace treaty with Augustus that benefitted her kingdom over Rome—a deal that was out-of-character for the Roman emperor.[6]

In the face of Roman conquest, Amanerinas kept her kingdom, successfully establishing a boundary between Kushite and Roman lands.[7] This exceptional ancient queen proved that she was a ruler who could courageously and astutely wage both war and peace.

Cleopatra
Metrodora

CLEOPATRA METRODORA

CA. 200–400 CE, GREEK

FIRST FEMALE AUTHOR OF A MEDICAL TREATISE

Cleopatra Metrodora, Greek physician and author of the oldest medical book known to be written by a woman, was practicing medicine and writing about her findings many centuries before most women had the chance to do so. She was among a group of early female medical practitioners who paved the way for generations of future female physicians.

It is distressing to acknowledge that it wasn't until 1849 that the first woman in America earned her MD,[1] especially when we place that "first" into a historical context. Nearly 5,000 years before Elizabeth Blackwell was allowed to become a physician in nineteenth-century New York, there was Merit-Ptah, an Egyptian woman who served as chief physician at the pharaoh's court in the twentieth-eighth century BCE, a time when women often worked as physicians and midwives.[2]

Merit-Ptah is one of "the most famous Egyptian doctors no one has ever heard of," holding the distinction as being the first woman mentioned in the study of science as well as the first female doctor known by name.[3] As chief physician, she would have been a teacher and supervisor of male students.[4] And she wasn't the only woman in ancient history to achieve exemplary status in the medical field. There is evidence suggesting that around 3000 BCE, a woman (whose name is unknown) ran a medical school at the Temple of Neith in Sais, a city in Lower Egypt.

Other noteworthy female medical scientists of the ancient era included botanist and medical researcher Artemisia II (ca. 350 BCE), who is credited with discovering wormwood as a treatment for various women's health problems, including delayed menses and prevention of miscarriage.[5] And her possible contemporary, Greek physician Agnodike (ca. fourth-century BCE), who was motivated to study medicine so that she could treat women who were dying in childbirth or of reproductive diseases who did not want to be treated by a male physician.[6] Unlike the more progressive Egyptian society into which Merit-Ptah was born, women were not allowed into Greek medical schools, forcing Agnodike to dress as a man in order to gain access to the medical classroom.[7] When she began to treat women, her gender identity was discovered, and she was put on trial for practicing medicine illegally.[8] Had it not been for the women of Athens, who protested at her trial, Agnodike could have been sentenced to death.[9] Instead, a groundbreaking law was passed allowing women to become physicians.[10]

Which brings us to Metrodora, who is justly honored for another first. Her treatise entitled *On the Diseases and Cures of Women* earned her the distinction of becoming the first female medical scholar.[11] This leading-edge work contains herbal remedies not found elsewhere in ancient Greek writing, assesses the causes of many female health problems, and was widely referenced by physicians in ancient Greece and Rome.[12] Influenced by the works of Hippocrates, Metrodora's scholarship would continue to be influential and later contribute to the medical education of physicians in medieval Europe.[13] A twelfth-century copy of *On the Diseases and Cures of Women* (in the Laurentian Library in Florence, Italy) reveals innovative prescriptions for the treatment of diseases of the uterus, stomach, and kidneys.[14]

How respected are Metrodora's findings today? According to scholars Gregory Tsoucalas and Markos Sqantzos, both of whom are on the faculty of medicine at the University of Thessaly, Larissa, in Greece, Metrodora's "education, skills, courage, innovation, nerve, and audacity" earn her "a place among the best in the history of surgery."[15] The professors assert that not only was Metrodora's *On the Diseases and Cures of Women* "constructed in such a way, as to describe in details all women diseases, in a similar pattern to a modern textbook" but she also "performed a series of innovative surgical operations" and her "breast and face reconstruction, resuturing of the vaginal hymen, and breast and uterine cancer excisions present great similarities to modern surgery."[16]

The professors' research revealed evidence that this female physician from the Byzantine era was incredibly ahead of her time and accomplished far more than she was ever given credit for:

> [She] was able to determine possible sexual abuse, mastering a method on how to diagnose virginity. She defined the way to diagnose and treat female sterility by administering herbal and chemical drugs, and also provided instructions for breastfeeding and breast milk production.... She had used intravaginal and intraureteral rowels to cure local infections, while she was able to perform embryotomias of the dead embryos to save the pregnant [mother]. She was also considered able to cure obesity, diseases of the kidney and stomach.
>
> [As] a surgeon, she was among the few to perform cosmetic operations, such as aesthetic breast and face reconstruction, and re-suturing of the vaginal hymen to create a sense of a new virginity for the abused, or sinful 'unlucky' women. In an effort to cure the most fatal of diseases, malignant ulcer, or scirrhous, or as named today cancer, she suggested surgical treatment for both the breast and the uterine cancer, following the Hippocratic dogma that any disease that can't be cured with a conservative way must be dealt with a scalpel and a flatiron to prevent both massive hemorrhage and infection of the surgical wound, those innovative surgical operations, were all procedures ahead of her era.[17]

Was Metrodora heralded by her contemporaries? Was she cited by other medical scholars of her day? Did her work even receive perfunctory acknowledgment while she was alive? The evidence is disheartening but not surprising. According to professors Tsoucalas and Sgantzos:

> *It is extremely unusual that neither Byzantine medical writers, such as Oribasius (ca 320 AD to 403 AD), Aëtius of Amida, Paul of Aegina (ca 620 AD to 690 AD), Pavlos Nikeos (ca 7th century AD) and Alexander of Tralles (ca 525 AD to 605 AD), nor Patriarch Photius the 1st (ca 810 AD to 893 AD) of Constantinople in his 'Bibliotheca,' or 'Myriobiblon,' have mentioned her work. Thus, Cleopatra Metrodora seems to have been completely unknown and forgotten for many centuries.* [18]

Despite the odds she confronted, stories of scholarly and professional contributions like Metrodora's serve as inspiration to young women pursuing medical careers.

Recent optimistic news that Metrodora would doubtlessly applaud: For the first time in US history, the number of women enrolling in medical schools exceeded the number of men, according to data released on December 18, 2017, by the Association of American Medical Colleges.[19] Out of the 21,338 new enrollees in 2017, women comprised 50.7 percent, compared to 49.8 percent in 2016.[20]

Sutayta Al-Mahamali

SUTAYTA AL-MAHAMALI
BIRTHDATE UNKNOWN–987, ARAB
ONE OF THE FIRST FEMALE MATHEMATICIANS
IN RECORDED HISTORY

We may be sending the inadvertent message to girls that they are not as good at math as boys. That was the finding by two Stanford scholars, whose paper was recently published in the journal *Cognitive Science*. An article about their findings reported that:

> While saying 'girls are as good as boys at math' is meant as encouragement, it can unfortunately backfire. Although well meaning, the statement commonly expressed by parents and teachers can subtly perpetuate the stereotypes they are trying to debunk ...

> On the surface, the sentence tries to convey that both sexes are equal in their abilities. But because of its grammatical structure, it implies that being good at math is more common or natural for boys than girls, the researchers said.[1]

Over a thousand years ago, a young Arab woman proved that being good at math was not gender specific.

In the tenth century, Baghdad was a vibrant cultural center for mathematicians, scientists, scholars, and researchers. Sutayta Al-Mahamali, the daughter of judge Abu Abdallah al-Hussein, was fortunate to have been born into a family of respected scholars who were her teachers and mentors. Her intellectual curiosity and brilliance resulted in a sharp legal mind and mathematical mastery for which she was respected throughout the city of Baghdad.[2]

More is known about her father, son, and grandson—well-regarded judges and scholars—than is known about Al-Mahamali. What we do know is that she "was widely consulted for her legal and mathematical insight, and that she solved problems of inheritance that imply an advanced knowledge of algebra" —a new field of study at that time.[3] Since "questions of inheritance, of how to correctly distribute the proceeds of an estate between people of varying relation to the deceased, were mathematical," a complex-yet-practical system of algebraic equations was used to "mathematize a web of competing claims on an estate."[4] Because she contributed to this new practical application of mathematics, Al-Mahamali's calculations influenced not only the field of mathematics but jurisprudence as well.

While there is no known record of her actual mathematical calculations, we know that Al-Mahamali made original contributions to the field of algebraic equations and to the theory of arithmetic because subsequent mathematicians cited her calculations and solutions to algebraic equations.[5] And renowned historians such as Ibn al-Jawzi, Ibn al-Khatib Baghdadi, and Ibn Kathīr praised her work.[6] She was known for her skills in solving individual problems as well as her ability to identify and create general solutions.[7] Her mathematical ingenuity is an example for young girls everywhere.

Mariam Al-Ijliya

MARIAM AL-IJLIYA

TENTH CENTURY, SYRIAN

DESIGNER OF ASTROLABES, USED TO DETERMINE THE POSITION OF THE SUN AND THE PLANETS

Credited with enhancing a valuable instrument called the *astrolabe*, Mariam Al-Ijliya achieved her notable accomplishment during an era known as the Islamic Golden Age, a period of strong economic, cultural, and scientific prosperity in the Muslim world spanning the eighth to fourteenth centuries.[1] According to the Institute for Astronomy at the University of Hawaii: "An astrolabe is a two-dimensional model of the celestial sphere. The name has its origins from the Greek words *astron* and *lambanien,* meaning 'the one who catches the heavenly bodies.' [It was] once the most used, multipurpose astronomical instrument.... [Its] portability and usefulness ... made it something like the multipurpose 'lap-top computer' of our predecessors."[2] Although the astrolabe originated in ancient Greece, it was refined by Arabic mathematicians, craftsmen, and astronomers—including Al-Ijliya—making it more accurate and versatile.[3]

Astrolabes were used to determine the position of the sun, moon, stars, and planets. And for Muslims, it was a vital tool used to determine prayer times and the initial days of Ramadan and Eid.[4]

Al-Ijilya learned about astrolabes from her father, who apprenticed with an astrolabe maker in Baghdad and in turn shared his knowledge with his daughter.[5] Working with precision and employing complex mathematical calculations, Al-Ijilya gradually mastered the designs and developed innovative enhancements to the astrolabe. Her work was admired by the Emir of Aleppo, Sayf Al Dawla, who consequently employed her in his court from 944–967.[6]

The creation and perfection of the astrolabe, including Mariam Al-Ijilya's improvements to this unique scientific instrument, "significantly advanced the early world. It [the astrolabe] promoted scientific and astronomic exploration, and cultivated new [techniques for] navigation and timekeeping."[7]

Although she lived eleven centuries ago, Al-Ijliya's scientific contribution should serve as an inspiration to girls and young women aspiring to a career in astronomy. During her lifetime, there were few women engaged in the study and practice of astronomy. Today, according to an article in *Astronomy & Geophysics*, approximately one-quarter of all professional astronomers are women. "In some countries there are none; elsewhere, they are the majority. There are countries, such as France, Romania and Argentina, that have more women astronomers, for reasons we do not fully understand: perhaps role models are effective once a critical number is reached, perhaps barriers came down when large numbers of scientists were needed."[8]

Rabi'a Balkhi

RABI'A BALKHI
TENTH CENTURY, AFGHAN
FIRST WOMAN POET OF NEW PERSIAN POETRY

hile the exact dates of her birth and death are unknown, Rabi'a Balkhi is believed to be the first woman poet in the history of New Persian poetry.

She was a native of Balkh in Khorasan (now part of Afghanistan), and likely lived at the same time as Abū 'Abdallāh Rūdakī (858–ca. 941), often considered the father of modern Persian poetry and founder of Persian classical literature.[1] It is said that he "was so amazed by [Rabi'a Balkhi's] wonderful poetry and upset by her tragic love story … that he revealed the secret of her love for [the slave] Bektash by quoting her poems which inadvertently caused her death when they were overheard by her jealous brother."[2]

While Rabi'a Balkhi may not be widely known outside the region, the dramatic story of her death and the depth of her poetic impulse are renowned and heralded in her native Afghanistan. According to the authors of *The Lives of Contemporary Afghan Women*, Rabi'a Balkhi's dying testimony to her abiding love for a person "beneath her station" in life continues to inspire the women of Afghanistan:

The resilience and resistance of Afghan women has a long and celebrated history dating back to at least the tenth century when Rabi'a Balkhi was jailed by her brother, the ruler of Balkh. According to legend, upon discovering her love poems to a Turkish slave, her brother ordered her wrists slashed before she was thrown into a steam bath. Her last act was to use her own blood to write another poem on her prison walls. Her tale and poem have been told and studied for centuries as part of the educated and folk culture of Afghanistan, which has a special regard for poets. Rabi'a Balkhi's name lives on in public institutions dedicated to women's advancement. This includes Rabi'a Balkhi High School, the alma mater of Massouda Jalal, former Women's Affairs Minister and the only woman to run against Hamid Karzai for president, and Rabi'a Balkhi Hospital in Kabul, the country's largest women's hospital.[3]

As part of the Afghan Women's Writing Project, a thirteen-year-old girl named Alia offered her impressions of Rabi'a Balkhi's story and testified to her lasting influence on girls and women in Afghanistan:

The first time I heard the story of Rabia, I couldn't believe that although she was one of the biggest personalities in her city, she did not have the freedom to tell people what she wanted. She became a victim of a culture in which a rich girl can't be with a poor boy. People thought this relationship was immoral ... Now Rabia Balkhi high school is one of the biggest schools of Afghanistan. It has about 4,000 students and has the best equality education for girls in Afghanistan.[4]

The following untitled poem by Rabi'a Balkhi (translated by author and poet Paul Smith) speaks mournfully of the suffering associated with love:

The wailing of a bird was kindling my love, increasing my pain and stirring my memory. It was late last night that the bird from a bough in deep lamentation cried, incessantly. I asked that bird, 'Why cry and moan in the dark of night while the stars shine brightly?' I weep because I'm separated from my love ... but why weep when you've a friend, tell me! When I shed tears of blood I don't complain: why cry when you do not bleed tears nightly?[5]

Liang Hongyu

LIANG HONGYU
1102–1135, CHINESE
GENERAL DURING THE SONG DYNASTY

How does a woman in tenth-century China become general of an army?

In the case of Liang Hongyu, her success as an army general had its roots in her family upbringing, her training as a wrestler, and her astute aptitude for military strategy.

Not much is known about Liang Hongyu's life, but we do know that she was born into a military family, the daughter of an army commander who had no reservations about teaching her martial arts. He introduced her to military tactics, weaponry, and strategy, training her from a young age to use weapons and strategize like a general.[1] After her father was killed in battle, she aspired to one day take his place as a commander in the Song army.[2] She pursued this dream following her marriage in 1121 to Han Shizhong, who became one of China's most celebrated generals and with whom she had at least two sons.[3]

It was alongside her husband that she found military success. The pair fought together in the Song army against invading Jin forces, her "quick mind, versatile tactics, and calmness in danger [complementing] his success."[4] After her husband and eldest son were captured by the Jin army, Liang Hongyu gathered her forces and set out on a rescue mission, only to be approached by Wu Zhu, commander of the Jin army. The commander "wished to discuss with her the release of her husband rather than fight her, since he feared her reputation as a valiant warrior-strategist."[5] Liang Hongyu refused his offers of Jin nobility in exchange for surrender, and though she lost the ensuing battle, she was "wildly acclaimed for her bravery and patriotism."[6]

Liang Hongyu's success as a female general in the Song dynasty is unusual. This was a period of burgeoning female subjugation in China, a time that would eventually extend into the even more oppressive Ming dynasty.[7] The cruel practice of foot binding, as well as a growing prostitution industry, threatened the freedom of women.[8] Liang Hongyu's achievements in a time of subjugation demonstrate her tenacity, strength, and bravery.

Liang Hongyu's illustrious military career fighting for the Song dynasty against the invasion of the Jin was commemorated in this poem by female poet Zheng Guangyi in 1574:

Thinking of Liang Hongyu at Huangtiandang

*Jade-white face and cloud coiffure brushed with the dust
of war,*

The little 'Lotus Batallion' clustered at river's edge.

*Carrying—not well-bucket and rice mortar—but the
drums of battle,*

Who would believe the hero was a fair maid?[9]

Alessandra Giliani

ALESSANDRA GILIANI

1307–1326, ITALIAN

ANATOMIST WHO INVENTED A TECHNIQUE
TO VIEW BLOOD VESSELS

At a time when women in most parts of the world were rarely allowed to pursue a higher education, Alessandra Giliani attended the University of Bologna around 1323. Her field of interest was anatomy, and one of her instructors was Mondino de Liuzzi, an anatomist and physician who "believed that to have a complete medical education, his students should know the human body by means of dissection."[1] Giliani became his prosector, an individual tasked with preparing a dissection for a demonstration, specifically in schools or hospitals.[2] She "developed a method for draining blood from vessels and replacing it with a colored dye, facilitating the observation of cardiovascular structures."[3]

In their article in the *Journal of the History of Medicine and Allied Sciences*, "A Brief Account of the Use of Wax Models in the Study of Medicine," authors Thomas N. Haviland and Lawrence Charles Parish offer more specific information about Giliani's significant contribution to the study of anatomy:

Wax representations were first employed in teaching anatomy early in the fourteenth century by a young female prosector for Mondino de' Luzzi (Mundinus) of Bologna (1270?–1326), Alessandra Giliani of Persiceto (d. 1326), who was apparently the pioneer in the wax injection technique ... According to M. Medici in his Compendio storico della scuola anatomica Bolognese (1857), she became most valuable to Mondino because: 'she would clean most skillfully the smallest veins, the arteries, all ramifications of the vessels without lacerating or dividing them ... she would fill them with various colored liquids which, after having been driven into the vessels, would harden without destroying the vessels, and she was also said to be a skillful modeler in wax.'[4]

It is important to note that there is dispute over Giliani's existence. It has been argued that lawyer, historian, and noted forger Alessandro Machiavelli (1693–1766) either invented or embellished Giliani's life and accomplishments.[5] This claim isn't without a basis: Machiavelli did indeed engage in forgery to enhance the life story of medieval Bolognese jurist and lecturer Bettisia Gozzadini (1209–1261).[6] Machiavelli did not invent

Gozzadini, however, but rather built upon her original sixteenth-century biography.[7] This suggests that he may have given Giliani a similar treatment. Assuming Giliani did exist, it is equally important to understand that her status as a woman (particularly a woman in the medical field) perhaps contributed to her limited historical record. This book accepts Giliani's existence as valid.

In her landmark multimedia installation entitled *The Dinner Party*, which was first exhibited in 1979 and presented a stunning symbolic history of women in Western Civilization through a series of place settings set on a triangular banquet table, artist Judy Chicago included Giliani as one of the 999 notable women represented in her piece. *The Dinner Party* is now permanently housed at the Brooklyn Museum within the Elizabeth A. Sackler Center for Feminist Art, which opened in 2007. The following excerpt from the biographical sketch of Alessandra Giliani appears in the exhibit at the museum: "Alessandra [Giliani] is said to have specialized in dissections and to have invented the technique of injecting colored dye to view the body's blood vessels."[8]

It is interesting to note the contrast between how Giliani's scientific contribution was described in 1857 by historian Medici versus how it was described in the 2007 citation at the Brooklyn Museum. Medici refers to Giliani's skillful cleaning of the veins and arteries before filling them with colored liquids. *The Dinner Party* description refers to Giliani as a specialist and an inventor. How often has the not-so-subtle choice of language served to minimize or downplay women's achievements?

Visual depictions of events and personalities can color our perceptions as well. In a plaque on the wall of a hospital church in Santa Maria del Mareto in Florence, Italy, which commemorates Giliani's scientific work,[9] she is depicted at the feet of her professor who sits high above her in a throne-like chair, holding a book. She has her hands inside the chest cavity of the cadaver, as she smiles up at her mentor. Giliani is performing a significant medical procedure but is portrayed as a mere child, enthralled by her regal superior. In fact, Alessandra Giliani was an innovator in the field of anatomy, whose pioneering techniques led to future advances.

Tan Yunxian

女性

TAN YUNXIAN

1461–CA. 1556, CHINESE

ONE OF THE EARLIEST FEMALE PHYSICIANS IN CHINA, AUTHOR OF *MISCELLANEOUS RECORDS OF A FEMALE DOCTOR*

Tan Yunxian gained the knowledge and skills necessary to become a physician in a rather unconventional manner. She was born into a family of medical practitioners: her great-grandfather had been a doctor, and his daughter (Tan Yunxian's grandmother) learned from him, with the daughter's husband reputedly marrying into the family to also learn medicine.[1] And because Tan Yunxian's grandparents respected her intellectual abilities, they passed on their medical knowledge to her.[2] She did not squander that valuable knowledge. Rather, she unknowingly made history.

Tan Yunxian lived during the Ming Dynasty at a time when Confucian ideology became conservative and oppressive of women.[3] Unlike male pupils, Tan Yunxian was unable to apprentice with a professional doctor, so she mostly worked as a nurse.[4] Confucianism prevented male doctors from touching their female patients, limiting their healing capabilities, allowing Tan Xunxian to work hands-on with women.[5]

Although there were likely other women doctors in ancient China, Tan Yunxian is the only one who left a record of her medical practice that has since been published in a book entitled *Miscellaneous Records of a Female Doctor*.[6] She practiced gynecology, pediatrics, and obstetrics. Because her manuscript survived, we are fortunate to have concrete evidence of the types of conditions and illnesses that she treated and the specific treatments she provided. According to Lorraine Wilcox, translator of *Miscellaneous Records*:

> At this time, a wealthy woman could not see a male doctor without having a male relative such as her father, husband, or son present. Modesty was the utmost female virtue. The male doctor questioned the husband, not the woman herself. He might not be allowed to see her face. He needed to ask for permission to feel her pulse.[7]

> [Tan Yunxian's] diagnostic questioning was careful and thorough, and Tan had a good rapport with the patients, so they told her details of their lives that explained their disease etiology. Tan could talk to patients in a way that male doctors could not . . . Patients received empathy and understanding from Tan.[8]

To some degree, women's attitudes with respect to being treated by a male gynecologist—in China and elsewhere—have not changed over the centuries. According to a study by the Shanghai Obstetrics and Gynecology Committee in 2012:

> Chinese women are still reluctant to consult male gynecologists, according to a recent survey conducted by the Shanghai Obstetrics and Gynecology Committee.
>
> Although regulations require that a nurse or a female doctor be present whenever a male doctor conducts examinations of a more intimate nature, over half of the women surveyed feel embarrassed by male gynecologists and approximately 60% would turn down the offer of a consultation with a male gynecology specialist.[9]

Like Tan Yunxian's patients and those in contemporary China, American women often feel more comfortable with female gynecologists. Dr. John Musich, chairman of the Council on Resident Education in Obstetrics and Gynecology, told the New York Times, "We can't force patients to see a particular gender, and there are women who feel that women are more sensitive as physicians to female complaints than men might be. It's reality, and we have to deal with it."[10] According to the American Congress of Obstetricians and Gynecologists, a little more than half of OB-GYNs in the US are women, but it's predicted that ten years from now, two-thirds of these physicians will be female.[11]

Tan Yunxian and other ceiling-shattering female physicians throughout the world paved the way for women who are drawn to the medical profession. In an article published by the National Center for Biotechnology Information, Tan Yunxian's work is summarized as follows:

> It was said that 'she always got wonderful therapeutic effects in treating those females who refused to see a male physician.' As one of the few women physicians in history, [her] 31 case reports [deal] with habitual abortion, menstrual disorders, postpartum diseases, and abdominal lumps ... From a clinical view point, though only a [small] number of case records are included, all the treatments are successful, with rich experiences and worthwhile for reference.[12]

Tan Yunxian knew that her experience as a female physician was unique, and she was committed to preserving and passing along the knowledge she learned and the skills she accumulated during her breakthrough medical career. Knowing that women were not allowed to publish books in China at that time, she nevertheless compiled thirty-one medical case studies into a book, instructed her son to cut printing blocks, and—undeterred by the misogynistic status quo—printed the book herself. The result is an extraordinary book documenting a groundbreaking and illustrious career.[13]

Gaitana

GAITANA

SIXTEENTH CENTURY, YALCÓN (INDIGENOUS COLOMBIAN)
RESISTANCE LEADER AGAINST SPANISH COLONIZATION

An astonishing sculpture in Neiva, Colombia, dramatically portrays a fierce battle between Spanish conquistadors and the indigenous Yalcón tribe of Colombia's Upper Magdalena Valley. An eagle-masked Yalcón fighter is shown with his bow pulled back, having just fired arrows that pierce the bodies of two Spanish horses and a centaur knight. At the center of the monument is a Spanish conquistador with a cross, a shield, and empty eye sockets, being dragged by a rope by a female Yalcón warrior with a "a compassionate motherly face yet in a powerful dress with a jaguar at her feet."[1]

There is no plaque explaining what is being depicted and who is being honored. But many Colombians know that the monument is a tribute to a sixteenth-century woman named Gaitana. She is especially known among the local indigenous community as the courageous leader who, in the mid-1500s, organized 6,000 Yalcón people to rise up against the Spanish conquistador Pedro de Añasco, who ruled over the indigenous population.[2]

De Añasco received an order to establish a Spanish settlement in the Yalcón region, where Gaitana was a local leader. Sent by Sebastián de Belalcázar, the Spanish conqueror of Nicaragua, Ecuador, and southwestern Columbia, de Añasco was to found Timaná, a village that would provide a trade route between the city of Popayán and the Magdalena River.[3] Not enough is known to say for certain what happened between Gaitana and de Añasco, but it is said that she disrespected his orders, and as a result de Añasco burned her son alive in her presence.[4]

Enraged by the murder, Gaitana assembled her indigenous people—equally infuriated by their Spanish overlords—in an act of independence-seeking rebellion.[5] After successfully attacking de Añasco and his men, the conquistador was captured, and subjected to torture at the hands of a vengeful mother: as punishment for de Añasco's brutal deeds, Gaitana tore his eyes out and dragged him by a noose until he died.[6]

By the time the Spanish arrived in Colombia in 1509, the indigenous population was flourishing, numbering between 1.5 to 2 million people belonging to several hundred tribes.[7] Although the Yalcón people perished, according to official data, indigenous peoples' population in Colombia is currently estimated at 1.5 million, which represents 3.4 percent of the national population, and among these people, sixty-five languages are spoken.[8]

Created in 1974 by sculptor Rodrigo Arenas Betancourt, the unnamed monument to Gaitana and to the indigenous peoples' struggle for self-determination and independence reminds twenty-first century Colombians of the courage of an oppressed population. Betancourt's stunning work connects this little-known piece of history to the larger issue of anti-colonialism—and keeps Gaitana's struggle alive.

Doña Grácia Mendes

DOÑA GRÁCIA MENDES
1510–1569, PORTUGUESE
HELPED JEWS ESCAPE THE INQUISITION

In the midst of the Spanish Inquisition, while Jews were being forced to renounce their faith in favor of Catholicism, one woman fought back. Doña Grácia Mendes, an intelligent and capable businesswoman, used her wealth and influence to protect *conversos*, Spanish and Portuguese Jews forced to convert to the Catholic faith in order to escape persecution.[1]

Not much is known about Mendes's early life. Born Beatrice Nasi in 1510, adopting the name Grácia around 1552, Mendes was from an eminent Spanish-Jewish family. It is possible that her Jewish parents fled Spain for Portugal in 1492, only to be forcibly baptized as Catholic five years later. At the age of eighteen, she married Francisco Mendes, a successful merchant who, alongside his brother, directed a trading empire.[2] Only twenty-five when her husband died, leaving her with a newborn child, Mendes inherited his vast wealth and influence. It was how she used that inheritance and power, however, that became her legacy.

Upon his death, Mendes took over her husband's business dealings along with her brother-in-law. Clearly, her husband was well aware of Mendes's impressive intelligence and expertise, as he had stipulated in his will that responsibility for the administration of his fortune was to be divided between his wife and his brother.[3] A "phenomenally successful businesswoman," Mendes continued overseeing the family's various enterprises on her own after her brother-in-law's death eight years after her husband's.[4] Shrewd at managing international commerce in wool, pepper, grain, cloth, and textiles, Mendes was equally astute in planning and arranging for her fellow conversos' escape.[5] This was the predominant project to which she was steadfastly committed.

As award-winning journalist and author Andrée Aelion Brooks points out, Mendes was able to turn her attention to a much more socially relevant mission than the overseeing of her inherited business:

> While steering Francisco's sprawling business interests, she would defy her enemies by spending most of her fortune on a humanitarian enterprise that would engross her more than the profitable royal loans, spice monopolies, syndications and currency arbitrage favored by her husband.
>
> The Inquisition, which would spread throughout the Catholic world, was just beginning its terror, torture and burning. She would become the self-appointed

protector and political liaison for its chief targets: the conversos.

These were the Spanish and Portuguese Jews who, like her own family, had been forcibly converted to Catholicism in the decades prior to her birth in 1510. These converts were being subjected to ethnic cleansing by Inquisition officials who were making wholesale arrests on the spurious charge that they had relapsed into Jewish practice, whether true or not.[6]

The foremost expert on the life of Mendes, Andree Aelion Brooks, delved into this remarkable Renaissance woman's history and discovered how she became a "Moses-like" leader to those seeking refuge during a dark time of tyranny and persecution:

To enable these conversos to undertake and survive the arduous journey to lands beyond the reach of the Inquisition was to embark upon a mission of Moses-like proportions. That she succeeded in saving thousands of them underscores her vital role at a crossroads of Jewish history.

Ultimately the conversos, and most of the openly professing Jews of the Eastern Mediterranean, would view Doña Gracia as their unquestioned leader. She would be revered as much for her wisdom and compassion as her capacity to stand up to tyranny; not to mention her willingness to give up her fortune to ensure the survival of this "remnant" of Israel, as her people were called in those days.

Here was a woman who made sure that she was constantly looking out for their welfare as they became a continual stream of frightened refugees, wandering stateless through the mountain passes, walled towns, hostile duchies and muddy roads of Europe.[7]

Oliva Sabuco

OLIVA SABUCO

1562–1622, SPANISH

PHILOSOPHER AND ORIGINATOR OF MIND-BODY DUALISM

We don't generally associate holistic health or the mind-body connection with the sixteenth century. But with the publication in 1587 of her treatise *Nueva filosofía de la naturaleza del hombre* (*New Philosophy of Human Nature*), Spanish philosopher **Oliva Sabuco** predated Descartes's mind-body dualism by fifty years and the popular mind-body connection philosophy of the late twentieth century by 400.

One of the first to espouse the concept of natural interaction between mind and body, Sabuco challenged the medical orthodoxy "by arguing for recognition of the symbiotic relationship between physical health and emotional well-being."[1]

Her landmark work is comprised of seven separately titled treatises:

- *Knowledge of One's Self*
- *Composition of the World as It Is*
- *Things That Will Improve This World and Its Nations*
- *Treatments and Remedies of Proper Medicine*
- *Proper Medicine Derived from Human Nature*
- *Brief Exposition on Human Nature: The Foundations of the Art of Medicine*

- *Proper Philosophy of the Nature of Composite Things, of Humans, and of the World, Unknown to the Ancients*

Having witnessed the failure of medicine to find a cure for the plague, Sabuco wanted to improve medical practice by focusing on the "power of the mind over the body in relation to disease."[2] Through her groundbreaking book, she sought to "promote health and prevent disease by expanding knowledge of the interrelationship between mind and body; the ultimate goal was to understand the function and form of the body in order to promote internal harmony and, thus, health."[3]

An academic and philosopher with a practical goal, Oliva Sabuco was influenced by "classical traditions in moral and natural philosophy, medicine, and cosmography … yet she 'synthesizes these traditions, disagrees with fundamental aspects of them, and carries them forward in a holistic philosophy of human nature that is part of a larger view of the cosmos and humans' place in it.'"[4]

First among modern philosophers to argue that the brain, not the heart, controls the body, her work also "anticipates the role of cerebrospinal fluid, the relationship between mental and physical health, and the absorption of nutrients through digestion."[5]

The interdisciplinary journal *Feminist Review* praised Sabuco's work as being "one of the pioneering volumes in psychosomatic medicine," also noting that, although Sabuco was one of the first philosophers to identify the mind-body connection, "because she was a woman in an era [when] males were the only ones with any real social value, her work was promptly dismissed."[6]

Sadly, the publication history of Sabuco's treatise backs up this widely held view. Initially, Sabuco's father, Miguel—a pharmacist—claimed that he had written her treatise.[7] It wasn't until the twentieth century that the treatise's authorship was debated again, and now it is once more accepted as Sabuco's work.[8]

Izumo no Okuni

IZUMO NO OKUNI
CA. 1572–CA. 1613, JAPANESE
ORIGINATOR OF KABUKI THEATER

*I*zumo no Okuni's unique creation became a classical Japanese dance-drama, but its unusual origins are reflected in the meaning of the word that is used to name it: *kabuki*. It is believed that kabuki theater originally derived its name from the "strange" and "unusual" actions of its early adopters.[1] Today, the art form of kabuki is now reflected in its individual characters (歌舞伎), which signify song (*ka*), dance (*bu*), and skill (*ki*).[2]

How did a young woman from humble beginnings come to create an innovative theatrical genre that would become one of Japan's defining cultural treasures?

The daughter of a blacksmith who worked near the Grand Shrine of Izumo, the oldest Shintō shrine in Japan, Okuni served at the temple as a *miko* or shrine maiden—one of many women who performed tasks ranging from cleaning to performing the sacred Kagura dance.[3] She allegedly gained a following during these ritual dances as temple congregants, as well as audiences in Kyoto, were drawn to her talent as a performer.[4]

In the early seventeenth century, Okuni organized a group of female dancers in Kyoto to perform dances and skits on a makeshift stage located near the Kamo River.[5] Unlike the more sedate and traditional Nō drama style,[6]

Okuni's productions were livelier, more provocative, and popular. For certain dances Okuni reportedly dressed as a man, and the troupe's sensual and uninhibited dance dramas quickly became famous throughout Japan, adopting the name *Okuni Kabuki*.[7]

Professor of East Asian languages and cultures, and director of the International Theatre Studies Center at the University of Kansas, Andrew T. Tsubaki, points to a specific scene in Okuni's productions that the average person would have found alluring. He implies that it was Okuni's skill in suffusing the dance-drama with emotional situations that resonated with her audiences and made her kabuki presentations so uniquely beloved:

> *The success of Okuni in establishing onna kabuki [women's kabuki] . . . was due to the creation of a dramatic scene in which a young man (played by a pretty woman) appears on his way to a teahouse; having arrived, he is entertained by odori [dancing] in a drinking party scene.*
>
> *[Okuni's kabuki performances exhibited] a softness and coquettishness that were completely foreign to the no. For eyes used to seeing a no performance, a kabuki*

presentation must have appeared thoroughly outside the norm.[8]

Employing themes based on everyday life and instilling the performances with emotional appeal and dramatic "coquettishness," Okuni was easily able to charm her audiences. The fact that ordinary people could relate to scenarios that were presented with such artistic excellence by Okuni's troupe of performers resulted in her kabuki productions gaining widespread notoriety and tremendous popularity.

However, in 1629, a decade or so after Okuni's death, women's participation in the performances were banned by the shogun (military ruler) Tokugawa Iemitsu. Iemitsu considered the provocative dances detrimental to the public's morality, especially considering that the performers were often also prostitutes.[9] Because of the ban on female kabuki performers, boys and young men began dressing as women to perform the female roles, although their participation was also banned by the shogun for moral reasons, resulting in older men dominating kabuki theater.[10]

Kabuki has gone through a number of creative transitions since the seventeenth century, but thanks to Izumo no Okuni, today kabuki is one of the most popular and iconic traditional Japanese drama styles; it has been recognized internationally as having lasting cultural significance. In 2005, the Kabuki theatre was proclaimed by the United Nations Educational, Scientific and Cultural Organization (UNESCO) as an intangible heritage possessing outstanding universal value, and in 2008 it was inscribed in the UNESCO Representative List of the Intangible Cultural Heritage of Humanity.[11]

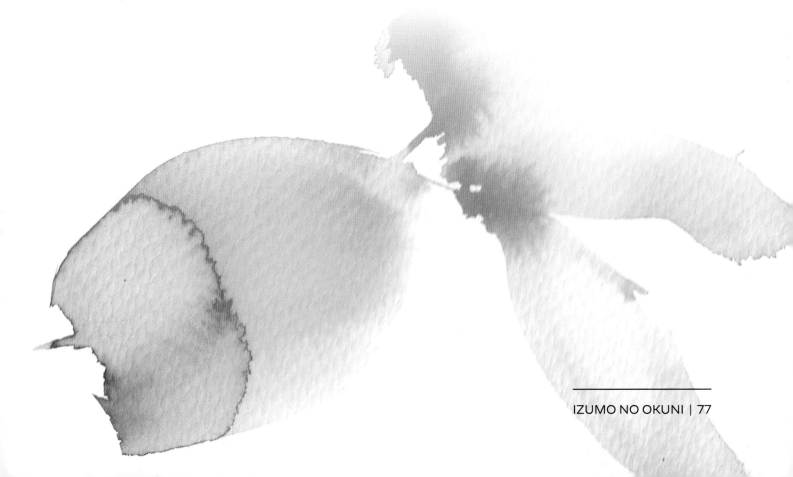

Michaelina Wautier

MICHAELINA WAUTIER

1604–1689, BELGIAN

BAROQUE PAINTER OF A DIVERSE
RANGE OF MASTERPIECES

*I*t took more than 350 years, but seventeenth-century Baroque artist Michaelina Wautier has received the attention and accolades she deserved. In 2018, the Museum aan de Stroom and the Rubens House in Antwerp, Belgium, mounted a groundbreaking exhibition, "Michaelina: Baroque's Leading Lady," heralding Wautier as "an artist who became popular in a period when female artists were very rare. Her work is so varied and unique that it defies all imagination when it comes to art history."[1]

Wautier was "popular" during her lifetime (in fact, she sold four paintings to Archduke Leopold Wilhelm of Austria),[2] but she was never accorded the admiration given to her male contemporaries whose talents she clearly matched. Not only was her work essentially ignored after her death, but for hundreds of years her paintings were misattributed to her brother Charles Wautier (1609–1703) or even to Italian Baroque painter Artemisia Gentileschi (1593–ca. 1652).[3]

Little is known about Wautier's life because, like with many historical women, it lacks documentation.[4] We know that she was born in Mons, Belgium, and moved to Brussels after 1640 with her younger brother, both remaining unmarried and living together in an upscale town house.[5]

While her biographical profile is scant, her paintings reveal her dazzling legacy. Distinguishing herself from other female artists of the day due to her diverse range of genres, Wautier painted intimate portraits, religious and mythological scenes, and large-format historical pieces, which were "a challenge that even many male painters resisted."[6] According to the Museum aan de Stroom:

> *Michaelina boasts a whole parade of masterpieces, ranging from impressive historical items to genre scenes, flower arrangements, and portraits, [her] absolute apotheosis is the monumental canvas known as the* Triumph of Bacchus … *In this large format work Michaelina showed no hesitation in revealing her knowledge of the male anatomy. Disguised as a half-naked possessed woman or 'bacchante': she also walks in this colourful parade of drunk accomplices and is the only one in the group to look spectators right in the eye.*[7]

Indeed, *The Triumph of Bacchus* masterfully reflects Wautier's familiarity with masculine anatomy and distinguishes her as one of the first female painters to paint a nude male.[8] Wautier's *The Triumph of Bacchus* is an extremely rare example of a woman painting an erotic scene, as for centuries female artists were discouraged and prevented from drawing nude models.[9] Therefore, while female nudes (painted by male artists) have long filled museums, those painted by women are much more difficult to find as "the erotic gaze of female artists was kept in check."[10]

Michaelina Wautier didn't keep her gaze in check, and we are grateful for that. Thankfully, recent exhibitions and scholarship are beginning to reflect her prolific career. Her achievements inspire contemporary women artists who are still forced to navigate a male-dominated art market.

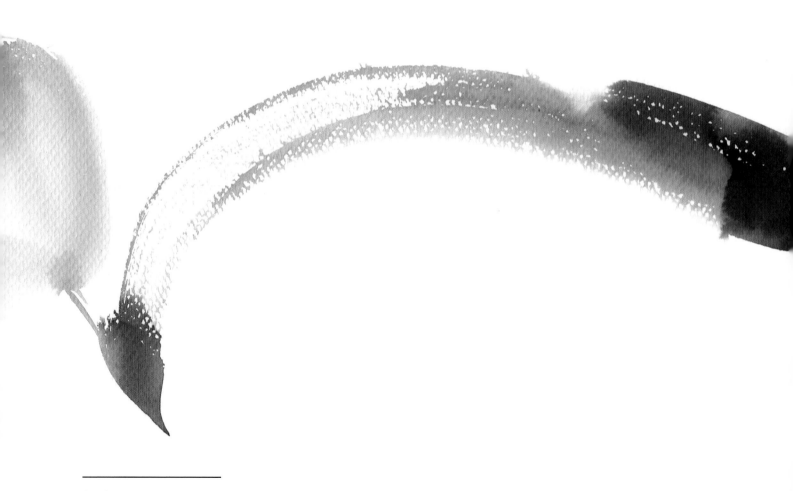

Barbara Strozzi

BARBARA STROZZI

1619–1677, ITALIAN

MOST PROLIFIC COMPOSER OF SECULAR VOCAL MUSIC IN MIDCENTURY VENICE

At a time when few women were afforded the opportunity to engage in a musical career, Barbara Strozzi, daughter of a household servant and a well-known poet,[1] became one of the most successful women composers of the seventeenth century. She was the most prolific composer—male or female—of printed secular vocal music in midcentury Venice.[2]

Strozzi's unlikely musical success didn't occur in a vacuum. Within the rich cultural environment of renaissance Venice, women from the more privileged classes often had the chance to pursue an intellectual or artistic path. And a number of them—along with Strozzi—achieved distinction, including:

- Moderata Fonte (1555–1592), author of *The Worth of Women*, published posthumously in 1600, which critiques the treatment of women and celebrates women's virtues and intelligence.[3]
- Lucrezia Marinella (1571–1653), poet, philosopher, and women's rights activist, best known as the author of the feminist treatise *The Nobility and Excellence of Women and the Defects and Vices of Men* (1600).[4]

- Arcangela Tarabotti (1604–1652), Benetictine nun and author, who wrote texts and conducted correspondence with political figures voicing her objections to patriarchy and misogyny.[5]
- Rosalba Carriera (1675–1757), celebrated artist who gained acceptance into Rome's Accademia di San Luca, popularized the use of pastels as a medium for serious portraiture and created portraits of prominent individuals, including the young Louis XV.[6]
- Gioseffa Cornoldi (birth and death dates unknown), publisher of the first Italian magazine specifically targeted for a female readership, *La donna galante ed erudita* (*The Elegant and Educated Woman*), initially published in 1786.[7]

Although Strozzi was born to servant Isabella Garzoni, she likely received ample encouragement and support from her mother's master and Barbara's father, poet Giulio Strozzi, who was well connected among cultural circles in Venice.[8] Even with that support, however, Barbara's achievements are particularly unusual in that her adopted father was not part of a musical family and her career existed outside of a court or a convent—the typical paths taken by European women of that era who had artistic or musical aspirations. In fact, over half of the female composers with music published before 1700 were nuns.[9] How did Strozzi, who was not affiliated with a convent, a court, or a musical family, gain entry and acceptance into the world of musical performance and composition?

Giulio Strozzi's connections were helpful. He saw to it that Barbara trained as a musician. She studied with singer and composer Francesco Cavalli, one of the most influential composers of opera in mid-seventeenth-century Venice. Secondly, Giulio belonged to a group of Venetian intellectuals, known as the Accademia degli Incogniti ("Academy of the Unknowns"), who met to discuss philosophy, religion, literature, music, and the arts. In 1637, he organized an offshoot of that group, referred to as the Accademia degli Unisoni ("Academy of the Like-Minded")—a musical salon over which Barbara, still a teenager, presided.[10] She not only performed arias and cantatas at these gatherings, she also proposed topics for the group's lively discussions.[11]

Barbara Strozzi's notoriety as a performer and salon hostess led to the accusation that she was a courtesan, a common assumption regarding female performers and musicians at the time.[12] But her reputation as a gifted composer was not diminished in the eyes of her admirers, and she clearly had an impact beyond her own musical career. In 1644 she published her first volume of madrigals. Eight more collections of her music—consisting of arias, cantatas, and ariettas—were published over the following twenty years.[13] Her works were dedicated to various royal or noble patrons, including the Grand Duchess of Tuscany, Ferdinand II of Austria, Eleanora of Mantua, and Nicolò Sagredo, a future doge of Venice.[14] Despite her prestigious patrons, however, Strozzi enjoyed little financial security, which may have been a motivating factor in the self-publication of her many compositions.[15]

Given her unprecedented level of achievement, Barbara Strozzi became a role model, along with certain other female singer-composers in seventeenth-century Italy, most notably Francesca Caccini (1587–after 1641), one of the highest paid performers at the Medici court in Florence.[16] Trailblazing female musicians such as Strozzi paved the way for other young women who sought a professional life in the musical arts. By 1700, twenty-three Italian female composers succeeded in having their music published.[17]

Beatriz Kimpa Vita

BEATRIZ KIMPA VITA

CA. 1684–1706, KONGOLESE

LEADER OF A MOVEMENT TO PRESERVE THE KONGOLESE KINGDOM AND RECOGNIZE THE HOLY FAMILY'S AFRICAN ORIGINS

When she was barely twenty years old, Beatriz Kimpa Vita instigated a political and religious movement advocating not only preservation of the Kongolese Kingdom but belief in the Holy Family's African origins. Her unusual inspiration for these convictions was the Catholic saint—Anthony.

Born around 1684 in the kingdom of Kongo, "the wealthiest and most powerful state in the Atlantic region of Central Africa during the fifteenth and sixteenth centuries,"[1] Beatriz Kimpa Vita came from a noble Kongolese background. Like all Kongolese, who were proud of their long-standing Catholic faith, she was baptized "as soon as a priest passed her town ... Christianity set true Kongolese aside from their neighbors, and in their view made them superior to the 'heathens,' even those to the north and east who spoke dialects of the same Kikongo language."[2]

The kingdom of Kongo experienced political upheaval for some time prior to Kimpa Vita's birth: "Portuguese military aggression emanating from the Angola colony to the south spurred the kingdom's disintegra-

tion, notably at the battle of Mbwila in 1665 at which Portuguese troops killed the Kongo ruler Antonio I. By the turn of the eighteenth century ... the kingdom had broken up into small territories ruled by warlords and members of the old Kongo nobility. Memories of Kongo's past glory remained, however, and a series of popular movements developed out of the Kongo people's desire to restore the kingdom to its former greatness."[3] Kimpa Vita's political perspective and inclinations were deeply rooted in this history.

Trained as a nganga marinda, an intermediary between the supernatural world and the community,[4] Kimpa Vita was a healer who developed the ability to communicate with spiritual forces. The event that would transform her into a revered spiritual and political advocate occurred in 1704 as she lay deathly ill: "For seven days she had been sick ... Then, suddenly, she became calm, and a clear vision appeared to her. It was a man dressed in the simple blue hooded habit of a Capuchin monk, so real that he seemed to be standing in the room with her. She turned to him transfixed."[5] He told her that he was sent from God to tell her that she should preach to her people, "to move the restoration of the Kingdom of Kongo forward."[6] With the words of this hooded monk, Kimpa Vita "felt herself recover ... full of resolve to complete the mission. Beatriz had been possessed by Saint Anthony."[7]

Her alleged visitation from Saint Anthony, as well as her recovery from near death, spurred Kimpa Vita on to organize for the cause of reunification of the Kingdom and to spread her newly realized religious beliefs. According to scholar Kathleen Sheldon, Kimpa Vita popularized a cult surrounding her inspiration, Saint Anthony, asserting that she had died only to be revived and possessed by the saint.[8] Under this guide she called for "reconciliation and restoration" of the kingdom of Kongo.[9] While her message of peace attracted a loyal following of "Antonians," she also incited frustration in the local Catholic leadership for her acceptance of black saints and assertion that Jesus Christ was Kongolese.

Inspired by her visitation from Saint Anthony, Kimpa Vita's radical new belief system went further, garnering fervent adherents and angry adversaries:

> Dona Beatriz also disclosed new versions of the Ave Maria and Salve Regina that were more relevant to Kongolese modes of thought. Although the movement

recognized papal authority, it was hostile to European missionaries, whom it considered corrupt and unsympathetic to the spiritual needs of Kongolese Catholics. Dona Beatriz and her followers briefly occupied Mbanza Kongo, from which she sent emissaries to spread her teachings and urge rulers of the divided Kongo territories to unite under one king. In 1706, however, she was captured by King Pedro II and burned as a heretic at the behest of Capuchin monks.[10]

Although her impassioned advocacy resulted in a violent death, Beatriz Kimpa Vita left behind a powerful legacy, as scholars continue to assess the cultural impact of her visionary religious beliefs:

> Her movement continued only until 1709, when her followers were decisively defeated by Portuguese King Pedro IV's army. Her vision and leadership, though short-lived, introduced intriguing ideas about African adaptations of Christian ideas to their own communities. As a woman she moved beyond the boundaries set by both the Kongolese society of her birth and by the increasingly influential European Catholic settlers.[11]

Eva Ekeblad

EVA EKEBLAD

1724–1786, SWEDISH

SCIENTIST WHO DISCOVERED A METHOD FOR MAKING FLOUR AND ALCOHOL FROM POTATOES

*I*n mid-eighteenth-century Sweden, potatoes were viewed as a luxury, grown in the greenhouses of the upper class. Even in that context, potatoes were considered food for animals, not humans.[1] But thanks to the scientific experimentation of a noblewoman who oversaw the management of her family's land, the humble potato would be transformed.

In 1746, when Eva Ekeblad was twenty-two years old, she used her kitchen as a laboratory and "deduced that the [potato] could be cooked, crushed and dried to make flour and therefore distilled to make clear spirits—a discovery that soon sparked a craze for potato-based vodka."[2] Ekeblad's discovery had far-reaching consequences for the Swedish population. By using potatoes to make alcohol rather than wheat, rye, and barley, the country's supply of those grains was more readily available for making bread—reducing the frequency of famines.[3] Eva's discovery had the clear benefit of famine reduction, relieving a terrible strain on the rural poor by turning the potato into one of Sweden's staple foods. However, the country then experienced a sharp increase in alcohol consumption.[4]

Potato-based alcohol, however, was not Ekeblad's only scientific contribution. Ahead of her time regarding the awareness of chemical toxicity, she "discovered a means of using soap to bleach cotton, yarn and other textiles in place of toxic dyes and later deployed her knowledge of potato flour to advocate its use in place of lead in cosmetics, a bid to reduce the latter compound's harmful impact on the skin."[5] She also found a replacement for the "dangerous chemicals used in wigs in the form of potato flour" and "advertised the potato plant by using its flowers to adorn her wigs."[6]

Eva Ekeblad was acknowledged by her peers during her lifetime, but in a limited and sexist manner. In 1748, at the age of twenty-four, she became the first woman scientist elected to the Royal Swedish Academy of Sciences. But in 1751, "the Academy referred to her as an honorary member because full membership was reserved for men."[7] It wasn't until nearly two centuries later that another woman, the Austrian nuclear physicist Lise Meitner, would receive full membership to the Academy.

Considering her groundbreaking scientific accomplishments, Ekeblad would likely be proud of the progress being made by women throughout the world in agricultural studies and careers. As an example of the increasing numbers of women earning degrees in agricultural fields: between 2004 and 2012 in the United States, there was a 98 percent increase in women earning bachelor's degrees in food science and technology fields, and a 49 percent increase in women earning bachelor's degrees in agricultural mechanization and engineering.[8]

On an international level, professor Robyn Alders of the University of Sydney offers the following insight in addressing the "essential role women play in feeding the world":

It's vital that we remember the role of women in global agriculture . . . Agriculture is the single largest employer in the world, providing livelihoods for 40 percent of today's global population . . . On average women make up 43 percent of the agricultural labour force in low-income countries, and over 50 percent in parts of Asia and Africa, yet they only own 20 percent of the land.[9]

Eva Ekeblad was fortunate enough to be a landowner, yet her agricultural discovery some 273 years ago had a beneficial impact on the rural poor of her country. Her innovative achievements serve as a unique inspiration to women entering the agricultural industries today.

Elizabeth Freeman

ELIZABETH FREEMAN

CA. 1742–1829, AMERICAN

SUCCESSFULLY FILED A LAWSUIT TO WIN HER FREEDOM

Born to enslaved African parents in Claverack, New York, around 1742, and after enduring enslavement herself for nearly forty years, Elizabeth Freeman initiated the first legal test of the constitutionality of slavery in Massachusetts.[1]

When she was six months old, Freeman and her sister were purchased by John Ashley of Sheffield, Massachusetts. Freeman would serve him until she was almost forty.[2] Freeman, who also used the nickname Mum Bett, was married and had a daughter; her husband, whose name is unknown, was killed fighting in the American Revolutionary War.[3]

How did Elizabeth Freeman conceive of the notion to file suit against her owner at a time when freedom for the enslaved population of the United States by means of the Emancipation Proclamation was still eighty-two years away?

Having been victimized her entire life by the injustice, horror, and cruelties of slavery, Freeman reached her tipping point when her sister was nearly struck by their mistress with a heated kitchen shovel. Freeman intercepted the blow—sparing her sister—and fled the house. Refusing to return to slavery, she turned to Theodore Sedgwick, a lawyer noted for his anti-slavery leanings,

and asked for his assistance in suing for her freedom.[4] Informing her decision to take Ashley to court and sue for her freedom was the fact that Freeman had recently attended a public gathering in Sheffield, Massachusetts, at which the newly ratified Massachusetts Constitution was read.[5] The reading included the Constitution's Bill of Rights, which states:

> *All men are born free and equal, and have certain natural, essential, and unalienable rights; among which may be reckoned the right of enjoying and defending their lives and liberties; that of acquiring, possessing, and protecting property; in fine, that of seeking and obtaining their safety and happiness.*
>
> —Massachusetts Constitution, Article I[6]

According to Catherine Sedgwick, daughter of Theodore Sedgwick, Freeman told the lawyer, "I heard that paper read yesterday that all men are created equal and that every man has a right to freedom. I'm not a dumb critter. Won't the law give me my freedom?"[7]

Sedgwick argued Freeman's case, which also included the case of a man named Brom, another of Ashley's slaves, before a county court. The jury ruled in favor of the plaintiffs, making the pair the first slaves to be freed under the 1780 Massachusetts Constitution.[8] This ruling not only set a precedent for future similar cases, such as the Quock Walker case,[9] but eventually resulted in the abolition of slavery in Massachusetts.[10]

After the court ruling, Elizabeth Freeman went to work for the Sedgwick family as their housekeeper, and later found outside employment as a popular midwife and nurse.[11] She died a free woman in 1829.

In their book, *Love of Freedom: Black Women in Colonial and Revolutionary New England*, the first study of black women in Colonial and Revolutionary New England, authors Catherine Adams and Elizabeth H. Pleck explain the significance of Elizabeth Freeman's story:

> *Like so many other women, she had a many-stranded definition of liberty, which included her belief in the ideals of the Declaration of Independence as well as in the opportunity to buy land, reunite her family, and live a Christian life. In freedom she found ways to express and combine multiple identities (racial, religious, familial, and occupational). No newspaper mentioned her suit at the time, but subsequently her neighbors and employers remembered her for her sterling character; other than [the poet Phillis] Wheatley, Elizabeth Freeman is the most famous black woman Patriot of the revolutionary era. For abolitionists her personal story of courage and extraordinary personal qualities undermined the argument that black people were intellectually inferior to whites and proved that blacks, just like whites, achieved their greatest potential from a life of freedom. The local people who recounted her life were important writers and abolitionists who supplied the words to prove that she believed in the abstract principle of inalienable rights of the individual.[12]*

Elizabeth Freeman's profound courage, wisdom, and belief in her "inalienable rights" continue to inspire women and men of the twenty-first century, including poet Gale Jackson, whose poem "elizabeth freeman's will" is a tribute to Freeman's strong character and determination:

elizabeth freeman's will
1742–1829

to my own daughter I leave a work apron
three pairs of cotton stockings
three sheets
three pillows of white
one handsome tablecloth
three quilts
a large woolen knit shawl
a short gown of africa that my mother has worn
my african father's long gown
the bill of rights I heard waiting table
and the god given right to dream of anything.[13]

Olympe
de Gouges

OLYMPE DE GOUGES
1748–1793, FRENCH
FEMINIST PLAYWRIGHT AND SOCIAL REFORMER

*I*t wasn't until 1944 that the French government allowed women the right to vote. But more than 150 years prior to that, a French woman was ardently advocating for women's rights. And she paid dearly for her advocacy.

Born Marie Gouze in southwestern France to working-class parents Anne Olympe Mouisset Gouze, a maidservant, and Pierre Gouze, a butcher, Olympe de Gouges wrote one of the defining manifestos championing equal rights for women: *The Declaration of the Rights of Woman and the Female Citizen* (1791).[1] But her humanistic ideology went beyond women's rights, as "her profound humanism led her to strongly oppose discrimination, violence and oppression in all its forms," including the slave trade in the French colonies.[2]

But before she began her illustrious career as a woman's advocate and playwright, Marie Gouze was an unhappily married woman at the age of sixteen, married off against her will.[3] In her semi-autographical novel, *Mémoire de Madame de Valmont contre la famille de Flaucourt*, she wrote, "I was married to a man I did not love, and who was neither rich nor well born. I was sacrificed without any justification that could outweigh the repugnance I felt for this man."[4] Her husband died shortly after they were

married, and in her early twenties Gouze moved to Paris, adopting her mother's middle name, Olympe, and exchanging her married name for the aristocratic-sounding "de Gouges."[5]

Once in Paris, with the support of Jacques Biétrix de Roziéres, a wealthy weapons merchant, de Gouges began educating herself on intellectual and political subjects and engaging with Parisian society.[6] She began writing novels and plays and, as psychology professor Joan Woolfrey explains, the focus of her literary work was reflective of her political and humanistic ideology. Unlike other female playwrights at the time, she was not only outspoken but did not resort to anonymity or to the use of a pseudonym:

> All of her plays and novels carry the theme of her life's work: indignation at injustice . . . While many of the plays by the dozen women playwrights that had been staged at the Comédie Française were published anonymously or under male pseudonyms, those playwrights who were successful on stage in their own names stuck to themes seen as suitable to their gender. Gouges broke with this tradition—publishing under her own name and pushing the boundaries of what

was deemed appropriate subject matter for women playwrights . . . Reviews of her early productions were mixed—some fairly favorable, others patronizing and condescending or skeptical of her authorship . . . Her later plays, more strongly political and controversial, were met with outright sarcasm and hostility by some reviewers: '[t]o write a good play, one needs a beard' wrote one critic.[7]

De Gouges was fearless in her dramatic portrayal of serious issues, including the inhumanity of slavery (her play *L'Esclavage de Nègres, ou l'Heureux naufrage/Black Slavery, or The Happy Shipwreck* was the first to feature a first-person perspective of the slave); divorce; the ability of priests and nuns to marry; girls sent to convents by force; the shameful practice of imprisonment for debt; and the double standard between sexes.[8]

The publication for which de Gouges is most well-known, *The Declaration of the Rights of Woman and the Female Citizen*, was written in 1791. It was a response to *The Declaration of the Rights of Man and of the Citizen*, a piece originally written in 1789 that later became the preamble to the French Constitution in September 1971.[9] Although women had hoped that the French Revolution would entitle them, as well as men, to enhanced human rights, the Constitution was, in fact "the death knell for any hopes of inclusion of women's rights under the 'Rights of Man.' . . . Forceful and sarcastic in tone and militant in spirit, [*The Declaration of the Rights of Woman*] takes up each of the seventeen Articles of the Preamble to the French Constitution . . . and highlights the glaring omission of the female citizen within each article."[10]

In this landmark document, as well as most of her literary and political writing, de Gouges "critiqued the principle of equality touted in France because it gave no attention to whom it left out, and she worked to claim the rightful place of women and slaves within its protection."[11]

Olympe de Gouges's lifetime of boldly advocating for women and other marginalized groups ultimately led to her violent death. In November 1793, just two years after the publication of the *Declaration of the Rights of Woman*, she was tried for and found guilty of treason, and was subsequently put to death by guillotine.[12] Because of her open and unreserved opinions on democracy, she was the only woman executed for sedition during France's bloody Reign of Terror (1793–1794).[13]

De Gouges saw injustice in society, and she wasn't afraid to criticize her country's participation in this injustice. Her bravery and candor ultimately cost her her life, but her words serve as a call to action even today, inspiring us to fight against inequality. De Gouges' voice is especially poignant in this excerpt from *The Declaration of the Rights of Woman* (translated from the French):

> *Man, are you capable of being just? It is a woman who poses the question; you will not deprive her of that right at least. Tell me, what gives you sovereign empire to oppress my sex? Your strength? Your talents? Observe the Creator in his wisdom; survey in all her grandeur that nature with whom you seem to want to be in harmony, and give me, if you dare, an example of this tyrannical empire. Go back to animals, consult the elements, study plants, finally glance at all the modifications of organic matter, and surrender to the*

evidence when I offer you the means; search, probe, and distinguish, if you can, the sexes in the administration of nature. Everywhere you will find them mingled; everywhere they cooperate in harmonious togetherness in this immortal masterpiece.[14]

Wang
Zhenyi

WANG ZHENYI
1768–1797, CHINESE
ASTRONOMER AND MATHEMATICIAN, EXPLICATED LUNAR AND SOLAR ECLIPSES

According to NASA historians, the ancient Chinese believed that "solar eclipses occur when a celestial dragon devours the sun" and that the same dragon attacks the moon during lunar eclipses.[1] In fact, the term for eclipse in ancient China was *shi*, which also means "to eat."[2] It was thought that banging loudly on drums during an eclipse would frighten the dragon away and prevent the sun or moon from being devoured.[3] In one reported event, "The Chinese Imperial Emperor Chung K'ang (2159–2146 BCE) learned of an eclipse when he heard much noise in the streets as his subjects tried to drive away the dragon that was eating the sun."[4]

Hundreds of centuries later, a young woman named Wang Zhenyi set the record straight by providing a mathematical, scientific explanation for solar and lunar eclipses. By applying hard mathematics to her work in astronomy, and by demonstrating the eclipse process in an accessible yet scientifically valid manner, Zhenyi set herself apart from her contemporaries.[5] As professor Barbara Bennett Peterson describes in her book *Notable Women of China*, Zhenyi was able to accurately describe a lunar eclipse through an experimental method:

She placed a round table in a garden pavilion, using it as a globe; from the ceiling beam she hung a crystal lamp on a cord, using it as the sun. On one side of the table she put a big round mirror as the moon and then she moved the three objects as if the sun, earth, and moon were moving according to astronomical principles. She could see how the lunar eclipse occurred by observing the relationship of the shining lamp with the reflecting mirror. Her article 'The Explanation of the Lunar Eclipse' was highly accurate.[6]

Born into a learned family, Wang Zhenyi's passion for mathematics and astronomy was nurtured early on by both her father and her grandfather. While still a teenager, she made friends with other female scholars and "began focusing on her studies in astronomy and mathematics, most of which were self-taught."[7] Being primarily self-educated, Wang Zhenyi understood the need to explain complex ideas and theories in a way that would be understandable to the average person, which explains why she was not only a scientist but also an educator.[8] She wrote texts specifically for beginners, revised the work of other scientists in order to make it more accessible, and "simplified a few dozen mathematical proofs in the process."[9] In addition to rewriting the famous mathematician Mei Wending's (1633–1721) *Principles of Calculation* into simpler language (retitling it as *The Musts of Calculation*), at the age of twenty-four Wang Zhenyi wrote a book entitled *The Simple Principles of Calculation.*[10]

Her other highly regarded publications include an article entitled "Dispute of the Procession of the Equinoxes," in which she explained and proved how equinoxes move and how to calculate their movement; "Dispute of Longitude and Stars"; "The Explanation of a Lunar Eclipse"; and "The Explanation of the Pythagorean Theorem and Trigonometry."[11]

A masterful scientist, mathematician, *and* educator? Yes. And also a poet. *And* an advocate for women's rights at a time in China—and elsewhere throughout the globe—when equality for women was not the cultural norm. Wang Zhenyi died at the age of twenty-nine. The following is an excerpt from one of her poems, reflecting the accomplishments of her own short life as well as her hopes for the lives of all women:

> *It's made to believe,*
> *Women are the same as Men;*
> *Are you not convinced,*
> *Daughters can also be heroic?*[12]

Marie-Sophie Germain

MARIE-SOPHIE GERMAIN

1776–1831, FRENCH

MATHEMATICIAN WHOSE WORK IN APPLIED MATHEMATICS WAS CRUCIAL TO THE BUILDING OF SKYSCRAPERS

Marie-Sophie Germain, commonly known as Sophie Germain, was so passionate about mathematics and so excited by the research taking place at the École Polytechnique in Paris that, despite the fact that women were typically not accepted in universities in eighteenth-century France, she borrowed lecture notes and corresponded with professors using a male pseudonym.[1]

Born into a wealthy family—her father was a silk merchant, politician, and director of the Bank of France—the young Germain was intellectually curious and took advantage of her father's extensive library, teaching herself mathematics as well as Latin and Greek so that she could read the classical mathematics texts.[2] With this self-taught educational foundation, Germain set her sights on the École Polytechnique, which opened in 1794, when she was eighteen.[3]

Using the pseudonym "M. Le Blanc" (the name of former student Monsieur Antoine-August Le Blanc), Germain corresponded with a number of mathematicians affiliated with the revered institution that she was unable to attend.[4] Among them were Joseph-Louis Lagrange and Carl Friedrich Gauss, both of whom were impressed with her insights and observations.[5] Noting the unique intelligence of M. Le Blanc, Lagrange requested a meeting with "him" and discovered that he was a she, and defied societal conventions to become the young woman's mentor.[6]

As for Carl Friedrich Gauss, with whom M. Le Blanc had corresponded regarding number theory, when he found out that his exceptional student was female, he responded:

> How can I describe my astonishment and admiration on seeing my esteemed correspondent M. LeBlanc metamorphosed into this celebrated person . . . when a woman, because of her sex, our customs and prejudices, encounters infinitely more obstacles than men in familiarising herself with [number theory's] knotty problems, yet overcomes these fetters and penetrates that which is most hidden, she doubtless has the most noble courage, extraordinary talent, and superior genius.[7]

Germain's fundamental mathematical pursuit was number theory, and her most significant contribution to the field dealt with Fermat's Last Theorem, on which she worked for many years.[8] Unfortunately, due to her gender and, thus, her lack of formal education, her remarkable theorem is known only because of a footnote in Adrien-Marie Legendre's treatise on number theory.[9]

Unconfined to one particular intellectual endeavor, Germain also became interested in the patterns produced by vibration, known as Chladni figures, submitting an essay to the Academy of Sciences [French Académie de Sciences] on these vibrations of elastic surfaces.[10] Germain's was the only such paper submitted, since the one other potential contestant was Denis Poisson (1781–1840), who was elected to the Academy and so became a judge instead of a contestant. Although the judges found errors in her work as it was first submitted, Germain continued to pursue the project, this time consulting with Poisson.[11] After twice resubmitting her work, she was finally awarded the prize in 1815, making Germain the Academy's first female prizewinner.[12]

Despite such an admirable achievement and her indisputable intellectual gifts, Germain was unable to fully pursue her mathematical interests. Not only was she, as a woman, barred from systematic education, but her gender also kept her from fully participating in the Academy, preventing her from attending its sessions and engaging directly in its discussions and interchange of current research.[13]

Sophie Germain's life was a testament not only to her brilliant mind but also to her ardent perseverance in the face of gender prejudice and discrimination. Despite facing numerous sexist obstacles, Germain dedicated herself to work that was "foundational to the applied mathematics used in construction of skyscrapers today, and was important at the time to the new field of mathematical physics, especially to the study of acoustics and elasticity."[14]

In 2003, the Sophie Germain Prize (Prix Sophie Germain) was initiated to honor a French mathematician for research in the foundations of mathematics. It is awarded annually by the Foundation Sophie Germain and is conferred by the French Academy of Sciences in Paris.

Jeanne Villepreux-Power

JEANNE VILLEPREUX-POWER
1794–1871, FRENCH
MARINE BIOLOGIST, INVENTOR OF THE AQUARIUM

Jeanne Villepreux-Power's unusual life journey took her from southern France to Paris to Sicily, reflecting her unlikely transformation from daughter of a village shoemaker, to elite dressmaker, to pioneering biologist and inventor.

Growing up in the small town of Juillac, Villepreux-Power learned to read and write, but had no formal education beyond that. At the age of eighteen, she made her way to Paris to find employment, making the trip by foot—over 400 kilometers (250 miles). Landing a job as a dressmaker, she gained notoriety for designing the wedding gown for the Bourbon princess, Caroline. Through her connections to such illustrious clientele, Villepreux-Power met her husband, James Power, a rich English merchant who was living in Messina, Sicily. From 1818 until 1843, the couple resided on the island of Sicily, where Villepreux-Power discovered her passion for the natural world and undertook a lifelong career as a marine biologist.[1]

That career began as the self-taught Villepreux-Power explored Sicily, recording and describing the region's flora and fauna.[2] She was particularly drawn to aquatic creatures, and looked for methods to study them more closely.[3] In the course of her research into the pelagic octopus or Argonauta argo, a type of mollusk, she was the first to discover how the animal reproduces and how it creates a shell casing around itself.[4] Her quest to understand this and other fascinating aquatic creatures led to "her greatest breakthrough: the invention of the aquarium."[5]

In order to observe live aquatic animals underwater, she created three different types of aquarium: a glass one of the type that we might recognise today, for use in her study; another made of glass, but surrounded by a cage, to submerge in the sea for studying small molluscs; and a third, a kind of cage for larger molluscs, which could be anchored at a chosen depth in the sea.[6]

Claude Arnal, of the Malacological[7] Society of London, in his essay "Jeanne Villepreux-Power: A Pioneering Experimental Malacologist," elaborates on Villepreux-Power's significant and fascinating scientific findings:

Jeanne, however, was not content with purely descriptive studies of dead specimens; she was excited by life and its mysteries. Living on the edge of the Mediterranean, she had everything at her disposal to undertake a study of aquatic life. In order to make good observations, she designed three different types of aquaria—one for use in a study, others anchored to the sea bed.

Between 1832 and 1843, Jeanne carried out experimental observations on the paper nautilus, Argonauta argo, tackling mysteries which had lain unresolved since the writings of Aristotle and Pliny the Elder. At the time there was dispute over whether the 'shell' was produced by the paper nautilus or was 'acquired,' like that of a hermit crab, and the creature was still said to use the membranes of the two un-suckered arms as sails, assisting motion by rowing with the six remaining arms. She showed that the young, lodged in the papery 'shell' of the mother develop their 'shells' as larvae, and that broken 'shells' would be rapidly repaired by a substance secreted from the membranes ('sails') of the un-suckered tentacles. She also reasoned that a minute organism resembling the small suckered arm of an octopus, found with the egg mass in the shell, was probably the male Argonauta: an hypothesis which was later confirmed.[8]

Arnal also pointed out Villepreux-Power's forward-thinking, practical contribution to aquaculture:

> *Jeanne also laid the foundations of aquaculture in Sicily. She suggested that the rivers might be re-populated with fish by feeding young caged fish until they were a suitable size for re-introduction to other, depopulated rivers.*[9]

Villepreux-Power is an excellent example of an early female scientist persevering in a male-dominated field. However, even today, women's participation in the discipline of marine science is rare. The Intergovernmental Oceanographic Commission of UNESCO (IOC-UNESCO) states that although the number of women involved in scientific careers has significantly increased in recent years, women are still underrepresented, particularly in marine science and ocean research.[10] IOC-UNESCO hopes that their Initiative for Women Marine Scientists will "encourage young women to pursue careers in science and in particular, science related to the ocean."[11]

Shanawdithit

SHANAWDITHIT

CA. 1801–1829, BEOTHUK (INDIGENOUS CANADIAN)

HER DRAWINGS DOCUMENT LITTLE-KNOWN BEOTHUK HISTORY AND CULTURE

The story of Shanawdithit is one of invaluable education and irreparable tragedy. A member of the Beothuk people, indigenous to Newfoundland, Canada, Shanawdithit documented her culture's language, customs, and even territories in interviews and sketches.[1] The last of her people, her death in 1829 signified the death of the Beothuk.[2]

Formal recognition of Shanawdithit's unique contribution to her country and her people came 171 years after her death. In 2000, she was recognized by the Historic Sites and Monuments Board of Canada as a national historic person,[3] and a statue of her, entitled *The Spirit of the Beothuk,* was erected at the Beothuk Provincial Historic Site near Boyd's Cove, a small rural town in Newfoundland where the Beothuk settlement was located.[4] In 2007, Shanawdithit was further honored with a monument in Bannerman Park in St. Johns, Newfoundland recognizing her importance to Canadian history.[5] In a ceremony led by aboriginal leaders at the monument's dedication, she was celebrated not only as a "representative of Newfoundland's aboriginal population, but also as a woman who by virtue of her personality left a lasting impression on the people around her."[6]

Indigenous people, and especially indigenous women, across the world and time have always been kept in the shadows of well-documented history. Thus, it is not surprising that it took so long for Shanawdithit's story to be acknowledged by the general public. In fact, had it not been for her artistic legacy, little would be known about the authentic history and culture of the Beothuk people, the original inhabitants of Newfoundland.

Europeans first arrived in Newfoundland long before Shanawdithit was born. After Europeans settled in the Newfoundland area in the 1500s, contact between settlers and the indigenous Beothuk was tense, and while they were initially cautious trading partners, the expanding European presence resulted in increasing hostility.[7] Beothuk and Europeans alike were killed in skirmishes, although evidence shows that Beothuk victims far outnumbered the European casualties.[8] Shanawdithit witnessed such horrors firsthand. In March 1819, she watched as her uncle, Chief Nonosbawsut, was murdered and her aunt Demasduit captured, only to be returned to her people in a coffin.[9] While descriptions of this gruesome attack vary, one account asserts that the husband was killed while attempting to rescue his wife, and his murderer stating, "it was only an Indian, and he wished he had shot a hundred instead of one."[10]

According to the Aboriginal Multi-Media Society of Alberta, "Between 1768 and 1823, the colonists took captive a number of Beothuk. The idea was to befriend them, win them over, and then send them back to their people to make a case for developing a peaceful relationship with the settlers. These attempts to build bridges between the two peoples, of course, failed. The European captors killed any Beothuk that got in the way of the kidnappings, and none of the captives was ever returned to his or her people."[11] The Beothuk population, estimated at about 300 in the mid-eighteenth century, quickly depleted, reaching less than one hundred members by 1811.[12]

In April 1823, English furriers captured Shanawdithit, her sister, and her mother—all of whom were in a state of starvation.[13] Only Shanawdithit, then approximately just twenty-three years old, survived.[14] She was taken in by the family of John Peyton Jr., and under the English name Nancy April served their household for five years.[15]

It was during her captivity, after losing her entire family and enduring a traumatic struggle for survival, that she contributed to the history of her people. In 1828, Shanawdithit was taken to the home of William Epps Cormack (1796–1868), a Scottish-Canadian explorer, philanthropist, author, and president of the Beothuk Institution.[16] It was Cormack who would study Shanawdithit to learn firsthand the culture and practices of the Beothuk—Shanawdithit drew sketches and diagrams illustrating her people's lifestyle as well as the horrific attacks and murders she witnessed.[17] She also provided integral information about her people's language, contributing to a list of Beothuk words that was previously added to by her late aunt Desmasduit while in captivity.[18]

Suffering from tuberculosis, Shanawdithit died on June 6, 1829, and with her death, the Beothuk people were officially declared extinct.[19] With her drawings depicting Beothuk life, Shanawdithit contributed vital information about her Beothuk culture to white society's previously inadequate knowledge of her people, an indigenous population eradicated as a result of European settlement. Today, Shanawdithit is honored as an indispensable historic voice in the preservation of her culture.

Maria Mitchell

MARIA MITCHELL
1818–1889, AMERICAN
FIRST AMERICAN WOMAN TO WORK AS A PROFESSIONAL ASTRONOMER AND FIRST WOMAN TO BE ELECTED TO THE AMERICAN ACADEMY OF ARTS AND SCIENCES

The third of ten children, Maria Mitchell was born on the Massachusetts island of Nantucket. As Quakers, her parents advocated equal education for girls, and her father—a schoolteacher, bank officer, and amateur astronomer—was instrumental in encouraging all of his children to take an interest in mathematics and astronomy, although it was Maria who was especially keen to learn from him.[1]

Throughout her early life, Mitchell engaged in astronomical observations with her father, and when she was twelve helped him "calculate the position of their home by observing a solar eclipse."[2] By the age of fourteen, "sailors trusted her to do vital navigational computations for their long whaling journeys."[3]

Mitchell essentially became an apprentice astronomer, continually learning from her father as they "'swept' the clear Nantucket night sky with the telescope in her rooftop observatory."[4] And it was on that very rooftop—above the Pacific National Bank on Nantucket's Main Street, where her father worked—that Mitchell made a name for herself.[5] According to the account published by the American Physical Society:

On the evening of October 1, 1847, Mitchell . . . went to the roof to begin her observations. She noticed a small blurry streak, invisible to the naked eye, but clear in the telescope, and she guessed at once that it might be a comet. Excited, she ran to tell her father. He wanted to announce the discovery right away, but she was more cautious. She recorded the object's position, and continued to observe it to be sure it was a comet.[6]

The comet that Mitchell discovered was later nicknamed "Miss Mitchell's Comet," formally known as C/1847 T1.[7] After publishing a notice of her discovery in *Silliman's Journal* (now known as *The American Journal of Science*) in 1848 and submitting her calculation of the comet's orbit, Mitchell was celebrated at the Seneca Falls Convention, the famous women's rights gathering in New York, for her discovery and calculation. She even received an award honoring her discovery by King Frederick VI of Denmark, bringing her international notoriety as America's first female professional astronomer.[8] However, her newfound fame was unwanted. At the time, Mitchell was working as the librarian at the Nantucket

Athenaeum, and she reportedly found the attention "irritating" because it made it difficult for her to work.[9]

Nonetheless, her reputation grew. Within a few years after her discovery, Mitchell became "one of America's first professional astronomers; as 'computer of Venus'—a sort of human calculator for the U.S. Navy's *The Nautical Almanac,* she calculated the planet's changing position."[10] In 1848 she became the first woman elected fellow of the American Academy of Arts and Sciences.[11] In 1850 she became a fellow of the American Association for the Advancement of Science.[12]

Maria Mitchell's exemplary accomplishments in the field of astronomy led to her being invited to join the founding faculty at Vassar College in 1865, where she was also named director of the Vassar College Observatory.[13] There "she had access to a twelve-inch telescope, the third largest in the United States, and began to spe-

cialize in the surfaces of Jupiter and Saturn. She defied social conventions by having her female students come out at night for class work and celestial observations, and she brought noted feminists to her observatory to speak on political issues, among them [poet and author] Julia Ward Howe. Mitchell's research and that of her students were frequently published in academic journals that traditionally only featured men."[14]

Maria Mitchell spent her later years mentoring the next generation of women astronomers from 1865 to her retirement in 1888.[15] Mitchell's career demonstrated her remarkable intelligence and commitment to encouraging women's participation in scientific fields. In her words: "The question whether women have the capacity for original investigation in science is simply idle until equal opportunity is given them."[16]

Eunice Newton Foote

EUNICE NEWTON FOOTE

1819–1888, AMERICAN

SCIENTIST WHO DISCOVERED THE
PRINCIPAL CAUSE OF GLOBAL WARMING

It is one of the most significant scientific findings to impact the survival of our planet, and yet it took more than 150 years for the scientist who made this vital discovery to be adequately acknowledged. Perhaps her gender had something to do with the long wait.

On August 23, 1856, at the Annual Meeting of the American Association for the Advancement of Science (AAAS), a paper was delivered entitled "Circumstances Affecting the Heat of the Sun's Rays." The paper "anticipated the revolution in climate science by experimentally demonstrating the effects of the sun on certain gases and [for the first time] theorizing how those gases would interact with Earth's atmosphere."[1] Its author, Eunice Newton Foote, was not permitted to read her own paper due to AAAS regulations regarding the distinctions between male and female members. Instead, professor Joseph Henry of the Smithsonian Institution presented her work.[2]

On May 17, 2018, 162 years later, at a symposium at the University of California, Santa Barbara (UCSB), entitled "Science Knows No Gender? In Search of Eunice Foote, Who, 162 Years Ago Discovered the Principal Cause of Global Warming,"[3] Foote was finally heralded as a groundbreaking scientist.

The UCSB symposium literature lays out the significance of Foote's momentous and increasingly relevant scientific contribution:

> [Eunice Foote] was the first person to demonstrate that CO2 is a greenhouse gas. She also was the first person to recognize that an atmosphere with more CO2 would lead to an earth with a higher temperature. In their own way, her discoveries rank in importance with Darwin's Origin of the Species for contemporary cultural and scientific debates, and though there are thousands of books written about Darwin, none exists regarding Eunice Foote.
>
> She remains totally unknown to this day solely because she was born a woman. Telling her story today has never been more compelling because it enhances the visibility of women in science, and their significant contributions. Setting the record straight about the importance of women in the history of science counters the mean notion that women are not as capable in math and science as men.

Eunice Foote's elegant and easily replicable experiments proved 162 years ago that carbon dioxide emissions cause global warming, and they illustrate the consequences of today's burning of fossil fuels. Foote clearly warned in 1856 that an atmosphere that contains more carbon dioxide will create a much hotter world.[4]

What were some of the specifics of Foote's "elegant experiments?" In her article "This Lady Scientist Defined the Greenhouse Effect but Didn't Get the Credit," *Smithsonian* journalist Leila McNeill explains:

Foote's paper demonstrated the interactions of the sun's rays on different gases through a series of experiments using an air pump, four thermometers, and two glass cylinders. First, Foote placed two thermometers in each cylinder and, using the air pump, removed the air from one cylinder and condensed it in the other. Allowing both cylinders to reach the same temperature, she then placed the cylinders with their thermometers in the sun to measure temperature variance once heated and under various states of moisture. She repeated this process with hydrogen, common air and $CO2$, all heated after being exposed to the sun.

Looking back on Earth's history, Foote explains that 'an atmosphere of that gas would give to our earth a high temperature ... At one period of its history the air had mixed with it a larger proportion than at present, an increased temperature from its own action as well as from increased weight must have necessarily resulted.' Of the gases tested, she concluded that carbonic acid trapped the most heat, having a final temperature of 125°F. Foote was years ahead of her time. What she described and theorized was the gradual warming of the Earth's atmosphere—what today we call the greenhouse effect.[5]

McNeill points out that "three years later, the well-known Irish physicist John Tyndall published similar results demonstrating the greenhouse effects of certain gases, including carbonic acid" and that his work "is widely accepted as the foundation of modern climate science, while Foote's remains in obscurity."[6]

Marianne North

MARIANNE NORTH
1830–1890, ENGLISH
BOTANICAL PAINTER, TRAVELED THE WORLD DOCUMENTING MORE THAN 800 PLANT SPECIES

Most people have heard of John James Audubon (1785–1851), who documented and painted 497 bird species throughout the United States and published his works of scientific art in an exquisite—and well-known—book entitled *Birds of America*.[1] But how many have heard of **Marianne North**, who documented and painted over 800 paintings of plant species while visiting seventeen countries on six continents?[2] Whose paintings can be found in the Marianne North Gallery at England's Royal Botanic Gardens at Kew, the only permanent space in Britain dedicated to a single female artist's works and one of the most important collections of botanical art in the world?[3]

Unlike most male naturalists of her time, North did not merely collect specimens; rather, she "painted what she saw with a scientific accuracy that would make her paintings vital botanical records."[4] And she traveled alone to do so—to North and Central America, South America, Europe, Asia, Australasia, and Africa.[5]

Marianne North was fascinated by plants as a child. Born into a well-connected and cultured family, she often visited the Palm House at Kew Gardens, as her father was a close friend of Sir William Hooker, the director of the Gardens.[6] It was there that she developed a love for exotic flora and the plants of the tropics. When near her holiday home in Norfolk, North would studiously and meticulously collect specimens of grasses and plants, hinting at her later career of scientific paintings.[7] Aware that their daughter displayed a talent for painting at an early age, North's family was supportive of her artistic interests as they considered painting a suitable hobby for a Victorian lady.[8]

But, as her artistic accomplishments would stunningly reflect, painting and botany were no mere hobbies for North. In her article for *The Guardian*, entitled "Travels with My Brush," journalist Ambra Edwards explains how North's career as a traveling botanical artist began with lessons in oil painting and grew to become a "vice" that brought her to a "state of ecstasy":

> *Like many women of her class, North had received lessons in flower painting, but in 1867 the Australian artist Robert Dowling . . . taught her to paint in oils. From that day, there was no stopping her. Oil painting, she declared, became a 'vice, like dram-drinking, almost impossible to leave off once it gets possession of one.'*

To the consternation of her family, she accepted an invitation to North America, where she planned to paint 'its peculiar vegetation on the spot in natural abundant luxuriance'. From there, she set off for Jamaica, arriving 'alone and friendless' on Christmas Eve 1871. North couldn't have been happier. She installed herself in a house in the Botanic Gardens, surrounded by orchids and palms. 'I was in a state of ecstasy' she wrote in her diary, 'and hardly knew what to paint first.'[9]

North America was just the beginning of Marianne North's ecstatic relationship with nature through her works of art. In just eight years, North traveled to America, Canada, Jamaica, Brazil, the Canaries, Japan, Singapore, Borneo, Java, Ceylon, and India, and—at the urging of Charles Darwin—she visited Australia and New Zealand as well.[10] Darwin "had insisted her life's work would not be complete until she had visited Australia."[11]

At a time when photography was not yet a practical option for capturing nature in all its colorful complexity, the scientific accuracy that North employed in documenting plant life throughout the world renders her paintings particularly valuable. Zoe Wolstenholme, gallery assistant at the Shirley Sherwood Gallery of Botanical Art, Kew Gardens, points out that "Marianne North's vibrant compositions defied the conventions of botanical illustration, taking specimens off the white page and returning them to their natural context surrounded by hovering humming birds, Buddhist temples, and doting insects."[12]

Marianne's core contribution to botanical art is that her elegant, scientifically accurate paintings not only depict the world's myriad flowers and plants, but also the specific and unique environments in which they thrive. As Ambra Edwards writes:

It is hard for us to appreciate the original impact of North's paintings, which would have been like images beamed from the surface of the moon. Even the eminent botanists of Kew, who would have known some plants from drawings or dried specimens, had little idea of the habitat in which they grew. North depicted not just the plant, but, for the first time, entire ecosystems.[13]

Though today we may not be able to grasp the original significance, both artistically and scientifically, of these paintings, North's accomplishments were exceptional, providing vital visual information about flora around the world and even helping botanists identify four new species.[14] Her legacy is inspirational: an independent woman in Victorian times, Marianne North was a trailblazer in botanical painting.

Savitribai Phule

SAVITRIBAI PHULE

1831–1897, INDIAN

GROUNDBREAKING ACTIVIST FOR WOMEN'S RIGHTS AND AGAINST THE CASTE SYSTEM; ESTABLISHED INDIA'S FIRST WOMEN'S SCHOOLS OPEN TO LOWER-CASTE STUDENTS

Social reformer and poet Savitribai Phule dedicated her life to empowering women and impoverished individuals. Born into a low-caste family of farmers in Naigaon, Maharashtra, Phule was married at the age of nine to a twelve-year-old boy, Jyotirao Phule, who would go on to share her dedication to improving the lives of women and those from the lower castes of India.[1]

Although Phule grew up in an era when girls were married off at a very early age, she and her husband later worked to change that tradition by creating an organization called Satyashodhak Samaj or the Truth-seekers' Society.[2] Aimed at eliminating discrimination and fostering the rights of women, the organization initiated the practice of *Satyashodhak marriage*, wherein couples took an oath of education and equality.[3] Phule and her husband "organized marriages without a priest, without dowry, and at a minimum cost. The wedding vows in these marriages were the pledges taken by both the bride and the bridegroom."[4]

Education for girls in India was paramount to Phule's goal of advancing women's rights. After her young husband taught her to read and write as a girl, and after six years of home study, Phule furthered her education so that she could become a teacher and forge a path toward her life's calling.[5] She completed teachers' training at Ahmednagar and in Pune, and became a qualified teacher in 1847—at the age of sixteen.[6] She and her husband then pioneered the campaign for women's education, starting the first school for girls at Pune in 1848.[7] Their students were from the *shudra-atishudra* community, the lowest rung of the caste ladder. According to an essay on Phule and her husband in the book *Equal Halves: Famous Indian Wives*:

> The Phules sought to revolt against the inhumane treatment meted out to women 'shudras' and 'atishudras' by educating them about structural exploitation. Having been denied the right to education for several centuries under an oppressive caste system and yet hesitant to accept the newly available Christian missionary education, the 'shudra atishudra' community must have felt right at home when two people from their [community] established a school that provided free

education . . . [Phule], a woman who had seen poverty, caste discrimination and life without education, was the perfect role model for her students.[8]

Phule's progressive work was not always well received, however, and in fact was often met with fury and outcries. After becoming the first woman teacher in India and building eighteen schools in her region, she attracted backlash, particularly from members of the upper castes.[9] She was subject to public abuse by her opposers, who would throw cow dung and mud at her while she walked to school.[10] This didn't discourage her; she carried a spare sari.[11]

Phule's interests weren't limited to educational reform; she also sought to solve women's issues. In nineteenth-century India, child marriage was rampant. Coupled with a high mortality rate, many young girls became widows before reaching puberty.[12] Such widows were required to shave their heads and live a simple life of austerity, even at such young ages.[13] It was Phule who, understanding the injustice of this practice, organized a strike against the barbers in order to end the practice of shaving young widows' heads.[14] Phule also understood women's risks of sexual exploitation and opened a care center for pregnant rape victims, protecting them from committing suicide or infanticide out of fear of social banishment.[15]

Though she lived nearly two centuries ago, Savitribai Phule's selfless actions toward education and equality are timelessly inspirational. Her attitude is especially poignant in her poetry, where she further articulated the need for women and those of the lower castes to speak out against societal injustice. In her own words:

Be self-reliant, be industrious,
Work—gather wisdom and riches.
All gets lost without knowledge
We become animals without wisdom
Sit idle no more, go, get education
End misery of the oppressed and the forsaken
You've got a golden chance to learn
So learn and break the chains of caste
Throw away the Brahman's scriptures fast.[16]

Mary Edwards Walker

MARY EDWARDS WALKER

1832–1919, AMERICAN

SURGEON; VOLUNTEER IN THE UNION ARMY DURING THE CIVIL WAR; ONLY WOMAN EVER TO RECEIVE THE MEDAL OF HONOR

American women have served their country in many capacities in conflicts throughout the nation's history, and the number of women in the military is only increasing.[1] As of 2019, women veterans were the fastest growing demographic treated by the U.S. Department of Veterans Affairs, representing 8.4 percent of American veterans and expected to increase to 20 percent in the next thirty years.[2] However, despite a significant (and climbing) presence in the U.S. military, only one woman has ever received the Congressional Medal of Honor—Mary Edwards Walker.[3]

Born in Oswego, New York, Mary Edwards Walker was the daughter of free thinkers who were not only abolitionists but also believed strongly in equal education for girls. It was thus appropriate for Mary to decide to go to medical school, especially since her father was a country doctor.[4] Despite attending Syracuse Medical College, the nation's first medical school and one that accepted both women and men, Mary was the only female in her class. She graduated in 1855, at the age of twenty-three, after three thirteen-week semesters of medical training, for which she paid $55 each.[5] Walker "is recorded as the first

female surgeon in the United States . . . [and] the second female graduate of an American medical school."[6]

Mary Edwards Walker broke the mold of the typical medical student, and she did so by challenging traditional women's attire. "Like her mother, she believed that the clothes women wore—the tight corsets and long, heavy dresses—were unhealthful and designed to limit activity. Walker wanted to be comfortable and active. So she wore a coat and trousers, sometimes with a skirt over the pants."[7]

The year following her graduation from medical school, Walker married Albert Miller, also a physician. Their wedding was progressive, as both Walker and Miller wore suits with top hats; Walker removed the word "obey" from her vows, and she refused to change her last name. All of these decisions were unusual for brides of her time.[8] The couple set up a joint medical practice, but "the public was not ready to accept a woman physician, and their practice floundered. They were divorced thirteen years later."[9]

When the Civil War broke out and Walker tried to join the Union Army, she was denied a commission as a medical officer, despite having been in private practice for many years.[10] Rejected as a medical officer because she was a woman, she was offered the role of a nurse but declined, choosing instead to volunteer as an unpaid civilian surgeon.[11]

In the face of blatant gender bias, Walker was officially appointed as a surgeon in 1863, becoming the first female surgeon in the United States Army.[12] The following year she was captured by the Confederate Army, remaining a prisoner of war for four months until she and other Union doctors were exchanged for Confederate medics.[13] After being released by the Confederates, Walker was assigned to work as medical director at a hospital for women prisoners in Kentucky.[14]

In addition to her barrier-breaking war work, Walker also worked to support women's rights and dress reform. Labelling women's fashion as restrictive and unhygienic, she adopted a uniform of trousers under a knee-length dress, and frequently was arrested for wearing men's clothes.[15] Though her masculine style often attracted harsh criticism, Walker once declared, "I don't wear men's clothes, I wear my own clothes."[16]

After leaving military service, Walker was awarded the Congressional Medal of Honor by President Andrew Johnson in November 1865. Because she had served as a civilian and not a commissioned officer, her medal (as well as those of 910 others) was rescinded in 1917, two years before her death. However, she refused to return the medal, and continued to wear it until she died.[17] Sixty years later, President Jimmy Carter saw that her achievement was restored, cementing her status as the only woman to hold a Medal of Honor. And rightly so—her wartime efforts as a female surgeon as well as her feminist work make Mary Edwards Walker an American hero.

Margaret E. Knight

MARGARET E. KNIGHT
1838–1914, AMERICAN
INVENTOR OF MORE THAN 100 MACHINES, INCLUDING THE PAPER BAG MACHINE

The most well-known names associated with the Industrial Revolution[1] are Eli Whitney (1765–1825), inventor of the cotton gin; James Watt (1736–1819), inventor of the steam engine; and Samuel Morse (1791–1872), inventor of the telegraph. These three gentlemen were indeed responsible for modernizing the world in major ways. But countless other inventions of the late-eighteenth and early-nineteenth centuries changed our lives in less-obvious ways. One such innovation was a machine that could manufacture flat-bottomed brown paper bags, more practical containers that would replace the inconvenient paper cones formerly used to carry groceries.[2] The inventor of this lifestyle-changing machine, as well as over a hundred others, had little formal education and began working in a cotton mill at age twelve, but was always "mechanically minded."[3] Her name was Margaret E. Knight.

As science and technology journalist Ryan P. Smith explains, Knight's early experiences in the mill inspired her to use her creativity and mechanical mindedness to come up with innovative design solutions:

In an unregulated, dangerous factory setting, the preteen toiled for paltry wages from before dawn until after dusk.

One of the leading causes of grievous injury at the mill, she soon observed, was the propensity of steel-tipped flying shuttles (manipulated by workers to unite the perpendicular weft and warp threads in their weaves) to come free of their looms, shooting off at high velocity with the slightest employee error.

The mechanically minded Knight set out to fix this, and before her thirteenth birthday devised an original shuttle restraint system that would soon sweep the cotton industry. At the time, she had no notion of patenting her idea, but as the years went by and she generated more and more such concepts, Knight came to see the moneymaking potential in her creativity.[4]

After leaving the mill in her late teens, Knight worked at a number of other technical jobs, including one at the Columbia Paper Bag Company in Springfield, Massachusetts. There, her job was to fold every paper bag by hand, which although inefficient, led to another "aha" moment for Knight: Why not invent a way to make the bags using an automated machine?[5] By 1870, her experiments had led to a machine that could make the square-bottomed bag we know today.[6]

Knight's new bag machine functioned so beautifully that an interloper named Charles Annan, who had seen her model while it was being built, decided to steal Knight's design and patent the bag machine under his own name. He didn't get away with it: Knight filed a successful patent interference lawsuit, won her case, and was awarded the patent in 1871.[7] It seemed Annan's argument relied on the court assuming Knight, as a woman, could not have invented such a complex machine. But, after Knight produced drawings, patterns, and even personal diary entries detailing her mechanical competence, the court declared that Annan was nothing but a fraud.[8] During the court case, Knight presented "her copious, meticulously detailed hand-drawn blueprints" in response to Annan's argument that "no woman could be capable of designing such a machine . . . Annan, who had no such evidence to offer himself, was quickly found to be a moneygrubbing charlatan."[9]

Margaret Knight's inventive mind was constantly coming up with ideas for new machines and products. Among her many inventions, for which she successfully would file over two dozen patents: a shoe-cutting machine; lid-removing pliers; a numbering machine; a window frame and sash, patented in 1894; and several devices relating to rotary engines, patented between 1902 and 1915.[10] What's more, unlike many women of the time, Knight refused to keep her gender anonymous. She used her full name on her first patent, instead of employing ambiguous initials, as was common for her contemporary female inventors.[11]

Though not a name often mentioned when discussing the Industrial Revolution, Margaret Knight's prolific career made her the nineteenth century's most famous female inventor.[12] An innovator unlike most of her contemporaries, Knight and her story show how anyone, including a woman born into factory life, can use their brilliance to improve lives for decades to come.

Bertha
von Suttner

BERTHA VON SUTTNER

1843–1914, AUSTRIAN

FIRST FEMALE RECIPIENT OF THE NOBEL PEACE PRIZE

Had Bertha von Suttner followed the path of most children of nobility, she might never have fulfilled her true calling as a novelist and peace activist. Although she was the daughter of Count Franz Joseph Kinsky, a retired high-ranking officer of the Habsburg Imperial Army, her noble beginnings gave way to a less-privileged life. Her father passed away shortly before her birth, leaving von Suttner, née Kinsky, to be raised by her mother, who had a penchant for gambling.[1] Kinsky eventually needed her own income and, at the age of thirty, took a position as governess and tutor to the four daughters of Baron Karl von Suttner. Following a romance with the girls' older brother, Arthur, and a broken engagement due to his parents' disapproval of Kinsky's advanced age (she was seven years Arthur's senior), she answered a newspaper advertisement for a job that would lead to one of her greatest achievements.[2]

The position was in Paris, as secretary to Alfred Nobel (1833–1896), the Swedish inventor of dynamite. While her stint as secretary to the famous inventor and philanthropist was relatively short, Kinsky developed a lasting friendship with Nobel, which would result in her convincing him years later to establish a peace prize.[3]

Returning to Austria from Paris, Kinsky eloped with Arthur von Suttner, and together they moved to the Caucuses as guests of her friend, Princess Ekaterina Dadiani.[4] It was there that she began writing for German-language literary papers, using the pseudonym B. Oulot, so that no one, not even her editors, could identify her as a female author.[5] She also spent her time reading Charles Darwin, Herbert Spencer, Immanuel Kant, and other influential thinkers.[6]

As von Suttner and her husband were living close to the Caucasian front during the Russo-Turkish War (1877–1878), she developed a keen awareness of the horrific costs of warfare, and in 1889 she published the antiwar novel *Die Waffen nieder!* (*Lay Down Your Arms*), about which Leo Tolstoy (1828–1910) wrote that he "wished it would do the same for repudiating war that Harriet Beecher Stowe's (1811–1896) *Uncle Tom's Cabin* had done to abolish slavery in the United States."[7] Von Suttner's previous employer, Alfred Nobel, commented that with her novel, she had "declared war on war."[8]

The book became extremely popular and was translated into twelve languages.[9] With the success of her novel, von Suttner launched the Austrian Peace Society in 1891 and began publishing a monthly peace journal with the same name as the title of her book: *Die Waffen nieder!* In numerous articles and appearances, she spoke out against fighting wars in order to resolve political conflicts—specifically, the Boer, US–Mexico, China–Japan, and Balkan wars. She attended annual Universal Peace Congresses as well as the First and Second International Hague Peace Conferences (1899 and 1907) and was vice president of the International Peace Bureau in Bern, Switzerland.[10]

For her impassioned efforts, she was both heralded and derided. Her character was often mocked by satirical caricaturists, who often painted her as a "naïve woman attempting to broker peace between warring nations."[11] At the same time, von Suttner commanded public attention like that given to prominent male politicians, unusual for a woman of her time.[12]

In an article in the International Encyclopedia of the First World War, historian Laurie Cohen assesses Bertha von Suttner's lasting legacy:

Bertha von Suttner devoted her life to attempting to prevent war . . . Her iconic call to 'lay down your arms'—written and shouted out to governments, civil servants, and to the public-at-large in lectures, journalistic articles and novels—seems just as relevant today . . . She envisioned a time when negotiations between conflicting states would replace battlefields, and disarmament and the end of conscription would supplant militaristic rhetoric and war industries . . . Hers was a call to always value life over death and human solidarity over human antipathy. As she wrote to Alfred Nobel (circa 1893): 'Progress towards justice is surely not a dream, it is the law of civilisation. The amount of savagery and stupidity in the world is certainly still very great, but the amount of kindness and gentleness and reason is growing every day.'[13]

After successfully encouraging Alfred Nobel to establish his prize for peace, Bertha von Suttner became the prize's first female recipient. In 1905, nine years after Alfred Nobel's death, Bertha von Suttner was awarded the Nobel Peace Prize for her tireless and trailblazing work to foster a culture of peace.

Augusta
Holmès

AUGUSTA HOLMÈS

1847–1903, FRENCH

COMPOSER OF OPERAS, CANTATAS, AND ORCHESTRAL WORKS

Writing in the journal *Harmonie et Mélodie*, renowned composer Camille Saint-Saëns offered this opinion of his less-renowned fellow composer Augusta Holmès: "Like children, women have no idea of obstacles, and their willpower breaks all barriers. Mademoiselle Holmès is a woman, an extremist."[1]

Perhaps Augusta Holmès interpreted Saint-Saëns pronouncement as a back-handed compliment: What artist *wouldn't* want to break creative barriers? Certainly, Camille Saint-Saëns was accurate in characterizing Holmès's musical path: it was indeed filled with obstacles, which she overcame brilliantly. Over her lifetime, Holmès wrote four operas, twelve symphonic poems, numerous other orchestral and oral pieces, and more than 120 songs.[2] She also wrote the lyrics to nearly all her music, as well as the libretto of her opera *La Montagne Noire* (1895).

A French citizen of Irish descent, Augusta Holmès was the only child of a retired Irish Army officer who left his homeland for France and a mother of mixed Scottish and Irish origins. Despite her parents' involvement in Parisian artistic circles, Holmès did not begin to study music until she was eleven, as her mother was unsupportive of her musical aspirations.[3] After her mother's death, Holmès began to study music with experts around the family's home in Versailles: she studied harmony and counterpoint with the organist of Versailles Cathedral, Henri Lambert; orchestration with Hyacinthe Klose, the director of the Regimental Band at Versailles; and voice with Guillot de Sainbris.[4]

According to composer, violinist, and music educator Elaine Fine:

> *Musical life at Versailles was centered around a military band, and Holmès was surrounded by wind players. Her orchestration teacher Klose (who also taught clarinet at the Paris Conservatory) encouraged Augusta to both write for and conduct the regimental band. The advantage of her early training writing for winds gave Holmès's orchestration interesting textures and a fresh voice against the organ-dominated colors of her contemporaries in France.*[5]

The creatively precocious Holmès began writing songs at age twelve. Thanks to the influence and mentorship of her godfather, French poet Alfred de Vigny, she already had a background in poetry and classics and spoke French, English, German, and Italian, so she was able to write most of the lyrics for her songs.[6] At fourteen, she began publishing her songs, three using the pseudonym Hermann Zenta, and four as A. Z. Holmes. (As with so many women in all fields of endeavor, admitting to being a woman could be perilous to one's career.) Most of her music published during her lifetime, however, was published under her own name.[7]

Around 1875, Holmès studied with César Franck (1822–1890), an important composer in the latter half of the nineteenth century, particularly in the realms of symphonic, chamber, organ, and piano music.[8] Both Franck and Richard Wagner (1813–1883), whose operatic piece *Das Rheingold* was particularly formative for her, were dominant creative influences, and she counted Hungarian composer Franz Liszt (1811–1886) among her admirers.[9] In the years following her time with Franck, Holmès composed many great works, including the symphonic poems *Pologne* and *Irlande*. She had a preference for epic themes, and in true Wagnerian fashion, often employed a large orchestra in her compositions.[10]

Holmès was commissioned to write a piece for the 1889 Paris Exposition, and the result was the dramatic *Ode triomphale*, a "behemoth" requiring a chorus of 900 singers and a 300-piece orchestra.[11] This grand spectacle was performed four times during the course of the Ex-

position, and Holmès worked for free, donating one performance's profits to the victims of a flood in Antwerp.[12]

Augusta Holmès shattered musical ceilings. While it was not uncommon in her day for women of the upper classes to learn music and play an instrument, composition was another matter altogether. As *New York Times* columnist Alice Gregory points out in her piece, "A History of Classical Music (The Women-Only Version)": "There is the notion, intractable for centuries, that women could perhaps be talented of body—with nimble fingers and a bell-like voice—but never of mind, which is, of course, where composition originates."[13] Holmès broke these gender barriers, illustrating her talent in her numerous compositions and overcoming obstacles in pursuit of her musical dream.

In describing a photograph of Augusta Holmès toward the end of her life, musicologist Karen Henson offers a poignant assessment of her stature as a composer:

> Among surviving portraits of Augusta Holmès is a photograph taken towards the end of her life . . . The setting is her home: possibly the main room, but more likely a study, since the picture is dominated by a grand piano at which the composer stands imperiously. Images such as this—emphasising professional zeal rather than feminine charm—were the exception in the representation of women composers at the end of the nineteenth century.[14]

Sofia Kovalevskaya

SOFIA KOVALEVSKAYA
1850–1891, RUSSIAN

MATHEMATICIAN WHOSE GROUNDBREAKING PAPER ON DIFFERENTIAL EQUATIONS BROUGHT HER RECOGNITION THROUGHOUT THE MATHEMATICAL COMMUNITY

Sofia Kovalevskaya was a woman of multidisciplinary talents: Not only a writer of novels and plays, she was also a pioneering mathematician who overcame gender bias in order to gain an education and engage in a mathematical career. Her perspective on mathematics was unique and profound, as evidenced by her words:

> It seems to me that the poet must see what others do not see, must see more deeply than other people. And the mathematician must do the same.[1]

The first woman to be awarded a doctorate at a European university and the first woman in Europe (outside of Italy) to hold a university chair in any discipline, Kovalevskaya's path to academic acceptance and achievement was not without barriers.[2] Although she came from a privileged background and enjoyed a good early education, she was often prevented from pursuing scholastic opportunities reserved for males.

Kovalevskaya was the daughter of an army general and a musically accomplished mother from a mathematical family, which may have shaped her own mathematical gifts.[3] With the encouragement of her paternal uncle, Kovalevskaya began studying mathematics as a girl, and although her father was initially against her mathematic education, he soon recognized her talent and aptitude, eventually allowing her to take private lessons.[4]

At the age of eleven, Kovalevskaya was introduced to calculus in a most unusual way: Her nursery room's wallpaper consisted of lecture notes on differential and integral analysis.[5] Kovalevskaya wrote in her autobiography:

> The meaning of these concepts I naturally could not yet grasp, but they acted on my imagination, instilling in me a reverence for mathematics as an exalted and mysterious science which opens up to its initiates a new world of wonders, inaccessible to ordinary mortals.[6]

Although Kovalevskaya was talented and passionate about mathematics, she was unable to further her education in Russia due to women being barred from attending universities. And in order to travel abroad, Kovalevskaya needed written permission from her father or husband.[7] So she married Vladimir Kovalevskij, a young paleontology student, and they moved to Germany in

1869 to enable Kovalevskaya to take advanced studies in mathematics.[8] With persistence she was able to obtain professors' permission to attend lectures at the University of Heidelberg, and over the course of three semesters she attended between eighteen and twenty-two hours per week of lectures.[9]

The following year, Kovalevskaya moved to Berlin to take private lessons with the noted mathematician Karl Weierstrass, a leader in modern analysis and professor of mathematics at the University of Berlin. The University would not allow women to enroll, but Weierstrass, impressed with Kovalevskaya's aptitude, tutored her privately for four years.[10]

Still in her early twenties, Kovalevskaya achieved a long-awaited goal. In 1874, she presented three papers—which addressed partial differential equations, the dynamics of Saturn's rings, and elliptic integrals—to the University of Göttingen as her doctoral dissertation. This impressive scholarly work earned her a doctorate in mathematics summa cum laude, making her the first woman in modern Europe to earn a doctorate in mathematics.[11]

Although she had earned her doctorate with honors, and had the enthusiastic support of Karl Weierstrass, Kovalevskaya was unable to secure an academic position. Yet again, the barrier preventing her from progressing as a mathematician was obvious: She was a woman.[12]

It wasn't until 1884 that Sofia Kovalevskaya finally secured a teaching position at the University of Stockholm. Six years later, after working in a sexist and hostile work atmosphere, the university finally awarded her a lifetime position as a professor.[13]

At the height of her mathematical career, in 1891, Sofia Kovalevskaya died of complications from a cold, pleurisy, or pneumonia.[14] She left behind a formidable academic legacy: besides publishing nine original articles, she was awarded the Prix Bordin of the French Academy of Sciences in 1888, an award so rare that it had only been given ten times in fifty years.[15] More than this, she was a woman of firsts, and by achieving academic success she set a precedent for women to follow in her path.

Bibi
Khanum
Astarabadi

BIBI KHANUM ASTARABADI

1858–1921, IRANIAN

AUTHOR OF THE FIRST DECLARATION OF WOMEN'S RIGHTS IN THE HISTORY OF MODERN IRAN AND ADVOCATE OF UNIVERSAL EDUCATION FOR GIRLS

Female authors, artists, and others who choose to remain anonymous or take on masculine pseudonyms often do so in order to prevent misogynistic preconceptions about their work. But there are men who choose anonymity for another reason: to spread hatred, contempt, or prejudice against women while remaining safely nameless. In today's online culture, we encounter such anonymous pronouncements in thousands of misogynistic postings.

Unfortunately, some things never change.

In 1887, a book entitled *The Education of Women* was published in Iran, written by "anonymous" and received with great interest by a certain segment of the Iranian population. At that time, some upper- and middle-class Iranian men and women were beginning to question traditional ideas about the role of women and their place in society. *The Education of Women* was an apparent response to this emerging consciousness. "In ten chapters, the anonymous author of *The Education of Women* not only wanted to educate women on how to behave properly toward their husbands, but also to put them in their place

because he considered the women of the Tehran upper class rather uppity."[1]

One courageous and astute woman fought back. Author, women's rights advocate, and mother of seven, Bibi Khanum Astarabadi wrote *The Vices of Men* in 1895, a critical response to what she called the "nonsensical argument" found in *The Education of Women*. With wit and forcefulness, she confronted the anonymous author's demeaning proclamations, including that woman is a being similar to a child, who must be educated by a man. Railing against the anonymous author's mean-spirited, patronizing attitudes toward women, Astarabadi's outrage includes this memorable line:

> When I perused these pages, I found that the author . . . has put forth an unrealistic criticism, senseless and more biting than the thorn of a thistle aimed at women.[2]

Combining the traditional florid language of the time and street Persian and slang words, *The Vices of Men* calls out the anonymous author of *The Education of Women*, thereby educating him as to his antiquated assessment of women's character and potential.[3] And "Anonymous" wasn't fooling anyone as to his gender; Astarabadi referred to the author as "this evil-natured man."[4]

Considered to be the first declaration of women's rights in the history of modern Iran, *The Vices of Men* spoke truth to power in an unprecedented, audacious manner. In one passage, Astarabadi protests the censorship of the Koran as she addresses Muhammad Baqer Majlisi, "the great Shi'ite theologian [who] even makes the teaching of the Koran to girls subject to censorship, leaving out the amorous story of Joseph and Potiphar's wife."[5]

It was Astarabadi's fervent belief that the only way to combat entrenched misogynistic values and assure that women develop their true potential is to offer girls an authentic education (not the type suggested in anonymous's book). Along with other intellectually oriented women who began to open schools for girls in Tehran in the early twentieth century, Astarabadi put her beliefs into action. In 1907, she founded the distinguished School for Girls (*Madreseh-ye Dooshizegan*) for girls ages seven through twelve. To respect religious sensitivities, all the teachers were women. The curriculum included reading, writing, history, geography, arithmetic, law, religion, and cooking.

An initial announcement for the school mentioned that "teaching will be adapted to the learning ability of each girl" and that a "discount is offered to those in reduced circumstances."[6]

While such an academic program hardly seems subversive, Astarabadi's relatively progressive school for girls and similar institutions were labeled by clerics as "centers for prostitution."[7] Those attending them faced various forms of hostility, leading some concerned parents to resort to home schooling. Despite such adverse consequences, however, the women's movement—including the movement for universal education for girls—forged ahead as advocates continued to subsidize girls' schools.

One citizen journalist, writing from within present-day Iran, poignantly expressed her gratitude to Astarabadi:

> All Iranian girls' schools owe pioneering educationalist Bibi Khanoom Astarabadi a debt of gratitude. Astarabadi took on the seemingly impossible task of setting up a school for girls in a reactionary society where women had no presence in public life and enjoyed few rights, if any. In many ways, she was a feminist—with a biting sense of humor.[8]

Diana Agabeg Apcar

DIANA AGABEG APCAR
1859–1937, ARMENIAN
FIRST FEMALE DIPLOMAT

According to a 2017 article entitled "Gender, International Status, and Ambassador Appointments" in the journal *Foreign Policy Analysis*, "The share of female ambassadors is low, glaringly so. Eighty-five percent of the world's ambassadors are male, making this high-prestige position yet another international post that is still dominated by men."[1]

Which makes Diana Agabeg Apcar's appointment in 1919 to the position of consul general of the Republic of Armenia in Japan exceptionally notable. Her courageous and outspoken advocacy on behalf of the Armenian people defines her story.

Diana Agabeg Apcar was a child of the Armenian diaspora. Born in Burma (Myanmar) to an Indian-Armenian father who migrated to Southeast Asia from Iran and an Armenian mother who was also from Iran, she was raised in Calcutta and attended a local convent school, becoming fluent in English, Armenian, and Hindustani. She married Michael Apcar, who was from a family of successful merchants in Southeast Asia. Together they moved to Japan to expand the family business.[2]

According to the historical summary posted on the Diana Apcar Organization's website, her life changed in 1909 with the horrific events unfolding in her ancestral homeland:

> Something changed for Diana after the massacre of approximately 30,000 Armenians in 1909, in Adana, Turkey. She began to focus her energy outward, calling attention to the plight of the Armenian people. She rejected political indifference to the pain and suffering of humanity . . . [writing] essays, letters, and books, pleading for compassion and action to divert an impending crisis.
>
> With the start of the genocide, and lack of response from world leaders, Diana's energy turned to rescuing and securing funds for the destitute. She was the American Red Cross coordinator in Japan, responsible for the Armenian refugees who found their way to Vladivostok, Siberia and Harbin, Manchuria. She solicited funds on their behalf and arranged their travel to Yokohama, where she housed them, found them jobs, and coordinated their travel documents and passage, primarily to the U.S. Hundreds of people passed through her care, staying with her in Japan for many months.[3]

Through articles, letters, books, and political essays, Apcar spoke out on behalf of the Armenian people and about "the right of self-determination and the evils of imperialism."[4] In one such work from 1912, entitled "Peace and No Peace," Apcar asserted:

> *The nations of Europe have cried out Peace! Peace! But the cry that has proceeded from their throats only, and not from their hearts; they have each and every one of them been desirous only to see the altars of greed and ambition broken down in the other men's countries, whilst eagerly stipulating to keep their own; and if Peace must come into the world, it can only come when the cry has gone forth from the hearts of the nation.*
>
> *The great Powers of Europe treat the small nations as billiard-players treat the balls on a billiard-table; they strike the helpless balls of the small nations with their political cues, and the balls have to go rolling here and there at the stroke of the players.*[5]

An excerpt from another 1912 essay, "The Peace Problem," continues to resonate in the twenty-first century:

> *There exists now in what are called the enlightened countries of the world a species of slavery that had never existed in the world before. . . . The nations of the powerful countries of Europe have now become the voluntary slaves of the gun-makers, and the financiers, the patrons of the gun-makers.*[6]

During her years in Japan, advocating for and assisting Armenians fleeing the genocide, Apcar interviewed refugees about their experiences living under and escaping Turkish and Russian oppression. Their stories were the inspiration for her book *From the Book of One Thousand Tales: Stories of Armenia and Its People, 1892–1922.*[7]

Apcar's formidable literary works challenging "the motives and decisions of major political powers,"[8] as well as her tireless dedication to advocating for the Armenian cause and aiding the Armenian people, led to her being appointed consul general for a country where she had never lived but to which she felt an unbroken connection.

When the Republic of Armenia gained independence on May 28, 1918, Armenia was not recognized by any international state. In 1920, through Apcar's efforts, Japan became one of the first nations to recognize the new republic's independence. By late 1920, however, the Republic of Armenia was conquered by the Soviet army, and Apcar's post was abruptly terminated.

Nonetheless, Apcar retains the distinction of being the first Armenian woman diplomat and the first woman to be appointed to a diplomatic post.

More importantly, she is revered by the Armenian community and others for her powerful writing and valiant outreach on behalf of an oppressed people:

> *This extraordinary woman worked tirelessly for justice for the oppressed, both through her writings and humanitarian efforts. . . . She campaigned on behalf of the Armenian people, whom she saw as political pawns in a game of brinkmanship between super-powers. She personally supported hundreds of destitute refugees from the crumbling Ottoman and Russian empires, after an arduous journey across Siberia to Japan; she housed, fed, and secured doc-*

umentation for hundreds of destitute souls escaping genocide, starvation, and the Bolshevik revolution. She overcame societal taboos and pressures of the time to become a respected leader in a male-dominated world....[9]

Nettie Maria Stevens

NETTIE MARIA STEVENS
1861–1912, AMERICAN
GENETICIST AND BIOLOGIST WHO DEVELOPED THE CONCEPT OF SEX DETERMINATION BY CHROMOSOMES

Nettie Maria Stevens's work proved that gender is determined by the male's chromosome (i.e., whether the sperm is carrying an X or Y chromosome). Without her work we might still be clinging to beliefs such as those of Aristotle, who thought that a father's body temperature during conception determined the child's sex, or nineteenth-century Europeans who believed that good nutrition led to a female child and poor nutrition to a male.[1]

Born in Cavendish, Vermont, Nettie Stevens was the daughter of a carpenter and small-property owner who was able to provide his family with a middle-class living. Nettie received her early education in the public schools of Westford, Massachusetts, impressing her teachers with an "exceptional ability in her studies.... After leaving the public schools, she entered Westford Academy, where she displayed the same clear-visioned aptitude."[2] At the age of nineteen, Nettie Stevens became a teacher:

Although teaching was not her first love, her enthusiasm for science made her a caring and dedicated teacher. She once told a hesitant student, 'How could you think your questions would bother me? They never will, so long as

I keep my enthusiasm for biology; and that, I hope will be as long as I live.'[3]

Nettie Stevens's sights were set on a higher education, a path that increasing numbers of gifted women in the United States were beginning to pursue.[4] Earning her living as a teacher, she continued to save, and at the age of thirty-five was able to enroll at newly established Leland Stanford University in Palo Alto, California.[5] While at Stanford, Stevens spent four summers conducting histological and cytological research at Stanford's Hopkins Marine Station.[6] In his autobiography, Stanford president and ichthyologist David Starr Jordan praised Stevens as "one of the ablest scientific investigators developed at Stanford."[7]

After receiving her BA in 1899 and her MA in 1900 from Stanford, Stevens moved back East to continue her education at Bryn Mawr College, earning her PhD in biology in 1903.[8] During her doctoral studies, she studied abroad at the Zoological Station in Naples, Italy, as well as the Zoological Institute of the University of Würzburg, Germany. Upon completing her degree, she remained at Bryn Mawr as a research fellow in biology and later as an associate in experimental morphology.[9]

It was during her time as a research scientist that Stevens studied the mealworm beetle and made her most influential scientific discovery. In her research, she was particularly interested in the process of sex determination:

> While studying the mealworm, she found that the males made reproductive cells with both X and Y chromosomes whereas the females made only those with X. She concluded that sex is inherited as a chromosomal factor and that males determine the gender of the offspring . . . At the time, the chromosomal theory of inheritance was not yet accepted, and it was commonly believed that gender was determined by the mother and/or environmental factors. Most scientists did not embrace Stevens's theory immediately.[10]

Not only did many scientists fail to readily accept Stevens's theory, but another scientist who also had been researching sex determination via chromosomes was initially credited with the discovery. The renowned biologist Edmund Beecher Wilson (1856–1939)—who taught at Bryn Mawr before Stevens attended—independently arrived at a similar conclusion as Stevens.[11] Although Wilson and Stevens published their related theories around the same time, making them co-discoverers of the same idea, the former often receives more credit due to his more substantial contributions in other scientific findings.[12] But it was Stevens who ultimately arrived at a more correct conclusion, as her research more clearly stated the connections between chromosomes and sex determination.[13]

Nettie Stevens died of breast cancer at the age of fifty, just nine years after completing her PhD and just after she received a research professorship at Bryn Mawr.[14] Her hard-won scientific career and her breakthrough discovery continue to impact geneticists and inspire scientists throughout the world. As Edmund Beecher Wilson wrote, Stevens was "not only the best of the women investigators, but one whose work will hold its own with that of any of the men of the same degree of advancement."[15]

Clelia Duel Mosher

CLELIA DUEL MOSHER

1863–1940, AMERICAN

PROFESSOR, PHYSICIAN WHO CONDUCTED THE FIRST AMERICAN STUDY OF VICTORIAN SEXUALITY

*L*ong before the well-known Kinsey Reports of 1948 and 1953, a survey conducted between 1892 and 1920 by Dr. Clelia Duel Mosher revealed the sexual attitudes and concerns of women born in the mid-1800s. Mosher never published her data, and it wasn't until 1973 that the survey was discovered—by accident.

Mosher's interest in science began at a young age. She was inspired by her father, Dr. Cornelius Mosher, who would bring her along for his medical rounds and introduced her to botany.[1] Her frail health worried him, but although he tried to dissuade her from pursuing a college education, Mosher was determined to pursue her scientific goals. In 1889, the twenty-five-year-old Mosher enrolled in Wellesley College, before transferring to the University of Wisconsin for her junior year, and finally entering Stanford in 1892 to earn her undergraduate and master's degrees in physiology.[2] While earning her master's degree, Mosher worked for the school in the department of hygiene, as an assistant teaching physiology, health, and exercise to female students.[3]

Her master's research at Stanford focused, in part, on the pain associated with menstruation and offered some groundbreaking conclusions: it confirmed that "women, just like men, breathe from the diaphragm," and that their "supposed 'monthly disability' was due to constrictive clothing, inactivity, and the general assumption that pain was an inevitable accompaniment to menstruation."[4] She also created a set of exercises, called "Moshering," that targeted menstrual pain and were designed to improve women's health.[5]

In 1896 Mosher attended Johns Hopkins University to obtain her MD, which she received in 1900. Although there were about 7,000 female doctors and surgeons in the United States (almost 6 percent of the total) by 1900, they continued to face discrimination. Mosher was told that men refused to work under her, and when she opened a private practice in Palo Alto, California, she struggled to be awarded grants for her studies and get patient referrals from male colleagues.[6] In 1910, when Stanford offered her an assistant professorship in personal hygiene as the women's medical adviser, Mosher accepted, happy to return to academia.[7]

It was at Stanford University that Mosher's survey was accidentally discovered by historian Carl Degler, who came across her papers as he was gathering research from the Stanford archives for an unrelated project. Among her files were questionnaires that surveyed forty-five women, most born before 1870, gathering their most private thoughts on sex during the Victorian era.[8]

Many of the survey responses differ considerably from the stereotypical Victorian attitudes about sex. For example, one respondent, born in 1844, considered sex "a normal desire" and remarked that "a rational use of it tends to keep people healthier," while another, born in 1862, noted that "the highest devotion is based upon it, a very beautiful thing, and I am glad nature gave it to us."[9] Stanford historian Estelle Freedman, coauthor of *Intimate Matters: A History of Sexuality in America*, called the discovery of Mosher's survey "a goldmine" for scholars: In Victorian times, when "the public ideal was that women should be very discreet, if not ignorant, about sexuality, [Mosher was] asking very modern questions. She's opening up an inquiry about what is the meaning of sexuality for women."[10]

The results of Mosher's survey were surprising. In summary, of this sample of Victorian women:

- 76 percent desired intercourse without influence from their husbands' interest
- 76 percent had experienced orgasm and 36 percent "always" or "usually" experienced orgasm

- 53 percent considered sexual pleasure to be for both women and men
- 84 percent used at least one method of birth control

Mosher's findings negate the traditional thought that Victorian women were sexually repressed. Her respondents did not support the stereotype that they reluctantly engaged in or rejected sexual relations, but rather exhibited a broader appreciation and acceptance of sex as a habit integral to a healthy and joyous life.[11]

Why was Dr. Mosher's sex survey never published—preventing her from being acknowledged during her lifetime for her pioneering research? Theories include a lack of time or the study's controversial subject matter as possible reasons for Mosher to not have published her research before her death in 1940.[12]

Nonetheless, Mosher's findings—finally published in 1980 as *The Mosher Survey: Sexual Attitudes of 45 Victorian Women*—are exceptionally valuable as a window into Victorian-era women's sexual attitudes. Although the survey respondents are not representative of every socioeconomic or ethnic group of American women of that time (they were all well-educated, middle-class, white women), Mosher's decision to ask "open-ended questions probing feelings and experiences" rather than "questions about physiology or mechanics" resulted in an intimate, nuanced, honest report.[13]

Zoila Ugarte de Landivar

ZOILA UGARTE DE LANDÍVAR
1864–1969, ECUADORIAN
FIRST FEMALE JOURNALIST IN ECUADOR
AND FEMINIST ADVOCATE

One of the first Latin American feminists of the late-nineteenth and early-twentieth centuries, Zoila Ugarte de Landívar—also referred to simply as Zoila Ugarte—was born in 1864 in El Guabo, Ecuador. Long before she was born, women throughout Latin America had been speaking out against economic and other gender inequities. Zoila Ugarte's stood out in her role of journalist.

Her career in journalism began in 1890, writing under the pseudonym "Zarelia" for *El Tesoro del Hogar*, a weekly periodical of literature, sciences, arts, and fashion.[1] Ugarte's early writings exhibited her unique literary style, which over the years would continue to distinguish her from her contemporaries.[2] In 1905, Ugarte founded the first Ecuadorian feminist magazine, *La Mujer*, as a platform for progressive and democratic ideas in pursuit of social rights.[3] A monthly publication featuring poets, writers, and feminist advocates, including early local feminists Mercedes González de Moscoso, María Natalia Vaca, Josefa Veintemilla, Antonia Mosquera, Dolores Flor, and Isabel Espinel, *La Mujer*'s printing press was shut down several times due to its politically controversial articles.[4]

Among the articles written by Ugarte were those defending a woman's right to education, while at the same time acknowledging a woman's traditional domestic role. In Ugarte's words, "Ignorance is no guarantee of happiness, and even if they say it, we will never be convinced that the educated woman is incapable of domestic virtues."[5] Her words reveal her ability to balance women's conventional duties with progressive feminist calls for social change, advocating for gender equality while recognizing women's differences.[6]

At the end of 1905 Ugarte was named honorary contributor to the newspaper *El Tipógrafo*, where she continued her feminist and leftist perspective with statements such as: "Women have the right to be given work because we need to live and cannot live or acquire amenities without working."[7]

Zoila Ugarte was a prominent literary presence in a number of other magazines and newspapers, including *El Demócrata (The Democrat)*, a publication dedicated to literature, art, and sociology; *La Mujer Ecuatoriana (The Ecuadorian Woman)*, published by the Feminist Center La Aurora in the city of Guayaquil; and *Páginas Literarias (Literary Pages)*, published in the city of Cuenca.[8]

In addition to her many journalistic pursuits, Ugarte also spent several years as head of the National Library, working there from 1912 to 1920 while she continued to publish her writings.[9]

Throughout her pioneering work as a journalist and feminist, Zoila Ugarte de Landívar espoused core truths about gender equality. One of the first Latin American feminists of the twentieth century, Ugarte is an inspiration for not only Ecuadorian women but for feminists around the world.

Alimotu
Pelewura

ALIMOTU PELEWURA

1865–1951, NIGERIAN

POLITICAL ACTIVIST AND LEADER OF THE LAGOS MARKET WOMEN'S ASSOCIATION, WHICH ADVOCATED AGAINST UNJUST TAXATION AND FOR WOMEN'S RIGHT TO VOTE

"No taxation without representation" is a slogan associated with American colonists during the 1700s, who protested that they were being unfairly taxed but not represented in the British Parliament that authorized those taxes. Less than 200 years later, their cry echoed again, this time by the voice of activist Alimotu Pelewura on behalf of her fellow female traders, or "market women," in Lagos, Nigeria.

Alimotu Pelewura was born in Lagos in 1865, a member of the Yorùbá people, an ethnic group concentrated in the southwestern part of Nigeria. At that time, the British had already formally annexed Lagos (in 1861), and Nigeria would later become a British protectorate, in 1900.[1]

The daughter of a fish trader, Pelewura followed in her mother's footsteps and engaged in fish trading as well.[2] She would go on to become the most important market woman in Lagos.[3] As anthropology professor Gracia Clark explains, the occupation of market woman is an integral part of the economies of Africa: "In the open marketplaces found in cities and villages throughout Africa, women traders usually predominate. This gives women considerable weight as economic actors, because these marketplace systems are the primary distributive networks in most parts of Africa."[4]

Throughout her career, Pelewura would use her influence in order to further the cause of justice and economic security for her women traders. She became president of the Lagos Market Women's Association (LMWA) after its founding in the 1920s, leading the LMWA in protests against imposed taxation and price controls.[5] Despite being illiterate, she was able to apply the same organizational skills from her work in the market to her position as president of the LMWA: "Lack of formal education was not an insurmountable problem; the important thing was knowing how to utilize the skills and advice of both her supporters and hired literate persons for the purposes of furthering market women's interests."[6]

Despite being an uneducated fish trader, Pelewura's position afforded her such power and influence that, as she opposed unfavorable policies imposed by the British, she became a "source of concern" to the colonial government.[7] Objecting to the imposed taxation and price control plan in 1932, she led a market women's protest that culminated in their demands being met:

> Rumor had spread throughout Lagos that the colonial government intended to levy a tax on Lagosian women . . . Immediately the market women organized a committee, with Pelewura as a member, went to the Government House to discuss the issue with the Administrator of the Colony, C.T. Lawrence. Lawrence assured the committee that the government had no intention of taxing the women of Lagos. Not until eight years later would the government attempt to tax the women, at which time Pelewura was in the forefront of the opposition to the taxation.[8]

Pelewura's leading role in pursuing economic justice for her fellow market women was ongoing. During World War II, she organized demonstrations protesting the British monopoly over food distribution and, in December 1940, led a group of about 7,000 women in protest of the taxation of women as well as a price control scheme.[9]

In her "caustic exchange" with the commissioner, Pelewura asserted that "it was the women of Lagos who bore the brunt of wartime hardship, having to feed and clothe unemployed husbands and relatives as well as to help their men pay income tax lest they be sent to prison for defaulting."[10] She concluded her argument with a declaration along the lines of "votes for women or alternatively no taxation without representation."[11] Later, when the commissioner of the Colony offered her a monthly allowance and a new, powerful position in exchange for her support of colonial policy, Pelewura stood by her people and responded with a "scathing rejection," refusing to "break and starve the country where she was born."[12]

In September 1945, at the end of the war, the government decontrolled food prices. It is not clear to what extent Pelewura's bold demands and pressure from the LMWA led to this success, but the group's advocacy represented the Nigerian awareness of colonial oppression and the women's power to stand up against it.[13] The other focus of the LMWA—women's suffrage—that happened in 1950 for those in southern Nigeria and in 1976 for those in the north.[14]

Pelewura's outspoken leadership on behalf of the working women of Lagos was formidable, and her legacy endures. Her ability to speak truth to power continues to inspire.

Alice
Hamilton

ALICE HAMILTON

1869–1970, AMERICAN

PIONEER IN THE FIELD OF OCCUPATIONAL HEALTH, FIRST WOMAN APPOINTED TO THE FACULTY AT HARVARD MEDICAL SCHOOL

In 1970, a few months after Alice Hamilton died at the age of 101, the United States Congress passed the Occupational Safety and Health Act, thereby establishing the Occupational Safety and Health Administration (OSHA), whose mandate is to ensure safety and health in the workplace.[1] Created because of public outcry against rising injury and death rates on the job, OSHA was a milestone in US history.

Had it not been for the lifelong efforts of Hamilton, that vital act may never have come to pass.

Born to an upper-class family as one of five children, Alice Hamilton grew up in Fort Wayne, Indiana, and was initially home schooled before completing her early education at a finishing school.[2] Her parents ensured she received decent schooling, but her pursuit of an education and career in medicine did not originate with an interest in science; rather, she had an earnest desire to be of use: "I chose medicine not because I was scientifically-minded, for I was deeply ignorant of science. I chose it because as a doctor I could go anywhere I pleased—to far-off lands or to city slums—and be quite sure I could be of use anywhere."[3]

After completing finishing school at Miss Porter's School in Farmington, Connecticut, she studied chemistry and physics with a high school teacher in Fort Wayne and anatomy and biology at Fort Wayne College of Medicine before enrolling at the University of Michigan's Medical School in 1890.[4] At the age of twenty four, she received her doctor of medicine from the University of Michigan, then completed an internship at the New England Hospital for Women and Children in Massachusetts, after which she studied bacteriology and pathology at universities in Munich and Leipzig.[5] Upon returning to the United States, she continued her postgraduate studies at the Johns Hopkins University Medical School.[6]

In 1897 Hamilton moved to Chicago, where she accepted a position as professor of pathology at the Woman's Medical School of Northwestern University.[7] It was at this time that she started observing workplace pollution negatively affecting workers' health.[8] In 1902, when the typhoid fever epidemic hit Chicago, Hamilton noticed how improper sewage disposal led to the spread of disease via flies, and her findings resulted in the restructuring of the Chicago Health Department.[9] She also noted that "the health problems of many of the immigrant poor were due to unsafe conditions and noxious chemicals, especially lead dust, to which they were being exposed in the workplace."[10]

An important factor in Hamilton's motivation and determination to improve public health in the workplace was her connection to Hull House, the Chicago settlement house founded by social reformer Jane Adams. Hull House was situated in an immigrant neighborhood in the Nineteenth Ward, a heavily populated area considered a slum in which polluted water, unsanitary living conditions, and overcrowded, rundown housing was rampant.[11] Hamilton herself was a resident of Hull House, enabling her to experience firsthand the hardships of the working poor:

> *Living side by side with the poor residents of the community, she became increasingly interested in the problems workers faced, especially occupational injuries and illnesses. The study of 'industrial medicine' (the illnesses caused by certain jobs) had become increasingly important since the Industrial Revolution of the late nineteenth century had led to new dangers in the workplace.*[12]

Her experiences at Hull House, namely her treatment of immigrants for diseases contracted at their dangerous workplaces, allowed Hamilton to make a name for herself in the new field of industrial toxicology.[13]

Although there was academic literature from abroad pertinent to this important new discipline, industrial medicine was relatively unstudied in America. Com-

mitted to shining a light on this critical set of health issues, Hamilton published her first article on the topic of occupational diseases in 1908.[14] Two years later, she was appointed director of the Occupational Disease Commission of Illinois, the first investigative body of its kind in the world, and studied "the extent of industrial sickness in the state, particularly the high mortality rates due to industrial poisoning in the lead and associated enamelware industries, rubber production, painting trades, and explosives and munitions."[15]

During the following decade Hamilton continued to investigate a range of occupational health issues for a number of state and federal health agencies. Then, in 1919, a *New York Tribune* headline announced the next phase in Alice Hamilton's commendable career: "A Woman on Harvard Faculty—the Last Citadel Has Fallen—The Sex Has Come Into Its Own."[16] Hamilton had been hired as assistant professor in the new Department of Industrial Medicine at Harvard Medical School, making her the first woman appointed to the school's faculty. While it was a well-deserved honor, Hamilton experienced gender-based discrimination, and was excluded from social events and the all-male graduation ceremonies.[17] From 1924 to 1930 she served as the only woman member of the League of Nations Health Committee, and after her retirement from Harvard in 1935, Hamilton was a medical consultant to the US Division of Labor Standards, retaining her connections to Harvard as professor emerita.[18]

A leading expert in the fields of occupational health and toxicology, Hamilton applied her scientific expertise to assist a population of people in hazardous environments who had been ignored. Her studies and advocacy made a lasting difference in the lives of workers throughout the United States and the world.

Privileged daughter, idealistic young woman, exemplary student, esteemed medical doctor and professor, occupational health pioneer, Hull House resident, and advocate for the working poor, Hamilton shared:

It was also my experience at Hull-House that aroused my interest in industrial diseases. Living in a working-class quarter, coming in contact with laborers and their wives, I could not fail to hear tales of dangers that workingmen faced, of cases of carbon-monoxide gassing in the great steel mills, of painters disabled by palsy, of pneumonia and rheumatism among the men in the stockyards.[19]

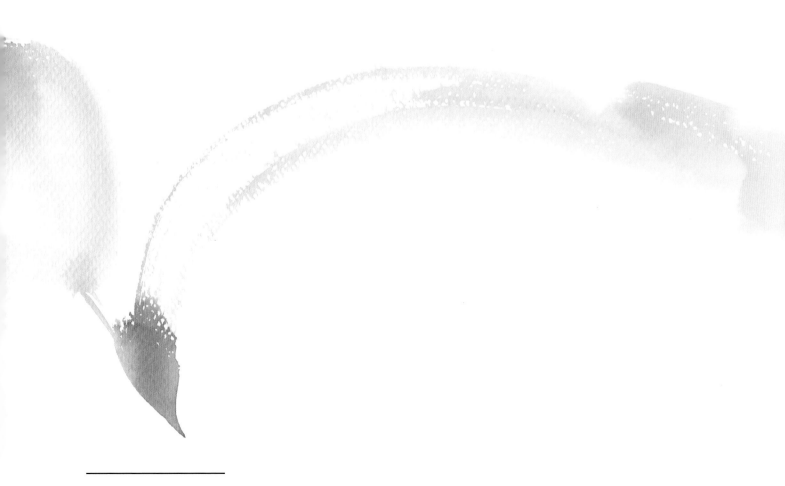

Marion Mahony Griffin

MARION MAHONY GRIFFIN
1871–1961, AMERICAN
ONE OF THE WORLD'S FIRST FEMALE ARCHITECTS, A MAJOR INFLUENCE ON FRANK LLOYD WRIGHT

Despite being one of the world's first female architects, Marion Mahony Griffin is not well known. Her work, however, was instrumental in building the reputation of one of the world's most celebrated architects: Frank Lloyd Wright (1867–1959).[1]

Marion Mahony was born in Chicago eight months before the great Chicago fire of 1871. After the fire, her family moved to Hubbard Woods, a neighborhood in the suburb Winnetka that resembled a "pioneer town."[2] Mahony would later describe enjoying a pastoral childhood where she had easy access to a natural world.[3] Her father was from Ireland, a "poet, journalist, and educator,"[4] and her mother was the daughter of a respected doctor with ties to liberal politics.[5] After the death of her father when Marion was eleven, her mother, Clara Mahony, took their five children and moved back to Chicago, where Clara became an elementary school principal. Clara also became a member of the prominent Chicago Woman's Club, and "traveled in a circle of female activists intent on women's voting rights and educational and labor reform."[6] From a young age, Mahony was surrounded by powerful women, fostering a progressive environment that served as a strong influence on the architect.[7]

It is likely that Mahony's cousin, Dwight Heald Perkins (1867–1941), who studied architecture at the Massachusetts Institute of Technology, was influential in inspiring her to enroll at MIT.[8] Mahony was also fortunate to have the support of Mary Hawes Wilmarth and her daughter Anna Wilmarth Ickes, whose wealth and influence allowed her to pursue her education in architecture.[9] In 1894, Mahony became the second woman to graduate from MIT's school of architecture.[10]

After graduating, she went to work for Perkins in a Chicago studio shared by several architects, one of whom was Frank Lloyd Wright. In 1895, Mahony became Wright's first employee.[11] She worked with Frank Lloyd Wright intermittently for the next fourteen years.[12] Her work with Wright was revolutionary, as at the time most architects refused to work with women, leaving even highly qualified female architects unable to gain experience.[13]

What was it like working for the celebrated Frank Lloyd Wright? Barry Byrne, another worker in Wright's team, notes that Mahony's skillful work gained the favor of the famed architect:

[Mahony] had unusually fine compositional and linear ability, with a drawing 'touch' that met with Mr. Wrights highly critical approval. She was the most talented member of Frank Lloyd Wright's staff, and I doubt that the studio, then or later, produced anyone superior.[14]

Byrne explains that Mahony won most of the informal competitions that Wright conducted among his employees to design the various details of his projects: stained glass, murals, mosaics, linens, and furnishings. Yet, despite her numerous contributions, Wright "sharply reprimanded anyone who referred to 'Miss Mahony's design' when her work appeared in later Wright commissions."[15] In other words, it seems that Wright felt perfectly entitled to claim Mahony's work as his own.

In fact, Mahony Griffin was later called upon to fill in for the renowned architect as his designer, again ensuring that his stellar reputation remained intact. Wright and a married client, Mamah Borthwick Cheney, left for Europe in 1909, leaving his business to be led by architect Hermann Von Holst (1874–1955). Mahony was hired as the practice's principal designer.[16] In this capacity, Mahony was the architect for a number of commissions Wright abandoned. She designed Millikin Place, a housing development in Decatur, Illinois, as well as the first (unbuilt) design for Henry Ford's Dearborn mansion in Michigan.[17]

It was during this time that Marion Mahony became Marion Mahony Griffin, marrying fellow architect Walter Burley Griffin in 1911. The pair established an office together, becoming collaborators on hundreds of projects throughout the US, Australia, and India, and even winning a competition to design the Federal Capital City of the Commonwealth of Australia.[18] Their partnership was characterized by Australian author Miles Franklin and Alice Henry, a feminist activist from Australia, as clearly synchronous: "It is plainly apparent that their ideals are happily interwoven."[19]

Walter Griffin died in 1937, leaving Mahony to complete their commissions in India and Australia. Shortly after his death, she returned to Chicago, and continued to be active in architectural work through writing, lecturing, and painting.[20] She died in 1961 at the age of ninety.

While Mahony may not have received due credit for her architectural artistry during her lifetime, astute critics are setting the record straight. Paul Kruty, architectural historian at the University of Illinois, Urbana-Champaign, asserts: "It is generally accepted that the rendering style through which Frank Lloyd Wright became known was Marion Mahony's."[21] Throughout her prolific career, Mahony broke gender barriers and created architectural history.

Charlotte Maxeke

CHARLOTTE MAXEKE

1874–1939, SOUTH AFRICAN

WOMEN'S RIGHTS ADVOCATE AND LEADER OF LIBERATION STRUGGLES IN SOUTH AFRICA

As a young woman, wherever she traveled, Charlotte Maxeke made an impression. With the singing voice of "an angel in heaven," she toured England with the African Jubilee Choir at the age of seventeen, performing for Queen Victoria.[1] She is said to have attended suffragette speeches by activists like Emmeline Pankhurst (1858–1928).[2]

On a choir tour to the United States, she was offered an opportunity to study at Wilberforce University in Ohio, which was not only affiliated with the African Methodist Episcopal Church,[3] but also the first college owned and operated by African Americans. It was there that she studied with American civil rights activist, sociologist, historian, Pan-Africanist, and author W. E. B. Du Bois (1868–1963), who influenced her future work as a leader and activist. When she received her bachelor of science from Wilberforce in 1901, Charlotte Maxeke became the first black South African woman to earn a college degree.[4]

Her travels yielded a solid educational and ideological foundation for the work she would undertake in the liberation struggles of South Africa.

As Zubeida Jaffer, author of *Beauty of the Heart: The Life and Times of Charlotte Mannya Maxeke*, explains, Charlotte Maxeke was "a remarkable woman who has long been written out of history and pushed aside in official school and university curricula."[5] Her notable accomplishments paved the way not only for the momentous political changes that later occurred in South Africa, but also for the country's first women's movement.

Upon obtaining her degree, Maxeke returned to South Africa to teach, devoting her work to uplifting and empowering black South Africans and participating in one of the first recorded women's movements.[6] In 1918, Maxeke founded the Bantu Women's League (BWL), a predecessor of the African National Congress Women's League (ANC), which focused on raising awareness of how South Africans "pass laws," an internal passport system that segregated the population, affecting the country's black women.[7] The pass became a symbol of oppression, as white men and women were not required to carry passes.[8] Maxeke was a leader in multiple protests against pass laws, such as one in 1913 in which protesters burned their passes (and were subsequently arrested), as well as another after the establishment of the BWL in which Maxeke led a group to the prime minister's office to protest.[9] Pass laws, especially their impact on black women, was a popular target for protests in the following years.

Such demands for women's freedom of mobility and fair pay were founded on Maxeke's long-held principles extolling social justice and women's rights. Jaffer states that Maxeke "and her contemporary circle of intellectuals were committed to crafting an inclusive society."[10] In her public debates she drew on her intellectual gifts to advocate for women and the working class. As scholar Thozama April of the Centre for Humanities Research at the University of the Western Cape explains:

In [Maxeke's] public engagements, she outlined the problems and the challenges of women in South Africa during the 1920s and 1930s. She deliberated and defined arguments about legislation relating to marriage, the relation of women to children, the politics of the employment of women, [and] women's mobility.[11]

Organizer of the women's anti-pass movement, founder of the Bantu Women's League, leader of a delegation to Prime Minister Louis Botha to protest passes for women, cofounder of the Industrial and Commercial Workers' Union, and speaker at the Women's Reform Club for the voting rights of women, Charlotte Maxeke used her intellect and her "angelic" voice to speak out and advocate for social change.[12] Charlotte Maxeke's Wilberforce University professor W. E. B. Du Bois had this to say about his former student:

[Charlotte Maxeke has a] a clear mind, [a] fund of subtle humour and a straight-forward honesty [of] character . . . I regard Mrs. Maxeke as a pioneer in one of the greatest of human causes, working under extraordinarily difficult circumstances to lead a people, in the face of prejudice, not only against her race, but against her sex. To fight not simply the natural and inherent difficulties of education and social uplift, but to fight with little money and little outside aid was indeed a tremendous task.[13]

Zitkala-Ša

ZITKALA-ŠA
1876–1938, YANKTON SIOUX (INDIGENOUS AMERICAN)
WROTE THE LIBRETTO FOR THE FIRST OPERA BY A NATIVE AMERICAN; FOUNDED THE NATIONAL COUNCIL OF AMERICAN INDIANS

As a young girl, Zitkala-Ša experienced the lack of educational opportunities and cultural appreciation afforded to Native Americans. As an adult, she would work to change these conditions as an activist, writer, and reformer.

Zitkala-Ša (Red Bird), also known as Gertrude Simmons Bonnin, was born to a Yankton-Sioux mother and a Euro-American father, and raised on the Yankton Reservation in South Dakota by her mother. At the age of eight, Zitkala-Ša was sent away from her reservation to attend Whites Manual Labor Institute, a Quaker missionary school in Wabash, Indiana.[1] She spent her lifetime writing about her experiences at such institutions, where the objective was to subjugate and "civilize" Native Americans. Those experiences contrasted to those within her own culture. In one autobiographical piece, she articulates that difference in stark poetic language:

The melancholy of those black days has left so long a shadow that it darkens the path of years that have since gone by. These sad memories rise above those of smoothly grinding school days. Perhaps my Indian nature is the moaning wind which stirs them now for their present record. But however tempestuous this is within me, it comes out as the low voice of a curiously colored seashell, which is only for those ears that are bent with compassion to hear it.[2]

Zitkala-Ša attended Earlham College in Richmond, Indiana, and graduated in 1897, after which she taught for two years at the Carlisle Indian Industrial School in Carlisle, Pennsylvania, despite her discomfort with the institution's policies. In addition to harsh disciplinary practices, the school also employed a Euro-American-centric curriculum that was designed to erase its students' Native American cultural identities.[3]

Still in her early twenties, Zitkala-Ša embarked on a fruitful writing career. In 1901, she published an anthology of Dakota stories, *Old Indian Legends*.[4] Around the same time, she began writing numerous autobiographical pieces and short stories, which were originally printed in the prestigious *Atlantic Monthly* magazine (and later published in a collection entitled *American Indian Stories* in 1921).[5] In her piece "Why I Am a Pagan," published in the *Atlantic Monthly* in 1902, she writes of her cousin's attempt to convince her to become a Christian and of her own enduring belief in the spiritual power and sanctity of nature:

> The little incident recalled to mind the copy of a missionary paper brought to my notice a few days ago, in which a 'Christian' pugilist commented upon a recent article of mine, grossly perverting the spirit of my pen. Still I would not forget that the pale-faced missionary and the hoodooed aborigine are both God's creatures, though small indeed their own conceptions of Infinite Love. A wee child toddling in a wonder world, I prefer to their dogma my excursions into the natural gardens where the voice of the Great Spirit is heard in the twittering of birds, the rippling of mighty waters, and the sweet breathing of flowers. If this is Paganism, then at present, at least, I am a Pagan.[6]

Zitkala-Ša's literary talents were not confined to books and articles. In 1913, a collaboration with Utah music instructor William F. Hanson established her as the first Native American to write a libretto for an opera. Together, the pair produced and staged *The Sun Dance Opera*, which merged traditional Plains Indian ritual with an operetta musical style and a melodramatic love triangle. This blending of cultural traditions was unique, as Dr. P. Jane Hafen of the University of Nevada, Las Vegas, explains:

> The composition of the opera presents the challenges of forging distinct and disparate cultures by harmonizing traditional Native melodies and perspectives into the pinnacle of artistic expression in western civilization: grand opera. Opera, literally the plural of opus or 'works' of artistic expression, provides a holistic context that represents varied and complex manifestations of culture. Visual presentation and costuming, singing, dancing, storytelling, and even incorporation of a trickster-like heyoka[7] depict aspects of Plains culture in *The Sun Dance Opera*. At the same time, an orchestral accompaniment and dramatic plot infuse elements of western civilization. As a classically trained musician, Bonnin used her skills to affirm her Sioux cultural identity and to engage the conventions of popular culture. Hanson used his fondness for Indian peoples and his association with them in what critics would now recognize as an artistic colonialism. The result is an uneasy duet of two cultures.[8]

This "uneasy duet" was due, at least in part, to Hanson's paternal-like overseeing of a performance of culture unrelated to his own, which contrasted with Zitkala-Ša's identity and cultural ownership.[9] But, it is likely that Zitkala-Ša viewed her participation in the project as empowering, as it gave her artistic control over presenting her cultural viewpoint, allowing her "personal and cultural validation."[10] In 1938, shortly after Zitkala-Ša's death, her opera was selected and performed by the New York Opera Guild as opera of the year.

Zitkala-Ša's creative accomplishments were informed by a profound connection to her Native American culture and its various communities, and that cultural bond inspired her to advocate for Indian rights throughout her life. She served as the secretary of the Society of the American Indian, was a liaison between the society and the Bureau of Indian Affairs, and edited the society's *American Indian Magazine*. Using her pseudonym Gertrude Bonnin, she coauthored *Oklahoma's Poor Rich Indians: An Orgy of Graft and Exploitation of the Five Civilized Tribes—Legalized Robbery*. Published by the Office of Indian Rights Association in 1924, the book exposed the mistreatment of the Native American population in Oklahoma. In addition, she founded the National Council of American Indians in 1926 and, as president, advocated for improved educational opportunities and health care, citizenship rights, and cultural recognition and preservation.[11] Throughout her career, she worked toward the advancement of her community and the protection of her heritage, and her poetic writings reflect her perspective. Such perspective is embodied by the opening lines of "Why I Am a Pagan":

> *When the spirit swells my breast I love to roam leisurely among the green hills; or sometimes, sitting on the brink of the murmuring Missouri, I marvel at the great blue overhead. With half closed eyes I watch the huge cloud shadows in their noiseless play upon the high bluffs opposite me, while into my ear ripple the sweet, soft cadences of the river's song.*[12]

Lise Meitner

LISE MEITNER

1878–1968, AUSTRIAN

PHYSICIST WHO LED IN THE DISCOVERY OF NUCLEAR FISSION

Born to Jewish parents in the intellectually and culturally vibrant city of Vienna, Lise Meitner's childhood was a treasured one, according to her biographer Ruth Lewin Sime. Meitner recalled "the unusual goodness of my parents, and the extraordinarily stimulating intellectual atmosphere in which my brothers and sisters and I grew up."[1] Her father, a lawyer, was able to provide all eight of his children with trips to the mountains, books, and music lessons. Meitner not only loved playing the piano but was also passionate about science and math, allegedly keeping a cherished math book under her pillow as a child.[2] All of the Meitner children, including the five girls, pursued an advanced education, under fortuitous timing as women were legally excluded from Austrian universities until 1897.[3]

Meitner had private instruction in physics and completed her rigorous final examinations at the Akademisches Gymnasium[4] in 1901.[5] Furthering her studies in physics, she went on to become the second woman to obtain a doctoral degree in physics at the University of Vienna in 1906.[6] Upon graduation, she spent a year teaching and becoming familiar with radioactivity research, unsure of

her future in Vienna.[7] With the financial support of her parents, she journeyed to Berlin in 1907 to continue her education, attending lectures by renowned physicist Max Planck at the Friedrich-Wilhelm-Universität.[8] She had to ask Planck for permission to attend his lectures, later noting that "he could have no very high opinion of women students, and possibly that was true enough at the time."[9]

Anxious to become involved in experimental physics, Meitner approached professor Heinrich Rubens, head of the experimental physics institute, who offered her a place in his laboratory.[10] It was likely through Rubens that she met Dr. Otto Hahn, with whom she would later engage in her most influential work on nuclear fission.[11]

When Hahn was appointed as head of radiochemistry at Kaiser Wilhelm Gesellschaft (KWG), a newly established independent research institute outside Berlin, Meitner became his salaried research assistant.[12] Together and independently for thirty years, they worked on exploring the physics and chemistry of radioactive substances, ultimately achieving important results in the new field of nuclear physics.[13] Their purpose was to "sort out and understand the confusing array of radioactive products that ensued … [when] bombarding uranium with neutrons."[14] In other words, they were attempting to solve the puzzle of nuclear fission.[15]

In 1938, Meitner's research with Hahn resulted in the discovery of nuclear fission in heavy nuclei. Coincidentally, that year Hitler's rise to power put all Jewish scientists at risk. "By the middle of 1938, it was clear that every day Meitner stayed [in Germany] she ran the risk of forced emigration or worse … she would have to leave—illegally … because her Austrian passport was no longer recognized and the Nazis refused to issue her legal documents."[16] Meitner was forced to escape to Sweden to live and work.[17]

A life begun with a treasured childhood, defined by an ongoing quest for scientific knowledge and breakthrough discovery, also entailed the flight of a refugee. Meitner continued her work in Sweden, became a citizen there in 1946, and conducted atomic research into her late eighties, including work on R1, Sweden's first nuclear reactor.[18]

But her major achievements were never properly acknowledged. Meitner had worked on the team that discovered nuclear fission of uranium and thorium and coined the term "nuclear fission" with her nephew, Otto Frisch. Yet, although she was awarded numerous honorary doctorates, medals, society memberships, and prizes, including the Enrico Fermi Prize, she did not share the Nobel Prize for Chemistry awarded to Hahn for their shared discovery of nuclear fission.[19] Her name was submitted ten times by Hahn to the Nobel Prize committee but was never accepted.[20]

Addressing the Austrian UNESCO Commission in 1953, Meitner offered these words to describe her profound connection to scientific inquiry:

> *Science makes people reach selflessly for truth and objectivity; it teaches people to accept reality, with wonder and admiration, not to mention the deep awe and joy that the natural order of things brings to the true scientist.*[21]

Lillian Gilbreth

LILLIAN GILBRETH

1878–1972, AMERICAN

PIONEER IN INDUSTRIAL-ORGANIZATIONAL PSYCHOLOGY

With a career spanning nearly seventy years, Lillian Gilbreth was a pioneering force in the field of industrial-organizational psychology, the scientific study of human behavior in the workplace, and engineering.[1] Gilbreth was a woman of "firsts": the first woman to receive the Hoover Medal for significant public service by an engineer, the first woman to become a member of the Society of Industrial Engineers, and the first female psychologist featured on a US postage stamp.[2] She was also an inventor of now-commonplace kitchen necessities such as the shelves inside refrigerator doors, an early electric mixer, and the foot pedal-operated trash can.[3]

Although her illustrious career was characterized by psychology and engineering, Lillian Gilbreth—born Lillie Moller in Oakland, California—initially favored poetry and music. Her BA at the University of California, Berkeley, was in literature, and when she graduated in 1900, she was its first female commencement speaker.[4]

Gilbreth intended to take graduate courses in literature with the well-known professor of dramatic literature Brander Matthews (1852–1929) at Columbia University before learning that Matthews did not allow women to attend his lectures.[5] Gilbreth instead studied with psychologist E. L. Thorndike, also at Columbia.[6] Still intending to pursue an academic program in literature, Gilbreth returned to Berkeley and completed her MA in literature in 1902.[7]

A year into her PhD studies, which included a minor in psychology, she met Frank Gilbreth, a wealthy construction company owner, through a mutual friend. After an instant connection, the couple were married in 1904. They would eventually have twelve children, two of whom would grow up to write the famous book *Cheaper by the Dozen* (1948) based on their large family.[8] The young family moved to Rhode Island in 1910, where Lillian, already a mother of four, attended Brown University and received her doctorate in 1915.[9]

The marriage became a turning point for Lillian professionally as well as personally. Despite not having a university education himself, her husband encouraged her to focus on scientific management and workplace efficiency, causing Gilbreth to change her major to psychology in order to help her husband's company once she obtained her PhD.[10] Her dissertation, published in 1914 with the title "The Psychology of Management," was "a manual for using psychological principles to increase industrial efficiency," building on the fields of industrial and management engineering.[11] Soon she and her husband became a pioneering team in the new discipline of organizational psychology, partners both at home and in work as they applied scientific management techniques to both their household and businesses.[12]

As the Association for Psychological Science points out, the husband-wife team was among the first to use film as a tool in their psychological and organizational analysis:

> Lillian and Frank Gilbreth were early adopters of film as a tool for analyzing how workers performed their jobs. They would film manufacturing workers, then review the film with the workers over cigars and quiz them on how the work could be improved. They studied worker motivation, including money and job satisfaction. They also installed suggestion boxes for worker feedback and added regular breaks for workers to improve morale and productivity. Their films also helped the team improve hospital efficiency and make jobs and household tasks easier and more accessible for disabled workers.[13]

The Gilbreths coauthored a number of books, but Lillian's name was excluded, as publishers feared the book's credibility would be questioned if a woman was acknowledged as its author. Instead, her husband, who had not been to college, was listed as the sole author, and Gilbreth was uncredited, despite possessing a doctorate and being one of the few specialists in industrial psychology.[14]

In 1928, Frank Gilbreth died unexpectedly, leaving Lillian to not only run their consulting business on her own but to care for and provide an income for her large family. She and Frank had previously offered training workshops in their home for managers looking to apply their scientific management techniques, and Gilbreth resumed these classes as they let her stay home with the children while she worked.[15] Initially some clients were reluctant to be trained by a woman, but eventually the workshops led to consulting work for companies like General Electric and Macy's department store in New York City, where she worked as a sales clerk to more fully understand how to help the employees.[16] As one of the first organizational psychologists to recognize and address fatigue and stress as detriments to productivity, she improved workers' schedules by introducing regular breaks and reduce workplace stresses such as a loud environment.[17] Eventually Gilbreth began offering training through universities and colleges, including Bryn Mawr, Rutgers, and Purdue. She became the first female professor in Purdue's engineering school in 1935.[18]

Lillian Gilbreth has been noted as being one of the first women to "have it all": a successful career as both an eminent specialist in engineering and industrial psychology, and a family-oriented mother of twelve.[19] She not only dedicated herself to her family but did so without compromising her pioneering work. While for years her work was considered adjunct to her husband's, her exhaustive career made her an undeniably influential force in her field. At the age of 76, in an interview with the *Minneapolis Tribune*, she offered this inspirational insight that mirrored her professional desire for improvement:

I think we all—and this goes even for newspaper reporters out traveling about the country—should always be on the lookout for new leaders, for young people with a new slant on things . . . We don't want these young people to think the past was perfect. We don't want them to sit here and let the world go to pieces.[20]

Lois Weber

LOIS WEBER

1879–1939, AMERICAN

ONE OF THE MOST SUCCESSFUL FILM DIRECTORS IN EARLY HOLLYWOOD

reta Gerwig, Sofia Coppola, Kathryn Bigelow, Jane Campion: successful film directors who also happen to be women, a distinction that is still appallingly rare in the twenty-first century. In fact, of the one hundred top-grossing films of 2018, women represented only 4 percent of directors.[1]

So how did Lois Weber, born in 1879, become one of the most successful Hollywood film directors in the early twentieth century, with the number one box-office film of 1916? And why have so few people heard of her?

The first American woman to direct a feature-length dramatic film (*The Merchant of Venice* in 1914) and the director of more than 130 short- and feature-length movies, Weber was ranked alongside D.W. Griffith and Cecil B. DeMille as the three "great minds" of the burgeoning film industry.[2] Her path to becoming a film director included professional experience as a concert pianist, classical singer, theatrical actress, director of *phonoscènes*,[3] and screenwriter.[4] In 1904, she married fellow actor Wendell Phillips Smalley, and by 1907 the pair had begun working in motion pictures together, often billed together as "The Smalleys."[5]

By 1916, Weber had established herself as the leader of the husband-and-wife duo, becoming the sole writer of the couple's film scripts, and was considered one of the top directors at the Universal Film Manufacturing Company.[6] At Universal, Weber directed "a series of high profile and often deeply controversial films on social issues of the day, including capital punishment in *The People vs. John Doe* (1916), drug abuse in *Hop, the Devil's Brew* (1916), poverty and wage equity in *Shoes* (1916), and contraception in *Where Are My Children?* (1916) and *The Hand That Rocks the Cradle* (1917)."[7]

In a 1913 issue of *Photoplay* magazine, Weber spoke of aspiring to produce work "that will have an influence for good on the public mind."[8] Her social consciousness and deeply held belief that movies could address serious issues while at the same time providing compelling entertainment motivated her creative efforts. Her talents and ideology are poignantly apparent in her 1916 film *Shoes*, as profiled in this summary by the film's current distributor, Milestone Film & Video:

> *Eva Meyer is [a] poor shop girl working at a five-and-dime. She is the sole wage earner for three younger*

sisters, a mother who struggles to hold everything together, and a father who prefers beer and penny dreadfuls to work. Each week, Eva returns to her cold-water flat and dutifully hands over her meager earnings to her mother. But her wages barely cover the grocer's bill and cannot provide for decent clothing. With only cardboard to patch the holes in the soles of her shoes, Eva's life becomes harder with each rainy day and every splinter. In constant pain and with no solution in sight, the disheartened girl considers the uninvited advances of Charlie, a cad with clearly dishonorable intentions . . .

So begins Lois Weber's SHOES, perhaps her finest masterpiece and one of the great feminist films in the history of cinema . . . Shoes is a plea for women's equality.[9]

Shoes was adapted from a short story by Stella Wynne Herron, who in turn was inspired by Jane Addams's 1912 book on prostitution, *A New Conscience and an Ancient Evil.*[10] Weber's cinematic interpretation of the harrowing struggles of one working-class woman, influenced by her own missionary work with young girls in the slums of New York, was not only a creative masterpiece, it was socially resonant, emotionally powerful, and hugely successful.[11]

After finding tremendous directorial success, and even earning the title of "the greatest woman director" in 1916, Weber left Universal in 1917 to establish her own company, Lois Weber Productions.[12] The business-savvy Weber was able to negotiate "extremely lucrative" distribution contracts with Universal; she was Hollywood's highest-paid director.[13]

In an era when films were often referred to as empty entertainment, Weber described, in her own words, her determination to "raise the standard" and "bring back refined audiences" to film, a desire that was reflected in her socially conscious and well-made movies.[14] At the time of her death in 1939, she was remembered primarily as a "star-maker," rather than her true position as one of Hollywood's most influential early directors.[15] After being rediscovered at the end of the twentieth century, her contributions are beginning to get rightful attention, allowing this incredible director to inspire today's film buffs, historians, and feminists.

Huda Sha'arawi

HUDA SHA' ARAWI
1879–1947, EGYPTIAN
FOUNDER OF THE EGYPTIAN FEMINIST UNION

To those from Western countries, the word *harem* may conjure a Hollywood image of exotic, scantily dressed women lounging on oversized pillows, at the beck and call of an entitled sultan. In fact, the word actually refers to women's quarters, a place where something forbidden is kept safe. The derivation of the word, according to the *Oxford Dictionary*: "from Arabic ḥaram, ḥarīm, literally 'prohibited, prohibited place' (hence 'sanctuary, women's quarters, women')."[1]

For Huda Sha'arawi, the daughter of an important Egyptian public servant, growing up within the harem system was not unusual. Egyptian women at the time were kept isolated and veiled, regardless of their economic status, and the young Sha'arawi spent her youth secluded in a harem.[2]

She would go on to spend her entire life speaking out against such isolation and advocating for the rights of all women.

Coming from an affluent family, Huda's education was extensive. A voracious student, she was tutored in several languages, including Arabic, Turkish, and French, and also studied grammar, calligraphy, piano, and poetry.[3] After studying the habits of poetess Sayyida Khadija, Sha'arawi concluded that "with learning, women could be the equals of men if not surpass them."[4] At the age of thirteen, she was married to her cousin, Ali Sha'arawi, who was more than thirty years her senior. They lived apart for seven years, during which time Huda concentrated on her studies, but in 1900 family pressure forced the couple to reconcile.[5] Despite their extreme age difference and the fact that it was an arranged marriage, Ali Sha'arawi, a leading political activist himself, supported his wife's activism and would often seek her council.[6]

The couple were both vocal advocates for Egyptian independence from Great Britain. Ali Sha'arawi was a founding member of the nationalist Wafd party, while Huda Sha'arawi founded and was president of the Wafdist Women's Central Committee, which became a proving ground for women's advocacy in Egypt.[7] This was not unusual at the time, as Egyptian women were openly engaging in political activism by publicly participating in the national movement, marking a turning point in Egyptian society.[8]

After the death of her husband, Sha'arawi began to focus heavily on women's equality, founding the Egyptian Feminist Union in 1923, an association that desired equality milestones like women's suffrage and broader educational opportunities.[9] She attended the International

Woman Suffrage Alliance Congress in Rome in 1923, and upon her return she decided to perform an act that was both personally meaningful and politically powerful: upon arriving at a busy Cairo train station, she publicly removed her veil, shocking those around her and causing a commotion. Women reportedly applauded her decision, with some even joining her in removing their veils.[10] Removing her face veil in public for the first time was her most well-known act of protest, becoming a symbol for her work striving for gender equality in Egypt.

For the rest of her life, Sha'arawi served as the prominent spokeswoman for women's rights in Egypt and the Arab world—organizing, publishing, and lecturing. Her beliefs are perhaps best summarized by her opening remarks at the Arab Feminist Conference in 1944, in which she passionately asserted:

> *Ladies and gentlemen, the Arab woman who is equal to the man in duties and obligations will not accept, in the twentieth century, the distinctions between the sexes that the advanced countries have done away with. The Arab woman will not agree to be chained in slavery and to pay for the consequences of men's mistakes with respect to her country's rights and the future of her children.*[11]

Maria Blanchard

MARÍA BLANCHARD

1881–1932, SPANISH

CUBISM'S TRANSCENDENT ARTIST

A complex and multifaceted visual art style, cubism emerged in the swell of avant-garde art movements dominating the early twentieth century. Spearheaded by the Spanish Pablo Picasso (1881–1973) and the French Georges Braque (1882–1963), cubism is characterized by a rejection of traditional painting norms that imitated natural perspective, modeling, and foreshortening.[1] Instead, cubist painters reduced and fractured their subjects into geometric forms, reconstructing them within a two-dimensional plane.[2] In other words, it was a groundbreaking, revolutionary, and incredibly challenging new style of art.

Spanish painter María Blanchard was not afraid of this challenge, creating works that uniquely addressed the challenges of cubism. But despite being considered equal, if not superior, to those of her fellow avant-garde artists, Blanchard is a relatively unknown name in art history.[3] Exhibitions and scholarships are just beginning to uncover this incredible woman artist and her distinctive oeuvre.

Born María Gutiérrez Cueto in the northern port city of Santander, Spain, and later adopting her grandmother's surname of Blanchard, María was born with physical deformities, causing her physical and emotional pain throughout her life.[4] Her growth was stunted, and she walked with a limp, resulting in her being teased as a child with the nickname "the witch."[5] Despite such formidable challenges, however, María was encouraged by her parents' love and support to study art, for which she had shown an aptitude as a young girl.[6]

In 1903, at the age of twenty-two, Blanchard moved to Madrid to study with artists Emilio Sala and Manuel Benedito.[7] After winning third prize at the Exposición Nacional de Bellas Artes, she was awarded an educational grant, enabling her to move to Paris and study at the Académie Vitti, where she discovered cubism and was influenced by artists like the Spanish painter Juan Gris (1887–1927).[8]

María Blanchard's artistic trajectory is astutely summarized in a narrative published by Madrid's Museo Nacional Centro de Arte Reina Sofía, Spain's national museum of twentieth-century art. In this overview of the museum's 2012–2013 exhibit of her work, Blanchard is described as "an original and decisive artist" who is "often obscured in art historiography":

> *Her pictorial work shows revealing connections with her tragic existence and situates her as an original and*

decisive artist, a contemporary—on equal terms—of other great figures by whom she is often obscured in art historiography.

Blanchard would achieve a perfect command of synthetic cubism, in which she uses a chromatic range that is sentimental and full of poetic plasticity.[9]

Exhibition Curator María Jose Salazar adds that although Blanchard's physical challenges impacted her life, "her strong character and tough existence earned her the respect of her colleagues, who came to accept her as an equal in an environment culturally dominated by men."[10] Salazar contends that María Blanchard "shows greater freedom in her interpretation of the subject matter" than the leading cubist artists of her day and that her work reflects "a highly personal form of Cubism which stands out for its formal precision, austerity and command of colour."[11] She further points out that cubist sculptor Jacques Lipchitz credited Blanchard for bringing expressiveness and feeling to cubism.[12] It is important to note, however, that her obscurity in art history was not due to her lack of originality and aptitude, but rather to the fact that, after her death, her family withdrew her paintings, leading to a lack of accurate documentation about her career.

Though her story is often overlooked, suffering from a lack of accurate documentation, María Blanchard remains one of the most significant cubist artists. Perhaps the highest compliment paid to Blanchard was that of one of her celebrated male counterparts, the Mexican painter Diego Rivera (1886–1957): "Her time in cubism produced the movement's best works, apart from those of our master, Picasso."[13]

Bessie Coleman

BESSIE COLEMAN

1892–1926, AMERICAN

FIRST AFRICAN AMERICAN PILOT

When considering famous American female aviators, many minds may immediately think of Amelia Earhart (1897–ca. 1937). While Earhart was a courageous and revolutionary figure in early aviation, she was not the first American woman to receive her pilot's license.[1] That honor belongs to Bessie Coleman.

Born to sharecroppers in Atlanta, Texas, the tenth of thirteen children, Bessie Coleman always dreamt of an opportunity to "amount to something," and worked hard to achieve her goal.[2] A voracious student, Coleman completed the eight grades offered in her one-room school and used her savings to enroll in the Colored Agricultural and Normal University in Langston, Oklahoma in 1910.[3] Unfortunately, she was forced to drop out after one term due to lack of funds, but that didn't stop her dreams—even if she wasn't certain what her success would look like.

Moving to Chicago to live with two of her older brothers, she worked as a manicurist on Chicago's south side.[4] But being a beautician was not what Bessie had in mind. She wanted to fly.

Not many American women had pilot's licenses in 1918, and the few who did were mostly wealthy and white.[5] Coleman was turned away by every flying school that she approached because of her race and gender.[6] Undeterred, she remembered what her brother, who had fought in World War I, told her about France; unlike the United States, women of any background in France were allowed to become pilots.[7]

Bessie learned French at a Berlitz school in Chicago and moved to France in 1920, becoming the only student of color in her class at the Caudron Brothers School of Aviation in Le Crotoy, France.[8] She had saved up from her jobs in Chicago, and she also received financial assistance for tuition from African American philanthropists such as Robert Abbott, founder of the *Chicago Defender*.[9]

Coleman learned how to fly in seven months, and was taught using a 27-foot biplane that often failed, sometimes while in the air.[10] While at school Coleman witnessed a plane crash that killed another student, which she recounted as being a "terrible shock."[11] On June 15, 1921, Bessie Coleman obtained her international pilot's license from the Fédération Aéronautique Internationale, making history as the first American woman to do so.

Upon her return to the United States in September 1921, Coleman was a celebrity, especially among African

Americans: "Scores of reporters turned out to meet her. The *Air Service News* noted that Coleman had become "a full-fledged aviatrix, the first of her race." She was invited as a guest of honor to attend the all-black musical *Shuffle Along*. The entire audience, including the several hundred whites in the orchestra seats, rose to give the first African-American female pilot a standing ovation."[12]

Her landmark achievement didn't automatically lead to an income, however. The savvy Coleman understood that a certain level of showmanship and entertainment was vital in forging a career, so in order to earn money she decided to become a "barnstormer," performing aerial acrobatics for audiences in "flying circuses."[13] Realizing that she lacked the technical skill to pursue such a dangerous profession, she returned to France for more training.

Upon returning to the United States, Coleman spent the next five years performing at countless air shows. The *Chicago Defender* publicized her first event at Curtiss Field on Long Island, promising that the "the world's greatest woman flier"[14] would do "heart thrilling stunts." The event was in honor of veterans of the all-black 369th Infantry Regiment of World War I, with over 3,000 people in attendance.

More exhibition flights followed—in Memphis, Chicago, and Texas—as well as a series of lectures in Black theaters in the southeast, as Coleman used her influence to encourage other African Americans to learn to fly, and also refusing to perform where African Americans were refused admission.[15] Realizing her position of prominence, her ultimate dream was to found a flying school for African Americans.[16] Keenly aware of the layers of prejudice that prevented African Americans from pursuing their goals, Bessie Coleman was quoted as saying, "The air is the only place free from prejudices. I knew we had no aviators, neither men nor women, and I knew the Race needed to be represented along this most important line, so I thought it my duty to risk my life to learn aviation."[17]

In fact, Bessie Coleman lost her life at the age of thirty-four doing what she had set out to do—making a difference by representing African Americans in a groundbreaking career. On April 30, 1926, as she was performing a practice flight for a May Day celebration in Jacksonville, Florida, her plane, with her mechanic and publicity agent William Will as pilot, unexpectedly went into a nosedive and plummeted to the earth, throwing Coleman from the plane to her death.[18]

Five thousand mourners attended Bessie Coleman's memorial service in Orlando, Florida, and an estimated 15,000 people paid their respects at her funeral in Chicago.[19] In 1929, her dream of flying school for African Americans was made reality thanks to American engineer and aviator William J. Powell (1897–1942), who established the Bessie Coleman Aero Club in Los Angeles, a school that educated and inspired future African American flyers.[20]

Every year on the anniversary of her death, African American pilots fly over Bessie Coleman's grave in Chicago, scattering flowers in her honor.[21]

Alice Ball

ALICE BALL

1892–1916, AMERICAN

CHEMIST WHO DISCOVERED A TREATMENT FOR LEPROSY

We too often fear what we don't understand, and for centuries leprosy was a misunderstood disease that was feared to be the result of a curse or a punishment from God. In Europe during the Middle Ages, for example, "leprosy sufferers had to wear special clothing, ring bells to warn others that they were close, and even walk on a particular side of the road, depending on the direction of the wind."[1] It wasn't until 1873 that science dispelled the superstitions and fears accompanying a diagnosis of leprosy, when a Norwegian doctor named Dr. Gerhard Hansen proved that leprosy was caused by a germ and was thus not hereditary and not the result of a curse or a sin.[2]

Still, the disease, known thereafter as Hansen's disease, is painful and debilitating. It can cause nerve damage, muscle weakness, paralysis, blindness, and disfigurement. By the early twentieth century, chaulmoogra oil (derived from the seeds of a tropical evergreen tree) was being used to treat the disease, but the results were inconsistent.[3]

Which is why Alice Ball's expertise as a research chemist was so significant.

Ball's interest in chemistry and awareness of chemical processes was likely nurtured by her family, several of whom were photographers, including her grandfather, J. P. Ball Sr., one of the first African Americans to learn the art of daguerreotype.[4]

Born in Seattle, Washington, in 1892, Alice Ball attended the University of Washington and graduated with two degrees: in pharmaceutical chemistry in 1912 and pharmacy in 1914. In the fall of 1914, she entered the College of Hawaii (later the University of Hawaii) as a graduate student in chemistry, and in 1915 she was the first African American and woman to graduate with a master of science degree in chemistry from that institution. She soon became the first woman to teach chemistry at the University of Hawaii, beginning in the 1914–1915 academic year.[5]

The subject of Ball's master's thesis (identifying the active components of the kava root) led to Dr. Harry Hollmann recruiting her to engage in research on the potential applications of chaulmoogra oil for the treatment of leprosy.[6] Hollmann, an assistant surgeon at Kalihi Hospital in Hawaii, one of the few facilities in Hawaii that treated patients with Hansen's disease, was impressed with Ball's work. Hollmann believed Ball could come up with a solution made from the active components of chaulmoogra oil that could be injected into patients with Hansen's disease without side effects.[7]

According to *National Geographic* medical writer Carisa Brewster, "Ball worked arduously, juggling teaching during the day and the chaulmoogra problem during every moment of her free time. In less than a year, she had found a way to create a water-soluble solution of the oil's active compounds that could be safely injected, with minimal side effects."[8]

Unfortunately, Alice Ball's groundbreaking research took a heavy toll on her health. While juggling her research and duties as chemistry instructor, Ball became ill. She died on December 31, 1916, at the age of twenty-four. According to her obituary, she was poisoned by the inhalation of chlorine gas during a class demonstration in Honolulu.

Ball never had the chance to publish her findings, but after her death, Arthur L. Dean, a chemist and the president of the University of Hawaii, refined her work, published the findings without giving credit to Ball, and began producing the injectable chaulmoogra extract.[9] Dean named the technique after himself but Ball's supervisor Hollmann set the record straight.[10] In a 1922 medical journal article, Hollmann clarified that Alice Ball created the chaulmoogra solution, and he referred to it as the "Ball Method."[11]

The Ball Method continued to be the most effective method of treatment for Hansen's disease until a new treatment was introduced to the market in the 1940s.[12]

It wasn't until long after her death that Ball received proper acknowledgment for her pioneering work in the treatment of Hansen's disease. In 2000, the University of Hawaii dedicated a plaque to her on the school's chaulmoogra tree,[13] and the former lieutenant governor of Hawaii, Mazie Hirono, declared February 29 Alice Ball Day. In 2007, ninety-one years after her death, Alice Ball was honored by the University of Hawaii board of regents with a medal of distinction.[14]

BEYOND ANONYMITY

In "A Letter to Virginia Woolf, On Translating *A Room of One's Own* into Romanian," Elena Marcu demonstrates that women throughout the world still relate to Judith Shakespeare and continue to be inspired by Virginia Woolf's protest:

> We know this girl, Shakespeare's sister. It is for her that we sometimes take to the streets today. It is for her that we translate this book in Romanian ... I went to the library the other day. A hundred years later and there are still fewer women on the shelves. But ... we are getting better, Virginia. We are getting closer.[1]

The ripple effects of Virginia Woolf's renowned assertion—"Indeed, I would venture to guess that Anon, who wrote so many poems without signing them, was often a woman"—frequently misquoted as "For most of history, Anonymous was a woman," still echo in the twenty-first century as women are forced to contend with many of the same dilemmas.

Why is it that the words of such a highly regarded author have been altered? What is the underlying significance of Woolf's phrase—and why does it continue to resonate nearly one hundred years after her essay was published?

I believe that women identify with the fundamental meaning of the "Anon" statement so profoundly that they feel compelled to use Woolf's words—albeit slightly modified—to define an indisputable truth: Throughout history, accomplished women have been disregarded. Throughout history, noteworthy women were overlooked and thus forgotten. Throughout history, remarkable, talented, brilliant women remained anonymous.

Virginia Woolf's original statement relates to her contention that female writers have historically been suppressed by culturally sanctioned misogynistic barriers. She creates a character named Judith Shakespeare, William's fictional sister, who was as talented and ambitious as her brother, in order to show that Judith would likely have been defeated by the sexist realities of the day. Woolf vehemently drives her thesis home in the following passage:

> Reviewing the story of Shakespeare's sister as I had made it ... any woman born with a great gift in the sixteenth century would certainly have gone crazed, shot herself, or ended her days in some lonely cottage outside the village, half witch, half wizard, feared and mocked at. For it needs little skill in psychology to be sure that a highly gifted girl who had tried to use her gift for poetry would have been so thwarted

and hindered by other people, so tortured and pulled asunder by her own contrary instincts, that she must have lost her health and sanity to a certainty.[2]

Readers extrapolate Judith Shakespeare's story and apply it to women in other cultures and circumstances. And they conclude that it has always been an uphill battle for women not only to achieve success, but also to be acknowledged for that success in a male-dominated world. Therefore, it is understandable that Virginia Woolf's quote reverberates in such a powerful manner with so many women and that her words are often tailored for use in the promotion of various women's causes. For example:

- The **Anonymous Is A Woman Theatre Company** in London states that, "Our job is to tell HERstory from history. Virginia Woolf said that everything attributed to 'anonymous' was actually written by a woman. Until we share an equal voice, we believe 'anonymous is a woman.' From the unsung heroes of our past to the high-profile trailblazers of today, we believe in women. In the 'bold spirit' of the women whose stories we tell, we create innovative work which fills our audiences with wonder."[3]

- The **Anonymous Was a Woman Program** awards grants to women artists. Started in 1996 as a response to the National Endowment for the Arts' decision to stop funding individual artists, the grants had long been awarded by a donor who chose to remain anonymous. But New York–based artist Susan Unterberg recently revealed herself as the funder in an article in the *New York Times*.[4]

- In **a fascinating column entitled "Anonymous Was a Woman,"** Fred R. Shapiro—editor of *The Yale Book of Quotations* and lecturer in legal research at Yale Law School—reveals many instances of men credited for famous quotations that were actually penned by women. For example: "I disapprove of what you say, but I will defend to the death your right to say it" was not written by French philosopher Voltaire, but by Evelyn Beatrice Hall (1868–1919), English author of *The Friends of Voltaire*, a book she published in 1906 under the pseudonym S. G. Tallentyre. The line is "Hall's own characterization of Voltaire's attitude."[5] And it was not Winston Churchill who coined the phrase "iron curtain" in his 1946 speech, it was Ethel Snowden (1881–1951), an English suffragette, who wrote in her 1920 book *Through Bolshevik Russia*: "We were behind the 'iron curtain' at last!"[6]

- **Virginia Woolf's altered quotation even appears on trendy T-shirts for sale online.** If you search the altered Anonymous quote, you'll find an array of T-shirts proclaiming, *For Most of History Anonymous Was a Woman*, proving there is a healthy market for those who want to wear their solidarity with Woolf's ideology.

Resisting misogyny, "second-sex" status, and "anonymity" are narratives reflected throughout this book. As we have witnessed in many of the stories, women frequently had to hide the fact that they were female (i.e., remain anonymous) in their pursuit of an education or career. When they didn't hide their female identity and managed to succeed in their chosen field of endeavor, they were often discounted or demeaned by their male contemporaries and the culture at large, thus rendering them historically "anonymous."

Throughout history women have struggled for equality and demonstrated resilience despite adversity. While they comprise half of the world's population and are deserving of the same rights and opportunities bequeathed to men, they continue to face daunting obstacles, preventing them from thriving, creating their own narrative, and succeeding at a level commensurate with their aptitude and skills. Although research has shown the enormous benefits of a more balanced and equitable world, as well as the manner in which inequality obstructs human potential, women have to continuously challenge and renegotiate a subordinate status—one that is rationalized and anchored in fictitious distinctions between the sexes. This is why it is critical to continuously challenge the validity of fabricated norms and to reframe gender equality as a human issue and not merely a "woman problem."

As we strive to advance beyond anonymity and achieve gender balance, it is imperative to abandon a debilitating cycle in which women and girls are held back from realizing their full potential—and to understand that the struggle we engage in on behalf of all humanity is fundamental to life itself.

Further Reading

Anderson, Becca. *The Book of Awesome Women: Boundary Breakers, Freedom Fighters, Sheroes, and Female Firsts.* Miami: Mango Publishing Group. 2017.

A collection of 200 inspiring women not often mentioned in history, from female trailblazers of the past to contemporary women in science, sports, cyberspace, politics, and the arts.

Chicago, Judy. *The Dinner Party.* New York: Penguin Books, 1996.

A detailed examination of the landmark multimedia exhibit showcasing the achievements of more than one thousand women throughout Western culture.

Howard, Sethanne. *The Hidden Giants: Women Hold Up Half the Sky, 4000 Years of Women in Science and Technology.* Washington, DC: Washington Academy of Sciences, 2012.

The history of over 4,000 years of women in the fields of science, technology, engineering, and mathematics.

Ignotofsky, Rachel. *Women in Science: 50 Fearless Pioneers Who Changed the World.* Berkeley: Ten Speed Press, 2016.

Highlights the contributions of fifty notable women to the fields of science, technology, engineering, and mathematics (STEM) from the ancient to the modern world.

Jewell, Hannah. *She Caused a Riot: 100 Unknown Women Who Built Cities, Sparked Revolutions, and Massively Crushed It.* Naperville, IL: Sourcebooks, 2018.

An empowering look at the epic adventures of one hundred brave and unconventional women.

Kristof, Nicholas D., and Sheryl WuDunn. *Half the Sky: Turning Oppression into Opportunity for Women Worldwide.* New York: Knopf, 2009.

A passionate call to arms against our era's most pervasive human rights violation: the oppression of women and girls in the developing world.

Lee, Mackenzi. *Bygone Badass Broads: 52 Forgotten Women Who Changed the World.* New York: Harry N. Abrams, 2018.

An engaging and witty recounting of the lives of fifty-two pioneering women whose successes have been ignored by mainstream history.

Miles, Rosalind. *Who Cooked the Last Supper? The Women's History of the World*. New York: Broadway Books, 2001.

Sets the record straight regarding women's place at the center of culture, revolution, empire, war, and peace. Includes stories of individual women who have shaped civilization and celebrates the work and lives of women around the world.

Sarkeesian, Anita, and Ebony Adams. *History vs Women: The Defiant Lives That They Don't Want You to Know*. New York: Feiwel and Friends, 2018.

Geared to a teen readership, inspiring stories of twenty-five remarkable women from around the world—from Mongolian wrestlers to Chinese pirates, Native American ballerinas to Egyptian scientists, and Japanese novelists to British Prime Ministers.

Schiebinger, Londa. *The Mind Has No Sex: Women in the Origins of Modern Science*. Cambridge, MA: Harvard University Press, 1991.

A comprehensive history of women's contributions to the development of early modern science.

Shen, Ann. *Bad Girls Throughout History: 100 Remarkable Women Who Changed the World*. San Francisco: Chronicle Books, 2016.

A beautifully illustrated coffee-table book featuring 100 women—pirates, artists, warriors, daredevils, scientists, activists, and spies—who helped shape history.

Wagman-Geller, Marlene. *Still I Rise: The Persistence of Phenomenal Women*. Miami: Mango Publishing Group, 2017.

Inspiring profiles of twenty-five extraordinary women, from Freedom Fighters to Nobel Prize winners, who overcame obstacles to make their mark in the world.

Women Who Launch: Women Who Shattered Glass Ceilings. Miami: Mango Media, 2018.

A collection of stories of trailblazing women—from the mid-nineteenth century to the present day—who launched some of the most influential brands, companies, and organizations in the world.

Notes

FEMALE ANONYMITY

1. Virginia Woolf, *A Room of One's Own* (Boston: Harvest/Harcourt, 1989), 41. *A Room of One's Own*, originally published in 1929, is based on two papers read to the Arts Society at Newnham and the Odtaa at Girton in October 1928. Newnham and Girton are women's colleges at the University of Cambridge.

2. Ibid.

3. Today, an increasing number of women in Iran continue to raise their voices, steadfast in their determination for freedom, human rights, and democracy. Their resilience and courageous struggle come at a high price, with the harsh sentences imposed for peaceful activism. Despite an uphill battle and four decades of discriminatory policies, they have excelled beyond their circumstances to become Olympic athletes, diplomats, award-winning scientists, filmmakers, authors, journalists, architects, artists, and even the first woman to ever win the Fields Medal (also known as the Nobel Prize of Mathematics), Professor Maryam Mirzakhani (1977–2017).

4. The London School of Economics Centre for Women, Peace and Security (LSEWPS) is an academic setting dedicated to developing strategies that promote justice, human rights, and participation of women in conflict-affected situations around the world.

For more information about the Centre, please visit their website: http://www.lse.ac.uk/women-peace-security.

5. UN Women Champions for Innovation support the programs of the Global Innovation Coalition for Change (GICC). More information about UN Women Champions for Innovation can be found on their website: https://www.unwomen.org/en/news/stories/2018/3/un-women-to-announce-champions-for-innovation. To learn more about the GICC, visit: https://www.unwomen.org/en/how-we-work/innovation-and-technology/un-women-global-innovation-coalition-for-change.

6. Bettany Hughes, "Why Were Women Written Out of History? An Interview With Bettany Hughes," *English Heritage*, February 29, 2016, http://blog.english-heritage.org.uk/women-written-history-interview-bettany-hughes/.

7. Woolf, *A Room of One's Own*, x-xi.

SHAKESPEARE'S SISTER

1. Woolf, A Room of One's Own, v.

2. Ibid., 48.

3. Ibid., 49.

4. Robert P. Irvine, *Jane Austen* (Abingdon: Routledge, 2005), 13–15.

5. When asked why she used only her initials as author of the Harry Potter books, Rowling responded that her publisher wanted the book to appeal to both boys and girls and felt that she should basically "disguise" the fact that she was a woman. But she added, "The book won an award and I got a big advance from America, and I got a lot of publicity…So I was outed as a woman." In Christine Amanpour and Eliza Mackintosh, "J.K. Rowling Wrote a Secret Manuscript on a Party Dress," *CNN*, July 10, 2017, https://www.cnn.com/2017/07/10/world/amanpour-j-k-rowling-interview/index.html.

6. Simone de Beauvoir, *The Second Sex*, trans. Constance Borde and Sheila Malovany-Chevalier (New York: Vintage Books, 2010), 71.

7. Christine de Pizan, *The Book of the City of Ladies* (New York: Penguin Classics, 2000), 141.

8. Stephanie Merrim, "Sor Juana Inés de la Cruz," *Encyclopaedia Britannica Online*, accessed September 26, 2019, https://www.britannica.com/biography/Sor-Juana-Ines-de-la-Cruz.

9. Ana Nogales, *Latina Power* (New York: Simon & Schuster, 2003), 122–23.

10. "A Nun Challenges the Patriarchy," *Women & the American Story Online*, trans. Michael Smith, https://wams.nyhistory.org/early-encounters/spanish-colonies/a-nun-challenges-patriarchy/.

11. Emilie L. Bergmann, et al., *Women, Culture, and Politics in Latin America*

(Berkeley: University of California
Press, 1992), 158.

12. François Poullain de la Barre, *Three
Cartesian Feminist Treatises*, trans. by
Vivien Bosley (Chicago: The University
of Chicago Press, 2002), http://
press.uchicago.edu/ucp/books/book/
chicago/T/bo3629107.html.

13. de la Barre, *Three Cartesian Feminist
Treatises*, 78.

14. Mary Wollstonecraft, *A Vindication of
the Rights of Woman* (London: Penguin
Books, 2004), 65, 72.

15. Wollstonecraft, *A Vindication of the Rights
of Woman*, 69–70.

16. Wendy Kolmar and Frances Bartkowski,
Feminist Theory: A Reader, 3rd ed. (New
York: McGraw Hill, 2010), ix, 7, 42.

17. Elizabeth Cady Stanton, "Seneca Falls
Keynote Address," speech presented at
Seneca Falls Convention, New York, July
19, 1848.

18. Kolmer and Bartkowski, *Feminist Theory*,
ix, 7, 36–37, 42.

19. Lori Ginzberg, author of *Elizabeth Cady
Stanton: An American Life*, in an interview
on "Morning Edition," National Public
Radio, July 13, 2011.

20. Brent Staples, "How the Suffrage
Movement Betrayed Black Women," *The
New York Times*, July 28, 2018, https://
www.nytimes.com/2018/07/28/
opinion/sunday/suffrage-movement-
racism-black-women.html.

21. Alice Janigro, "Ida B. Wells,"
*Women's Suffrage Celebration Coalition
of Massachusetts Online*, http://
suffrage100ma.org/ida-b-wells/.

22. Ibid.

23. Charlotte Perkins Gilman, *Women and
Economics* (Boston: Small, Maynard &
Co., 1893).

24. Kolmer and Bartkowski, *Feminist Theory*,
7, 32–45.

25. Nel Noddings, *Women and Evil*
(Berkeley: University of California
Press, 1989), 3, 59.

26. Virginia Woolf, *Selected Essays* (New
York: Oxford University Press, 2009),
141.

27. *Woolf, Selected Essays*, 142.

28. *Woolf, Selected Essays*, 144.

29. Betty Friedan, "The Feminine
Mystique," in *The Essential Feminist
Reader*, ed. Estelle B. Freedman (New
York: The Modern Library 2007), 274,
278.

30. Lindsey Blake Churchill, "The Feminine
Mystique," *Encyclopaedia Britannica*
(online), accessed September 26, 2019,
https://www.britannica.com/topic/
The-Feminine-Mystique.

31. Shoghi Effendi, *God Passes By*
(Wilmette, Illinois: Bahai Publishing
Trust, 1971), 75; N. Motahedeh, "The
Mutilated Body of the Modern Nation:
Qurrat al-Ayn Tahirah's Unveiling and
the Iranian Massacre of the Babi's,"
*Comparative Studies of South Asia and the
Middle East* 8, no. 2 (1998): 38–50.

32. Effendi, *God Passes By*, 75; Motahedeh,
"The Mutilated Body of the Modern
Nation," 38–50.

33. Susan Gammage, "A Gathering of
the Poems of Tahirih," *Nine Star
Solutions*, September 11, 2011,
https://www.ninestarsolutions.
com/?s=The+Morn+of+Guidance.

34. *Indian Literature: An Introduction*, ed.
Anjana Neira Deve, Bajrang Bihari
Tiwari, and Sanam Khanna (London:
University of Delhi, Pearson/Longman,
2005), 133.

35. Rosalind O'Hanlon, *A Comparison
Between Men and Women: Tarabai Shinde
and the Critique of Gender Relations in
Colonial India* (Delhi: Oxford University
Press, 1994), 87–93.

36. Kishida Toshiko was born Toshiko
Kishida and also wrote under the name
Shōen.

37. Kishida Toshiko, "Daughters in Boxes,"
in *The Essential Feminist Reader*, ed.
Estelle B. Freedman (New York: The
Modern Library, 2007), 100.

38. Jad Adams, *Women and the Vote: A World
History* (Oxford: Oxford University
Press, 2016), 383.

39. Francisca Diniz, "Equality of Rights,"
in *The Essential Feminist Reader*, ed.
Estelle B. Freedman (New York: The
Modern Library, 2007), 112.

40. Ibid., 114.

41. Ibid.

42. Toril Moi, *Simone de Beauvoir: The
Making of an Intellectual Woman*, 2nd ed.
(New York: Oxford University Press,
2008), 75.

43. de Beauvoir, *The Second Sex*, 159.

44. Ibid., 721.

45. Ibid., 283.

46. Audre Lorde, *Sister Outsider: Essays and
Speeches* (Berkeley: Crossing Press, 2007),
124–33.

47. Alice Walker, *In Search of Our Mothers'
Gardens: Womanist Prose* (New York:
Harvest/Harcourt, Inc., 2004), 235.

48. "(1981), Audre Lorde, 'The Uses of
Anger: Women Responding to Racism,'"
BlackPast, August 12, 2012, https://
www.blackpast.org/african-american-
history/speeches-african-american-
history/1981-audre-lorde-uses-anger-
women-responding-racism/.

49. Ibid., 237.

50. Marianne Schnall, "Conversation with
Alice Walker," *feminist.com*, December
12, 2006, https://feminist.com/
resources/artspeech/interviews/
alicewalker.html.

WOMEN BY THE NUMBERS

1. Gender equality refers to men and women having equal rights, responsibilities, and opportunities that are not dependent on their gender. Gender equality should concern and engage both women and men as it is a human rights concern.

2. A. W. Geiger, Kristen Bialik, and John Gramlich, "The Changing Face of Congress in 6 Charts," *Pew Research Center*, 2019, https://www.pewresearch.org/fact-tank/2019/02/15/the-changing-face-of-congress/.

3. "Women of Color in Elective Office 2019," *Center for American Women and Politics*, accessed September 26, 2019, http://www.cawp.rutgers.edu/women-color-elective-office–2019.

4. Susan Franceschet and Karen Beckwith, "Spain's Majority Female Cabinet Embodies Women's Rise to Power," *The Conversation*, July 13, 2018, http://theconversation.com/spains-majority-female-cabinet-embodies-womens-global-rise-to-power-98433.

5. Gender parity is a statistical measure that compares indicators among women, such as education or income, to the same indicators among men. Unlike gender equality, gender parity provides specific numerical values to help understand relative equality between the sexes.

6. Hadra Ahmed and Kimiko de Freytas-Tamura, "Ethiopia Appoints Its First Female President," *The New York Times*, October 25, 2018, https://www.nytimes.com/2018/10/25/world/africa/sahlework-zewde-ethiopia-president.html.

7. Fatima Faizi and David Zucchino, "700 Afghan Women Have a Message: Don't Sell Us Out to the Taliban," *The New York Times*, February 28, 2019, https://www.nytimes.com/2019/02/28/world/asia/afghanistan-women-taliban.html.

8. All statistics, facts, and figures were current as of the writing of this book.

9. *The Global Gender Gap Report 2018* (Geneva: World Economic Forum, 2018), 7.

10. Ibid., 7.

11. Ibid., 18–20.

12. Ibid., 10.

13. Ibid.

14. *The Global Gender Gap Report 2015*, (Geneva: World Economic Forum, 2015), 8.

15. *The Global Gender Gap Report 2018*, 7.

16. Ibid., 15.

17. Saadia Zahidi, "Accelerating Gender Parity in Globalization 4.0," *World Economic Forum*, June 18, 2019, https://www.weforum.org/agenda/2019/06/accelerating-gender-gap-parity-equality-globalization-4/.

18. *The Global Gender Gap Report 2018*, 8.

19. Ibid.

20. Ibid., vii.

21. Casey Hicks, Jacque Smith, and Amanda Wills, "All the Countries that had a Woman Leader Before the U.S.," *CNN Politics*, updated January 28, 2019, https://www.cnn.com/interactive/2016/06/politics/women-world-leaders/.

22. The G20 members are Argentina, Australia, Brazil, Canada, China, France, Germany, India, Indonesia, Italy, Japan, Republic of Korea, Mexico, Russia, Saudi Arabia, South Africa, Turkey, the United Kingdom, the United States, and the European Union. These members represent the world's largest advanced and emerging economies, encompassing approximately two-thirds of the global population, 85 percent of global gross domestic product, and more than three-quarters of global trade. See http://g20.org.tr/about-g20/g20-members/.

23. French attorney Christine Lagarde served as Chairperson of the International Monetary Fund (IMF) since 2011. In 2019 she stepped down from her position at the IMF after her nomination to be the next head of the European Central Bank (ECB).

24. Kevin Liptak, "Where are the Women? Fewest Female Leaders in G20 Photo," *CNN Politics*, November 30, 2018, https://www.cnn.com/2018/11/30/politics/g20-women-fewest-photo/index.html.

25. A. W. Geiger, Kristen Bialik, and John Gramlich, "The Changing Face of Congress in 6 Charts," *Pew Research Center*, February 15, 2019, http://www.pewresearch.org/fact-tank/2019/02/15/the-changing-face-of-congress/.

26. "Iran Elections: Rouhani Notes Record 6% Women Elected," *BBC.com*, May 1, 2016, https://www.bbc.com/news/world-middle-east-36182796.

27. *The Global Gender Gap Report 2018*, 20.

28. *A Quantum Leap for Gender Equality: For a Better Future of Work for All* (Geneva: International Labour Organization, 2019), 8.

29. *Women, Business and the Law 2019* (Washington, DC: The World Bank), 13.

30. Ibid.

31. Ibid., 8.

32. Ibid.

33. Ibid.

34. Ibid., 3.

35. "An improvement and yet…still only 6 countries offer equal legal rights to

women, World Bank reports," *Women in the World*, February 28, 2019, https://womenintheworld.com/2019/02/28/an-improvement-yet-still-only-6-countries-offer-equal-legal-rights-to-women-world-bank-reports/.

36. Kristalina Georgieva, Twitter post, February 27, 2019, 1:14 p.m., https://twitter.com/KGeorgieva/status/1100866909510209555.

37. Stephen J. Rose, PhD, and Heidi Hartmann, PhD, "Still A Man's Labor Market: The Slowly Narrowing Gender Wage Gap," *Institute for Women's Policy Research*, November 26, 2018, 15.

38. Chandra Childers, Heidi Hartmann, Ariane Hegewisch, and Jessica Milli, "Pay Equity & Discrimination," *Institute for Women's Policy Research (IWPR)*, https://iwpr.org/issue/employment-education-economic-change/pay-equity-discrimination/.

39. Ibid.

40. *A Quantum Leap for Gender Equality*, 12.

41. Ibid., 13.

42. Ibid.

43. Christopher Ingraham, "The World's Richest Countries Guarantee Mothers More than a Year of Paid Maternity Leave. The U.S. Guarantees Them Nothing," *The Washington Post*, February 5, 2018, https://www.washingtonpost.com/news/wonk/wp/2018/02/05/the-worlds-richest-countries-guarantee-mothers-more-than-a-year-of-paid-maternity-leave-the-u-s-guarantees-them-nothing/?utm_term=.553c88f56364.

44. Jeanette Settembre, "These Women Had to Crowdfund Their Maternity Leave," *Marketwatch*, February 15, 2018, https://www.marketwatch.com/story/these-women-had-to-crowdfund-their-maternity-leave-2018-02-15-8883850.

45. Ingraham, "The World's Richest Countries."

46. Rose and Hartmann, "Still A Man's Labor Market," Highlights.

47. *Women, Business and the Law 2018*, 20.

48. "Protecting Women from Violence: Key Facts for this Indicator," *Women, Business and the Law 2018, World Bank Group*, accessed September 26, 2019, http://pubdocs.worldbank.org/en/289441522241133897/WBL-fact-sheet-protecting-women-from-violence-FINAL-PDF.pdf.

49. "Legal Barriers," *Women's Workplace Equality Index*, accessed September 26, 2019, https://www.cfr.org/interactive/legal-barriers/.

50. Ibid.

51. "What is the Impact of Child Marriage?" *Girls Not Brides*, accessed September 26, 2019, https://www.girlsnotbrides.org/what-is-the-impact/.

52. *Women, Business and the Law 2018* (Washington, DC: The World Bank), 14.

53. Ibid.

54. Ibid., 2.

55. *The Global Gender Gap Report 2018*, 9–12.

56. "Legal Barriers," *Women's Workplace Equality Index*.

57. Ibid.

58. *Women, Business and the Law 2018*, 1.

59. "Facts and Figures: Peace and Security," *UN Women*, updated October 2019, https://www.unwomen.org/en/what-we-do/peace-and-security/facts-and-figures.

60. Dana Olson, "Do Female Founders Get Better Results? Here's What Happened on my Quest to Find Out," *Pitchbook*, January 23, 2018, https://pitchbook.com/news/articles/do-female-founders-get-better-results-heres-what-happened-when-i-tried-to-find-out.

61. "Number of female held CEO positions in FTSE companies in the United Kingdom (UK) as of June 2019," *Statista*, August 9, 2019, https://statista.com/statistics/685ista208/number-of-female-ceo-positions-in-ftse-companies-uk.

62. Chad M. Topaz, Bernhard Klingenberg, Daniel Turek, et al., "Diversity of Artists in Major U.S. Museums," *PLOS ONE* 14(3): e0212852 (2019), https://doi.org/10.1371/journal.pone.0212852.

63. "Assessing Gender Gaps in Artificial Intelligence," World Economic Forum, accessed September 27, 2019, http://reports.weforum.org/global-gender-gap-report-2018/assessing-gender-gaps-in-artificial-intelligence/.

64. Caitlin Mullen, "On National STEM Day, Diversity Still an Issue," *Bizwomen, The Business Journals*, November 8, 2018, https://www.bizjournals.com/bizwomen/news/latest-news/2018/11/on-national-stem-day-diversity-still-an-issue.html?page=all.

65. "International Women's Day: Top 10 Universities led by Women," *The World University Rankings*, March 8, 2019, https://www.timeshighereducation.com/student/best-universities/top-10-universities-led-women.

66. "Summary Profile: College Presidents, by Gender," *American Council on Education*, accessed September 27, 2019, https://www.aceacps.org/summary-profile-dashboard/.

67. "Nobel Prize Awarded Women," *The Nobel Prize, Nobel Media AB 2019*, July 22, 2019, https://www.nobelprize.org/prizes/lists/nobel-prize-awarded-women-3-2/.

68. "What is the Impact of Child Marriage? *Girls Not Brides.*

69. Ibid.

70. "Committee Rejects Bill to Ban Child Marriage in Iran," *Center for Human Rights in Iran,* December 28, 2018, https://iranhumanrights.org/2018/12/outrage-after-judicial-parliamentary-committee-rejects-bill-to-ban-child-marriage-in-iran/.

71. Ibid.

72. "Iran Child Marriage Rates," *Girls Not Brides,* accessed September 27, 2019, https://www.girlsnotbrides.org/child-marriage/iran/.

73. "Child Marriage: Latest Trends and Future Prospects," *UNICEF,* July 2018, 4.

74. Ibid.

75. Sarah Ferguson, "What You Need to Know About Child Marriage in the U.S.," *Forbes,* October 29, 2018, https://www.forbes.com/sites/unicefusa/2018/10/29/what-you-need-to-know-about-child-marriage-in-the-us–1/#382f56825689.

76. Eric Adler, "Missouri Governor Signs Law Banning Marriage of 15-Year-Olds," *The Kansas City Star,* July 13, 2018, https://www.kansascity.com/news/politics-government/article214840670.html.

77. Hannah Al-Othman, "These British Women Narrowly Escaped Being Forced into Marriage. They Say the Government Must Act Now," *BuzzFeed News,* November 10, 2018, https://www.buzzfeed.com/hannahalothman/forced-marriage-bill-tory-latham-legal-age-home-office.

78. Quentin T. Wodon and Benedicte Leroy de la Briere, *Unrealized Potential: The High Cost of Gender Inequality in Earnings (English)* (Washington, DC: World Bank Group, 2018), 1.

79. Ibid., 2.

80. Ibid.

81. Ibid.

82. Larry Elliott, "More Women in the Workplace Could Boost Economy by 35%, says Christine Lagarde," *The Guardian,* March 1, 2019, https://www.theguardian.com/world/2019/mar/01/more-women-in-the-workplace-could-boost-economy-by-35-says-christine-lagarde.

83. Christine Lagarde, "Women's Empowerment: An Economic Game Changer," speech presented at *Glamour Magazine* lunch, Los Angeles, November 14, 2016, https://www.imf.org/en/News/Articles/2016/11/14/SP111416-Womens-Empowerment-An-Economic-Game-Changer.

84. Ed Yong, "What We Learn From 50 Years of Kids Drawing Scientists," *The Atlantic,* March 20, 2018, https://www.theatlantic.com/science/archive/2018/03/what-we-learn-from-50-years-of-asking-children-to-draw-scientists/556025/

85. Ibid.

86. Ibid.

87. David Miller, PhD, is a researcher at American Institutes for Research focusing on STEM education who, in 2018, along with his colleagues, analyzed five decades of data from seventy-eight studies where more than 20,000 children were collectively asked to draw scientists.

88. Yong, "What We Learn From 50 Years of Kids Drawing Scientists."

89. Corlia Meyer, Lars Guenther, and Marina Joubert, "The Draw-A-Scientist Test in an African Context: Comparing Students' (Stereotypical) Images of Scientists Across University Faculties," *Research in Science & Technological Education* 37, no. 1 (2019): 1–14, https://doi.org/10.1080/02635143.2018.1447455.

90. Laura Beth Kelly, "Methods and Strategies: Draw a Scientist, Uncovering Students' Thinking about Science and Scientists," *Science and Children* 56, no. 4 (2018): 86, https://www.questia.com/read/1G1-561732858/draw-a-scientist-uncovering-students-thinking-about.

91. Kelly, "Methods and Strategies: Draw a Scientist."

92. Magnea Marinósdóttir and Rósa Erlingsdóttir, "This Is Why Iceland Ranks First for Gender Equality," *World Economic Forum,* November 1, 2017, https://www.weforum.org/agenda/2017/11/why-iceland-ranks-first-gender-equality/.

93. "For analytical purposes, *WESP* [the United Nations World Economics Situation and Prospects report] classifies all countries of the world into one of three broad categories: developed economies, economies in transition and developing economies. The composition of these groupings… is intended to reflect basic economic country conditions." In "Country Classification," *World Economic Situation and Prospects 2014* (New York: United Nations, 2014), https://www.un.org/en/development/desa/policy/wesp/wesp_current/2014wesp_country_classification.pdf.

94. Lori Beaman, Esther Duflo, Rohini Pande, and Petia Topalova, "Female leadership raises aspirations and educational attainment for girls: A policy experiment in India," *Science Magazine* 335, no. 6068 (2012):

582–586, http://gap.hks.harvard.edu/female-leadership-raises-aspirations-and-educational-attainment-girls-policy-experiment-india.

95. Ibid.

96. Ibid.

YINYANG AND THE ECONOMICS OF GENDER BALANCE

1. Katja Iverson, "7 Charts That Show Gender Inequality Around the World," *World Economic Forum*, August 21, 2017, https://www.weforum.org/agenda/2017/08/charts-gender-inequality-women-deliver.

2. "Gender Equality," *United Nations*, accessed September 27, 2019, https://www.un.org/en/sections/issues-depth/gender-equality/.

3. Kate Kelly, "40 Years Later, the ERA Is Still Not a Part of the Constitution," interview by Amna Nawaz, *PBS NewsHour*, January 29, 2019, https://www.pbs.org/newshour/show/forty-years-later-the-era-is-still-not-a-part-of-the-constitution.

4. *Global Gender Gap Report 2018*, viii.

5. Ibid.

6. Scott E. Page, *The Diversity Bonus: How Great Teams Pay off in the Knowledge Economy* (Princeton: Princeton University Press, 2017).

7. Page, *The Diversity Bonus*, 14.

8. Ibid.

9. Shane Parrish, "Scott Page: Becoming A Model Thinker," *The Knowledge Project with Shane Parrish*, episode #55, April 2, 2019, https://fs.blog/scott-page/.

10. Ban Ki-moon, "Secretary-General's remarks at March for Gender Equality and Women's Rights," speech presented at the March for Gender Equality and Women's Rights, New York, March 8, 2015, https://www.un.org/sg/en/content/sg/statement/2015-03-08/secretary-generals-remarks-march-gender-equality-and-womens-rights.

11. "Q&A with Scott E. Page: An Interview with Scott E. Page Author of *The Diversity Bonus*," *Princeton University Press*, accessed September 27, 2019, https://press.princeton.edu/interviews/qa–11077.

12. Larry Fink, "Larry Fink's 2018 Letter to CEOs: A Sense of Purpose," *BlackRock*, 2018, https://www.blackrock.com/corporate/investor-relations/2018-larry-fink-ceo-letter.

13. Ibid.

14. Larry Fink, "Chairman's Letter to Our Shareholders," *BlackRock*, 2018, https://www.blackrock.com/corporate/investor relations/larry fink chairmans-letter.

15. Stephen Turban, Dan Wu, and Letian Zhang, "Research: When Gender Diversity Makes Firms More Productive," *Harvard Business Review*, February 11, 2019, https://hbr.org/2019/02/research-when-gender-diversity-makes-firms-more-productive.

16. Caitlin Mullen, "On National STEM Day, Diversity Is Still an Issue," *The Business Journals, Bizwomen*, November 8, 2018, https://www.bizjournals.com/bizwomen/news/latest-news/2018/11/on-national-stem-day-diversity-still-an-issue.html?page=all.

17. Greg Satell, "Why We Need Women to Have a Larger Role in Innovation," *Inc.*, November 17, 2018, https://www.inc.com/greg-satell/why-we-need-women-to-have-a-larger-role-in-innovation.html.

18. Robin R. Wang, *Yinyang: The Way of Heaven and Earth in Chinese Thought and Culture* (New York: Cambridge University Press, 2012), 104.

19. Nicola Davis, "Girls Believe Brilliance Is a Male Trait, Research into Gender Stereotypes Shows," *The Guardian*, January 27, 2017, https://www.theguardian.com/education/2017/jan/26/girls-believe-brilliance-is-a-male-trait-research-into-gender-stereotypes-shows.

20. "Women in Science, Technology, Engineering, and Mathematics (STEM): Quick Take," *Catalyst*, June 14, 2019, https://www.catalyst.org/research/women-in-science-technology-engineering-and-mathematics-stem/.

21. Page, *The Diversity Bonus*, 5.

22. Ibid., 221.

23. For the purposes of this book, the Chinese term *yinyang* is used (with the exception of direct quotes when it may appear in the conventional way, "yin and yang" or "yin-yang"). The combined term *yinyang* "reflects the Chinese usage in which the terms are directly set together and would not be linked by a conjunction." In Wang, *Yinyang*, 6.

24. Wang, *Yinyang*, 6.

25. Joseph K. Kim and David S. Lee, *Yin and Yang of Life: Understanding the Universal Nature of Change* (Encino: Heal and Soul, LLC., 2008), 1.

26. Ibid.

27. "Yin Yang Laozi," from Wikimedia Commons, accessed October 9, 2019, https://commons.wikimedia.org/wiki/File:Yin_yang_laozi.jpg.

28. Kim and Lee, *Yin and Yang of Life*, 2.

29. Ibid.

30. Martin, Palmer, *Yin & Yang: Understanding the Chinese Philosophy of Opposites and How to Apply It to Your Everyday Life* (London: Judy Piaktus Publishers, 1997), ix.

31. Page, *The Diversity Bonus*, 216–17.

32. Vivian Hunt, Sara Prince, Sundiatu Dixon-Fyle, and Lareina Yee, *Delivering Through Diversity* (New York: McKinsey & Company, 2018).

33. Ibid., 1.

34. Marcus Noland and Tyler Moran, "Study: Firms with More Women in the C-Suite Are More Profitable," *Harvard Business Review*, February 8, 2016, https://hbr.org/2016/02/study-firms-with-more-women-in-the-c-suite-are-more-profitable.

35. Robin R. Wang, "Dong Zhongshu's Transformation of *Yin-Yang* Theory and Contesting of Gender Identity," *Philosophy East and West* 55, no. 2 (April 2005): 209–10.

36. Lao-Tzu, *Tao Te Ching: A New English Version*, trans. Stephen Mitchell (New York: HarperCollins, 2006).

37. Wang, "Dong Zhongshu's Transformation," 209–10.

38. Wang, *Yinyang*, 109.

39. Ibid., 6.

40. Erin Cline, "What Can We Learn from Ancient Chinese Views of Marriage?" *Berkley Center for Religion, Peace, and World Affairs, Georgetown University*, November 13, 2014, https://berkleycenter.georgetown.edu/forum/what-can-we-learn-from-ancient-chinese-views-of-marriage.

41. Maoshing Ni, *The Yellow Emperor's Classic of Medicine, a New Translation of the Neijing Suwen* (Boston: Shambhala, 1995), 17.

42. Robin R. Wang, "Zhang Shiying and Chinese Appreciation of Hegelian Philosophy," *ASIANetwork Exchange: A Journal for Asian Studies in the Liberal Arts*, 22(1) (2015): 94.

43. "Cheney, Ednah (Dow) Littlehale," *Encyclopedia.com*, updated August 23, 2019, https://www.encyclopedia.com/arts/news-wires-white-papers-and-books/cheney-ednah-dow-littlehale.

44. Ednah Dow Cheney, *Reminiscences of Ednah Dow Cheney (Born Littlehale)* (Boston: Life & Shepard Publishers, 1902), 227.

45. Kim and Lee, *Yin and Yang of Life*, 32.

46. "The Jungian Model of the Psyche," *Journal Psyche*, accessed September 25, 2019, https://journalpsyche.org/jungian-model-psyche/.

47. Kim and Lee, *Yin and Yang of Life*, 13.

48. de Beauvoir, *The Second Sex*, 766.

FORGOTTEN INNOVATORS

1. According to a study by economists from Harvard University, the London School of Economics, and MIT entitled *Who Becomes an Inventor in America*, "If young girls were exposed to the same number of female inventors as boys were to male inventors… their invention rates would skyrocket by 164%, knocking out 55% of the gender gap." In "Childhood Surroundings Matter More than Genes for Would-Be Inventors," *The Economist*, December 4, 2017, https://www.economist.com/united-states/2017/12/04/childhood-surroundings-matter-more-than-genes-for-would-be-inventors.

En Hedu-Anna

1. "Mercury Crater-naming Contest Winners Announced," *International Astronomical Union*, April 29, 2015, http://www.iau.org/news/pressreleases/detail/iau1506/.

2. En Hedu-Anna may also be spelled as En'hedu'anna or Enheduanna.

3. Sethanne Howard held positions with US national observatories, NASA, the National Science Foundation, the US Navy, and the US Nautical Almanac Office. While her primary research focused on galactic dynamics, she also was passionate about the history of women in science.

4. Sethanne Howard, "En'hedu'anna—Our First Great Scientist," *Women in Astronomy* (blog), posted by Joan Schmeltz, May 6, 2013, http://womeninastronomy.blogspot.com/2013/05/enheduanna-our-first-great-scientist.html.

5. Emily Temple-Wood, "It's Time These Ancient Women Get Their Due," *Nautilus* (blog), April 12, 2016, http://nautil.us/blog/its-time-these-ancient-women-scientists-get-their-due.

6. Cuneiform is one of the earliest systems of writing and was created by the Sumerians and characterized by wedge-shaped marks on clay tablets, made with a stylus of a blunt reed. The name *cuneiform* means "wedge shaped."

7. Howard, "En'hedu'anna—Our First Great Scientist."

8. Ibid.

9. Ibid.

10. Her sacred private quarters in the temple were called the *gipar*.

11. Betty De Shong Meador, *Inanna, Lady of Largest Heart: Poems of the Sumerian High Priestess Enheduanna*, (Austin: University of Texas Press, 2000), 72.

12. Howard, "En'hedu'anna—Our First Great Scientist."

13. Sethanne Howard, "Science Has No Gender: The History of Women in Science," *Journal of the Washington Academy of Sciences* 93, no. 1 (Spring 2007): 1.

Tapputi-Belatekallim

1. Gabriele Kass-Simon and Patricia Farnes, eds., *Women of Science: Righting the Record*, First Midland Book Edition (Bloomington: Indiana University Press, 1993), 301.

2. Zing Tsjeng, *Forgotten Women: The Scientists* (London, England: Cassell, 2018), excerpted in "Forgotten Women in Science: Tapputi-Belatekallim," *Cosmos Magazine*, March 16, 2018, https://cosmosmagazine.com/chemistry/forgotten-women-in-science-tapputi-belatekallim.

3. Erin Branham, "The Scent of Love: Ancient Perfumes," *The Iris* (blog), May 1, 2012, http://blogs.getty.edu/iris/the-scent-of-love-ancient-perfumes/.

4. Tsjeng, *Forgotten Women: The Scientists*.

5. Enfleurage is a process that uses odorless fats that are solid at room temperature to capture the fragrant compounds exuded by plants.

6. "The Lost History of Women in Chemistry: The First Perfumer," *Death/Scent*, March 8, 2016, https://deathscent.com/2016/03/08/the-lost-history-of-women-in-chemistrythe-first-perfumer/.

7. Martin Levey, *Early Arabic Pharmacology: An Introduction Based on Ancient and Medieval Sources* (Leiden: Brill Archive, 1973), 8–9.

8. "Tapputi Belatekallim, The First Chemist," *Girl Museum*, January 31, 2017, https://www.girlmuseum.org/tapputi-belatekallim/.

9. Tsjeng, *Forgotten Women: The Scientists*.

Kentake Amanerinas

1. Kathleen Sheldon, *African Women: Early History to the 21st Century*, (Bloomington: Indiana University Press, 2017), 6–7; "Kingdom of Kush," *New World Encyclopedia*, accessed October 9, 2019, http://www.newworldencyclopedia.org/entry/Kingdom_of_Kush.

2. "Kingdom of Kush," *New World Encyclopedia*.

3. Robert B. Jackson, *At Empire's Edge: Exploring Rome's Egyptian Frontier* (Yale University Press, 2002), 147–148.

4. Ibid., 148–149.

5. The Meroitic War is named after the Kushite capital of Meroë. See Joshua J. Mark, "Meroe," *Ancient History Encyclopedia*, August 11, 2010, https://www.ancient.eu/Meroe/.

6. Ibid.

7. Sheldon, *African Women*, 7.

Cleopatra Metrodora

1. Graduating from New York's Geneva Medical College in 1849, Elizabeth Blackwell became the first woman in America to earn the MD. See "Dr. Elizabeth Blackwell," *Changing the Face of Medicine*, accessed September 30, 2019, https://cfmedicine.nlm.nih.gov/physicians/biography_35.html.

2. Emily Temple-Wood, "It's Time These Ancient Women Get Their Due," *Nautilus*, April 12, 2016, http://nautil.us/blog/its-time-these-ancient-women-scientists-get-their-due.

3. Joshua J. Mark, "Female Physicians in Ancient Egypt," *Ancient History Encyclopedia*, February 22, 2017, https://www.ancient.eu/article/49/female-physicians-in-ancient-egypt/.

4. Ibid.

5. Jeanne Achterberg, *Woman as Healer* (Boulder: Shambhala, 1991), 32.

6. Temple-Wood, "It's Time These Ancient Women Get Their Due."

7. Ibid.

8. Ibid.

9. Ibid.

10. Ibid.

11. Ibid.

12. Ibid.

13. Lecia Bushak, "The Most Influential Women in Medicine: From the Past to the Present," *Medical Daily*, March 4, 2014, https://www.medicaldaily.com/most-influential-women-medicine-past-present–270560.

14. Judy Chicago, *The Dinner Party* (New York: Viking Penguin Books, 1996), 59.

15. Gregory Tsoucalas and Markos Sgantzos, "Aspasia and Cleopatra Metrodora, Two Majestic Female Physician-Surgeons in the Early Byzantine Era," *Journal of Universal Surgery* 4, no. 3 (August 10, 2016): 4.

16. Ibid., 1–2.

17. Ibid., 3.

18. Ibid., 2.

19. "More Women Than Men Enrolled in U.S. Medical Schools in 2017," *Association of American Medical Colleges*, December 18, 2017, https://news.aamc.org/press-releases/article/applicant-enrollment-2017/.

20. Ibid.

Sutayta Al-Mahamali

1. Alex Shashkevich, "Some Well-Meaning Statements Can Spread Stereotypes Unintentionally, New Stanford Study Says," *Stanford News*, July 10, 2018, https://news.stanford.edu/2018/07/10/well-meaning-statements-can-spread-stereotypes-unintentionally/.

2. Dale DeBakcsy, "The Algebraist of Baghdad: Sutayta Al-Mahamali's Medieval Mathematics," *Women You Should Know*, November 1, 2017, https://womenyoushouldknow.net/sutayta-al-mahamalis-mathematics.

3. Ibid.

4. Ibid.

5. DeBakcsy, "The Algebraist of Baghdad"; Salim Al-Hassani, "Women's Contribution to Classical Islamic Civilisation: Science, Medicine and Politics," *Muslim Heritage*, accessed October 9, 2019, https://muslimheritage.com/womens-contribution-to-classical-islamic-civilisation-science-medicine-and-politics/.

6. Madiha Sadaf, "Muslim Women and the History of Science," December 18, 2017, *About Islam*, https://aboutislam.net/science/science-tech/muslim-women-history-science.

7. DeBakcsy, "The Algebraist of Baghdad."

Mariam Al-Ijliya

1. George Saliba, *A History of Arabic Astronomy: Planetary Theories During the Golden Age of Islam* (New York: New York University Press, 1994), 245, 250, 256–57.

2. "Astrolabe History," *University of Hawaii Institute for Astronomy*, updated April 18, 2000, https://www.ifa.hawaii.edu/tops/astl-hist.html.

3. "How Astronomers and Instrument Makers in Muslim Civilisations Expanded Our Knowledge of the Universe," *Muslim Women's Council*, September 23, 2014, http://www.muslimwomenscouncil.org.uk/uncategorized/how-astronomers-and-instrument-makers-in-muslim-civilisation-expanded-our-knowledge-of-the-universe/.

4. Charvi Kathuria, "Tech Women: Meet Mariam Astrulabi, the Woman Behind Astrolabes," *She the People*, December 2, 2017, https://www.shethepeople.tv/news/tech-women-meet-mariam-astrulabi-the-woman-behind-astrolabes.

5. Ibid.

6. Brandi Neal, "7 Amazing Inventions by Muslim Women You've Probably Never Heard About," *Bustle*, March 27, 2017, https://www.bustle.com/p/7-amazing-inventions-by-muslim-women-youve-probably-never-heard-about-47168.

7. Nageen Khan, "Astrolabes and Early Islam: Mariam 'Al-Astrolabiya' Al-Ijliya," *Why Islam*, December 6, 2014, https://www.whyislam.org/muslim-heritage/astrolabes-and-early-islam-mariam-al-astrolabiya-al-ijliya/.

8. Helen Walker, "She is an Astronomer," *Astronomy & Geophysics* 50, issue 3 (June 1, 2009): 3.25, https://doi.org/10.1111/j.1468-4004.2009.50325.x.

Rabi'a Balkhi

1. "A Thousand Years of the Persian Book: Classical Persian Poetry," *Library of Congress*, accessed October 9, 2019, https://www.loc.gov/exhibits/thousand-years-of-the-persian-book/classical-persian-poetry.html.

2. *The Qit'A: Anthology of the 'Fragment' in Arabic, Persian and Eastern Poetry*, trans. Paul Smith (Victoria, Australia: New Humanity Books, 2012), 155–56.

3. Jennifer Heath and Ashraf Zahedi, eds., *Land of the Unconquerable: The Lives of Contemporary Afghan Women* (Berkeley: University of California Press, 2011), 77.

4. "The Story of Rabia Balkhi," *Afghan Women's Writing Project*, August 27, 2013, http://awwproject.org/2013/08/the-story-of-rabia-balkhi/.

5. Smith, *The Qit'A*, 159.

Liang Hongyu

1. Barbara Bennett Peterson, *Notable Women of China: Shang Dynasty to the Early Twentieth Century* (Abingdon: Routledge, 2015), 270.

2. Ibid.

3. Ibid.

4. Ibid., 271.

5. Ibid.

6. Ibid.

7. Ibid., 272.

8. Ibid., 272–273.

9. Kang-i Sun Chang and Haun Saussy, eds., *Women Writers of Traditional China: An Anthology of Poetry and Criticism* (Stanford: Stanford University Press, 1999), 391.

Alessandra Giliani

1. Artineh Hayrapetian et al., "Female Anatomists and their Biographical Sketches," *International Journal of History and Philosophy of Medicine* 5 (2015): 1–2. https://www.ijhpm.org/index.php/IJHPM/article/view/96.

2. It was common for anatomists to begin their medical careers as prosectors assisting lecturers and demonstrators. The act of prosecting differs from that of dissecting.

3. Hayrapetian et al., "Female Anatomists and Their Biographical Sketches," 2.

4. K. E. Lander, "Study of Anatomy by Women Before the Nineteenth Century," *Proceedings of the Third International Congress of the History of Medicine* (Antwerp: Imprimerie De Vlijt, 1922), 132–34.

5. Anthony Grafton, *Forgers and Critics: Creativity and Duplicity in Western Scholarship* (Princeton: Princeton University Press, 1990), 138, note 5.

6. Paula Findlen, "Inventing the Middle Ages: An Early Modern Forger Hiding in Plain Sight," in *For the Sake of Learning* (Leiden: Brill, 2016), doi: https://doi.org/10.1163/ 9789004263314_050.

7. Ibid., 895–96.

8. "The Dinner Party: Alessandra Giliani," *Brooklyn Museum*, accessed September 30, 2019, www.brooklynmuseum.org/eascfa/dinner_party/heritage_floor/alessandra_giliani.

9. Hayrapetian et al., "Female Anatomists and Their Biographical Sketches"; Fielding H. Garrison, *An Introduction to History of Medicine*, 4th ed. (Philadelphia: W.B. Saunders Company, 1929).

Tan Yunxian

1. Patricia Ebrey, Anne Walthall, and James Palais, *Pre-Modern East Asia: To 1800: A Cultural, Social, and Political History, Volume I: To 1800*, 2nd ed. (Boston: Houghton Mifflin Company, 2009), 231.

2. Ibid.

3. Peterson, *Notable Women of China*, 272.

4. Olivia Bullock, "Badass Ladies of Chinese History: Tan Yunxian," *The World of Chinese*, September 19, 2014, https://www.theworldofchinese.com/2014/09/badass-ladies-of-chinese-history-tan-yunxian/.

5. Ibid.

6. Tan Yunxian, *Miscellaneous Records of a Female Doctor*, trans. Lorraine Wilcox (Portland: The Chinese Medicine Database, 2015).

7. Ibid., 23.

8. Ibid., 20.

9. Liu Yunting, "Most Chinese Women Reluctant to See Male Gynecologists," *Women of China*, May 17, 2012, http://www.womenofchina.cn/html/node/140990-1.htm.

10. Tamar Lewin, "Women's Health Is No Longer a Man's World," *The New York Times*, February 7, 2001, https://www.nytimes.com/2001/02/07/us/women-s-health-is-no-longer-a-man-s-world.html.

11. Alex Olgin, "Male OB-GYNs Are Rare, but Is That a Problem? April 12, 2018, *NPR*, https://www.npr.org/sections/health-shots/2018/04/12/596396698/male-ob-gyns-are-rare-but-is-that-a-problem.

12. Zheng J., "Tan Yunxian, a Woman Physician of Ming Dynasty, and her Nu yi za yan (Random Talks of a Woman Physician)," *PubMed*, https://www.ncbi.nlm.nih.gov/pubmed/11624101.

13. Bullock, "Badass Ladies of Chinese History: Tan Yunxian."

Gaitana

1. "La Gaitana Monument," *Atlas Obscura*, accessed October 9, 2019, https://www.atlasobscura.com/places/la-gaitana.

2. Ibid.

3. "Biografía de Pedro de Añasco," *El Pesante Educación*, February 16, 2017, https://educacion.elpensante.com/biografia-de-pedro-de-anasco/.

4. "Biografía de Pedro de Añasco," *El Pesante Educación*; Marta Herrera Ángel, "La Gaitana," *Banrepcultural*, accessed October 9, 2019, http://enciclopedia.banrepcultural.org/index.php?title=La_Gaitana.

5. La Gaitana Monument," *Atlas Obscura*.

6. "Biografía de Pedro de Añasco," *El Pesante Educación*; "La Gaitana Monument," *Atlas Obscura*.

7. Rex A. Hudson, ed., *Colombia: A Country Study*, 5th ed. (Washington, DC: Library of Congress Federal Research Division, 2010), 82.

8. "The Indigenous Peoples of Columbia," *International Work Group for Indigenous Affairs (IWGIA)*, accessed October 9, 2019, https://www.iwgia.org/en/colombia.

Doña Grácia Mendes

1. Conversos were also called Crypto-Jews, Marranos, and Secret Jews.

2. H. P. Solomon and Leoni A. Leone, "Mendes, Benveniste, De Luna, Micas, Nasci: The State of the Art (1522–1558)," *The Jewish Quarterly Review* 88, nos. 3–4 (1998): 135–211.

3. Miriam Bodian, "Doña Gracia Nasi," *Jewish Women's Archive Encyclopedia*, accessed October 9, 2019, https://jwa.org/encyclopedia/article/nasi-dona-gracia.

4. Renée Levine Melammed, "His Story/Her Story: Doña Gracia Nasi, 1510–1569," *The Jerusalem Post*, February 18, 2011, https://www.jpost.com/Jewish-World/Judaism/His-StoryHer-Story-Dona-Gracia-Nasi-1510-1569.

5. Ibid.

6. Andrée Aelion Brooks, *The Woman Who Defied Kings: The Life and Times of Doña Gracia Nasi, a Jewish Woman Leader During the Renaissance* (Saint Paul: Paragon House, June 15, 2000), as excerpted in "The Woman Who Defied Kings: The Life and Times of Doña Gracia Nasi," Andrée Aelion Books, www.andreeaelionbrooks.com/_the_woman_who_defied_kings__the_life_and_times_of_do_a_gracia_nasi__35636.htm.

7. Ibid.

Oliva Sabuco

1. "The Dinner Party: Oliva Sabuco," *Brooklyn Museum*, accessed September 30, 2019, https://www.brooklynmuseum.org/eascfa/dinner_party/heritage_floor/oliva_sabuco.

2. Oliva Sabuco de Nantes Barrera, *New Philosophy of Human Nature: Neither*

Known to nor Attained by the Great Ancient Philosophers, Which Will Improve Human Life and Health, trans. and ed. Mary Ellen Waithe, Maria Colomer Vintro, and C. Angel Zorita (Urbana: University of Illinois Press, 2007), 20.

3. Michele L. Clouse, review of *New Philosophy of Human Nature: Neither Known to nor Attained by the Great Ancient Philosophers, Which Will Improve Human Life and Health* by Oliva Sabuco de Nantes Barrera, Isis 99, no. 2 (June 2008): 393–94.

4. Oliva Sabuco de Nantes Barrera, *New Philosophy of Human Nature*, 20.

5. Ibid.

6. "New Philosophy of Human Nature," *University of Illinois Press*, accessed September 30, 2019, https://www.press.uillinois.edu/books/catalog/38gxq6sc9780252031113.html.

7. "Sabuco, Oliva de Nantes Barrera (1562–1625)," *Encyclopedia.com*, updated September 27, 2019, https://www.encyclopedia.com/women/encyclopedias-almanacs-transcripts-and-maps/sabuco-oliva-de-nantes-barrera-1562-1625.

8. Ibid.

Izumo no Okuni

1. Louis Frédéric, "Kabuki," *Japan Encyclopedia*, trans. Käthe Roth (Cambridge: The Belknap Press of Harvard University Press, 2002).

2. The Editors of Encyclopaedia Brittanica, "Kabuki: Japanese Arts," *Encyclopaedia Britannica*, accessed October 9, 2019, https://www.britannica.com/art/Kabuki.

3. Stuart D. B. Picken, *The A to Z of Shinto* (Lanham: The Scarecrow Press. 2006), 140.

4. YABAI Writers, "The Life and Work of Izumo no Okuni," *Yabai*, accessed October 9, 2019, http://yabai.com/p/4170.

5. The Editors of Encyclopaedia Brittanica, "Okuni: Kabuki Dancer," *Encyclopaedia Britannica*, accessed October 9, 2019, https://www.britannica.com/biography/Okuni.

6. The Nō, or Noh, drama style is a traditional Japanese theatre form and one of the oldest surviving drama styles in the world. Unlike Western actors who enact a story, Nō performers use their visual appearances and movements to suggest a story's essence, resulting in a performance that is closer to a visual simile or metaphor than an action-based play. See The Editors of Encyclopaedia Brittanica, "Noh Theatre: Japanese Drama," *Encyclopaedia Britannica*, accessed October 9, 2019, https://www.britannica.com/art/Noh-theatre.

7. The Editors of Encyclopaedia Brittanica, "Okuni: Kabuki Dancer."

8. Andrew T. Tsubaki, "The Performing Arts of Sixteenth Century Japan: A Prelude to Kabuki," in *A Kabuki Reader: History and Performance*, ed. Samuel L. Leiter (New York, London: M.E. Sharpe, 2002), 13–14.

9. The Editors of Encyclopaedia Brittanica, "Okuni: Kabuki Dancer."

10. Ibid.

11. "Kabuki Theatre," *UNESCO*, accessed October 9, 2019, https://ich.unesco.org/en/RL/kabuki-theatre-00163.

Michaelina Wautier

1. "Michaelina: Baroque's Leading Lady," *Museum aan de Stroom*, June 1–September 2, 2018, https://www.mas.be/en/michaelina.

2. Katlijne van der Stighelen, *Michaelina Wautier, 1614–1689: Glorifying a Forgotten Talent* (Leuven: Exhibitions International, 2018), 41.

3. Julie Baumgardner, "Michaelina Wautiers' Paintings Were Attributed to Her Brother for Hundreds of Years," *Observer*, April 6, 2017, https://observer.com/2017/04/michaelina-wautiers-tefaf-2017/.

4. van der Stighelen, *Michaelina Wautier*, 3.

5. "Michaelina: Baroque's Leading Lady," *Museum aan de Stroom*.

6. Ibid.

7. "Michaelina: Baroque's Leading Lady," *Museum aan de Stroom*.

8. Pierre Dambrine, "Michaelina Wautier (1617–1689), une femme peintre tombée dans l'oubli," March 15, 2018, http://www.wukali.com/Michaelina-Wautier-1617-1689-une-femme-peintre-tombee-dans-l-oubli-3219#.XZvMJ0ZKiCg.

9. Talia Lavin, "10 Amazing Female Artists and Their Male Muses," *Huffington Post*, updated December 6, 2017, https://www.huffingtonpost.com/2015/02/13/female-artists-male-muses_n_6669670.html.

10. Lavin, "10 Amazing Female Artists and Their Male Muses."

Barbara Strozzi

1. It is generally acknowledged that Barbara Strozzi was the illegitimate child of Giulio Strozzi.

2. Beth L. Glixon, "New Light on the Life and Career of Barbara Strozzi," *The Musical Quarterly* 81, no. 2 (1997): 311.

3. "The Worth of Women," *The University of Chicago Press Books*, accessed October 9, 2019, https://www.press.uchicago.

edu/ucp/books/book/chicago/W/
bo3683460.html.

4. "Lucrezia Marinella," *Stanford
Encyclopedia of Philosophy,* revised
February 2, 2018, https://plato.
stanford.edu/entries/lucrezia-
marinella/.

5. "What It Was Like to Be a Woman in
Venice at the Time of the Republic,"
Venezia Autentica, accessed October 9,
2019, https://veneziaautentica.com/
woman-during-republic-venice/.

6. "Rosalba Carriera," *National Museum
of Women in the Arts,* accessed October
9, 2019, https://nmwa.org/explore/
artist-profiles/rosalba-carriera.

7. *Venezia Autentica,* "What It Was Like to
Be a Woman in Venice at the Time of
the Republic."

8. Beth L. Glixon, "New Light on the Life
and Career of Barbara Strozzi," *The
Musical Quarterly* 81, issue 2 (July 1,
1997): 312

9. Merry E. Wiesner-Hanks, *Women and
Gender in Modern Europe,* 3rd edition
(Cambridge: Cambridge University
Press, 2008), 186.

10. Rebecca Cypess, "Barbara Strozzi:
Italian Singer and Composer,"
Encyclopaedia Britannica, accessed
October 9, 2019, https://www.
britannica.com/biography/Barbara-
Strozzi.

11. Ibid.

12. Glixon, "New Light on the Life and
Career of Barbara Strozzi," 312.

13. Cypess, "Barbara Strozzi: Italian Singer
and Composer."

14. "Barbara Strozzi," *Music Academy Online,*
accessed October 9, 2019, https://
www.musicacademyonline.com/
composer/biographies.php?bid=134.

15. Cypess, "Barbara Strozzi: Italian Singer
and Composer."

16. Wiesner-Hanks, *Women and Gender in
Modern Europe,* 186.

17. Ibid.

Beatriz Kimpa Vita

1. Alexander Ives Bortolot, "Women
Leaders in African History: Dona
Beatriz, Kongo Prophet," *Metropolitan
Museum of Art,* October 2003, https://
www.metmuseum.org/toah/hd/
pwmn_4/hd_pwmn_4.htm.

2. John K. Thornton, *The Kongolese Saint
Anthony: Dona Beatriz Kimpa Vita and
the Antonian Movement, 1684–1706,*
(Cambridge: Cambridge University
Press, 1998), 17.

3. Bortolot, "Women Leaders in African
History."

4. Ibid.

5. Thornton, *The Kongolese Saint Anthony,*
10.

6. Ibid.

7. Ibid., 10–11.

8. Sheldon, *African Women,* 32–33.

9. Ibid., 33.

10. Bortolot, "Women Leaders in African
History."

11. Sheldon, *African Women,* 33.

Eva Ekeblad

1. Joe Sommerlad, "Eva Ekeblad: Who was
the pioneer scientist we have to thank
for vodka?" *Independent,* July 10, 2017,
https://www.independent.co.uk/news/
science/eva-ekeblad-swedish-scientist-
google-doodle-potatos-vodka-flour-
starch-a7832971.html.

2. Ibid.

3. "Eva Ekeblad: Swedish Agronomist,
and Scientist," *Learning History,* July 10,
2019, https://www.learning-history.
com/eva-ekeblad-swedish-agronomist-
scientist/.

4. Sommerlad, "Eva Ekeblad"; Sonali
Kokra, "6 Cool Facts About Eva

Ekeblad, the Scientist Who Made Vodka
from Potatoes," *Huffington Post,* October
7, 2017, https://www.huffingtonpost.
in/2017/07/10/6-cool-facts-about-
eve-ekeblad-the-scientist-who-made-
vodka-fro_a_23023277/.

5. Sommerlad, "Eva Ekeblad."

6. Kokra, "6 Cool Facts About Eva
Ekeblad."

7. Ibid.

8. Emma Hopkins, "Female Students
in Agriculture," *Agricultures
Magazine,* May 12, 2016, citing U.S.
Department of Agriculture's Food and
Agricultural Education Information
System, https://web.archive.org/
web/20181113195152/https://
ag.purdue.edu/agricultures/Pages/
Spring2016/02-Female-Students.aspx.

9. Robyn Alders, "The Role of Women
in Global Agriculture," *The University
of Sydney,* March 7, 2017, https://
sydney.edu.au/news-opinion/
news/2017/03/07/the-role-of-
women-in-global-agriculture.html.

Elizabeth Freeman

1. "Africans in America: Elizabeth Freeman
(Mum Bett)," PBS, accessed October
17, 2019, https://www.pbs.org/
wgbh/aia/part2/2p39.html; Catherine
Adams and Elizabeth H. Pleck, *Love
of Freedom: Black Women in Colonial and
Revolutionary New England* (Oxford:
Oxford University Press, 2010), 128.

2. "Africans in America: Elizabeth Freeman
(Mum Bett)," *PBS.*

3. Mary Wilds, *Mumbet: The Life and Times
of Elizabeth Freeman: The True Story of a
Slave Who Won Her Freedom* (Greensboro:
Avisson Press, 1999), 13–14, 20.

4. "Africans in America: Elizabeth Freeman
(Mum Bett)," *PBS.*

5. Adams and Pleck, *Love of Freedom,* 139.

6. "Massachusetts Constitution," *The 191st General Court of the Commonwealth of Massachusetts,* accessed October 17, 2019, https://malegislature.gov/laws/constitution.

7. Wilds, *Mumbet: The Life and Times of Elizabeth Freeman,* 64.

8. "Africans in America: Elizabeth Freeman (Mum Bett)," *PBS.*

9. Quock Walker, an American slave, sued for and won his freedom in June 1781 based on a new Massachusetts Constitution (1780), which declared all men to be born "free and equal." Walker was born in central Massachusetts near the town of Barre in 1753 to slaves Mingo and Dinah who were Ghanaian-born. See Samuel Momodu, "Quock Walker (1753–?)," *BlackPast,* October 11, 2016, https://blackpast.org/aah/walker-quock-1753.

10. "Africans in America: Elizabeth Freeman (Mum Bett)," *PBS.*

11. Ibid.

12. Adams and Pleck, *Love of Freedom,* 128.

13. Gale Jackson, "elizabeth freeman's will 1742–1829," *The Kenyon Review* 14, no. 1 (1992): 4.

Olympe de Gouges

1. Joan Woolfrey, "Olympe de Gouges (1748–1793)," *Internet Encyclopedia of Philosophy* (online), https://www.iep.utm.edu/gouges/.

2. Clarissa Palmer, "Welcome to Olympe de Gouges," *Olympe de Gouges,* accessed October 17, 2019, https://www.olympedegouges.eu/.

3. Jone Johnson Lewis, "Biography of Olympe de Gouges, French Women's Rights Activist," *ThoughtCo.,* updated May 15, 2019, https://www.thoughtco.com/olympe-de-gouges-rights-of-woman-3529894.

4. Olympe de Gouges, "Mémoire de Madame de Valmont," trans. Clarissa Palmer, accessed October 17, 2019, https://www.olympedegouges.eu/mme_valmont.php.

5. Woolfrey, "Olympe de Gouges (1748–1793)."

6. Ibid.

7. Ibid.

8. Ibid.

9. Ibid.

10. Ibid.

11. Ibid.

12. Clarissa Palmer, "Welcome to Olympe de Gouges."

13. Ibid.

14. Olympe de Gouges, "Declaration of the Rights of Women, 1791," *College of Staten Island, City University of New York,* accessed October 17, 2019, https://csivc.csi.cuny.edu/americanstudies/files/lavender/decwom2.html.

Wang Zhenyi

1. "Eclipse 101: Eclipse History," *NASA,* accessed September 30, 2019, https://eclipse2017.nasa.gov/eclipse-history.

2. Ibid.

3. Ibid.

4. Ibid.

5. Olivia Bullock, "Badass Ladies of Chinese History: Wang Zhenyi," *The World of Chinese,* October 17, 2014, http://www.theworldofchinese.com/2014/10/badass-ladies-of-chinese-history-wang-zhenyi.

6. Peterson, *Notable Women of China,* 344.

7. Lily Xiao Hong Lee, Clara Lau, and A. D. Stefanowska, *Biographical Dictionary of Chinese Women: The Qing Period, 1644–1911,* vol. 1 (Abingdon: Routledge, 1998), 230–31.

8. Bullock, "Badass Ladies of Chinese History: Wang Zhenyi."

9. Ibid.

10. Peterson, *Notable Women of China,* 344.

11. Ibid., 343.

12. Ibid., 345.

Marie-Sophie Germain

1. Jone Johnson Lewis, "Biography of Sophie Germain: Pioneer Woman in Mathematics," *ThoughtCo.,* updated July 3, 2019, https://www.thoughtco.com/sophie-germain-biography-3530360.

2. Lewis, "Biography of Sophie Germain."

3. Lewis, "Biography of Sophie Germain"; J. William Moncrief, "Sophie Germain," in *Mathematics, Volume 2: Macmillan Science Library,* Barry Max Brandenberger, ed. (New York: Macmillan Reference USA, 2000), 103.

4. Simon Singh, "Math's Hidden Woman," *PBS Nova,* WGBH Educational Foundation, October 27, 1997, https://www.pbs.org/wgbh/nova/article/sophie-germain/.

5. Ibid.

6. Mary W. Gray, "Sophie Germain," in *Complexities: Women in Mathematics,* eds. Bettye Anne Case and Anne M. Leggett (Princeton: Princeton University Press, 2005), 68.

7. Nick Mackinnon, "Sophie Germain, or, Was Gauss a Feminist?" *The Mathematical Gazette* 74, no. 470 (1990): 349.

8. Singh, "Math's Hidden Woman."

9. Barry A. Cipra, "A Woman Who Counted," *Science* 319 no. 5865 (2008): 899.

10. Vesna Crnjanski Petrovich, "Women and the Paris Academy of Sciences," *Eighteenth-Century Studies* 32, no. 3 (1999): 384.

11. Gray, "Sophie Germain," 71.

12. Petrovich, "Women and the Paris Academy of Sciences," 384.

13. Ibid.

14. Lewis, "Biography of Sophie Germain."

Jeanne Villepreux-Power

1. Claude Arnal, "Jeanne Villepreux-Power: A Pioneering Experimental Malacologist," *The Malacological Society of London*, accessed September 30, 2019, http://www.malacsoc.org.uk/malacological_bulletin/BULL34/JEANNE.htm.
2. "Jeanne Villepreux-Power," *Epigenesys: Advancing Epigenetics Towards Systems Biology*, accessed September 30, 2019, https://www.epigenesys.eu/en/science-and-you/women-in-science/682-jeanne-villepreux-power.
3. Ibid.
4. Ibid.
5. Ibid.
6. Ibid.
7. Malacology is the branch of invertebrate zoology that deals with the study of the *Mollusca* (mollusks).
8. Arnal, "Jeanne Villepreux-Power."
9. Ibid.
10. "Gender Mainstreaming in Marine Science," *UNESCO*, accessed September 30, 2019, http://www.unesco.org/new/en/natural-sciences/priority-areas/gender-and-science/cross-cutting-issues/gender-mainstreaming-in-marine-science/.
11. Ibid.

Shanawdithit

1. George M. Story, "Shawnadithit," *The Canadian Encyclopedia*, updated June 20, 2019, https://www.thecanadianencyclopedia.ca/en/article/shawnadithit.
2. Ibid.
3. Merna Forster, "A Canadian Tragedy: Shanawdithit, ca. 1801–1829," *100 Canadian Heroines: Famous and Forgotten Faces* (Toronto: Dundurn Group, 2004), 236.
4. Graham Gibbs, *Five Ages of Canada: A History from Our First Peoples to Confederation* (Victoria: Friesen Press, 2016), 31.
5. Ramona Dearing, "Call for Statue in St. John's to Remember Shanawdithit, Last of her People," *CBC News*, June 19, 2018, https://www.cbc.ca/news/canada/newfoundland-labrador/shanawdithit-beothuk-statue-1.4710707.
6. "Last of Beothuk Honoured in New Monument," *CBC News*, July 13, 2007, https://www.cbc.ca/news/canada/newfoundland-labrador/last-of-beothuk-honoured-in-new-monument-1.635655.
7. "Shanawdithit: The Last of the Beothuk People," *Windspeaker.com*, October 18, 2017, https://windspeaker.com/news/womens-history-month/shanawdithit-the-last-of-the-beothuk-people/
8. Ibid.
9. Forster, "A Canadian Tragedy," 234.
10. Ibid.
11. "Shanawdithit," *Windspeaker.com*.
12. Ibid.
13. Story, "Shawnadithit"; Forster, "A Canadian Tragedy," 235.
14. Forster, "A Canadian Tragedy," 235.
15. "Shanawdithit," *Windspeaker.com*; Forster, "A Canadian Tragedy," 235.
16. Forster, "A Canadian Tragedy," 235.
17. Ibid.
18. "Shanawdithit," *Windspeaker.com*.
19. "Death of Shawnadithit, Last of the Beothuk," *Canadian Museum of History*, June 6, 2017, https://www.historymuseum.ca/blog/death-of-shawnadithit-last-of-the-beothuk.

Maria Mitchell

1. "Maria Mitchell," *National Women's History Museum*, ed., Debra Michaels, 2015, https://www.womenshistory.org/education-resources/biographies/maria-mitchell; Beatrice Gormley, *Maria Mitchell: The Soul of an Astronomer* (Grand Rapids: William B. Eerdmans Publishing Co, 2004), 4–6.
2. "About Maria Mitchell," *Maria Mitchell Association*, accessed October 17, 2019, http://www.mariamitchell.org/about/about-maria-mitchell.
3. Ibid.
4. Renee Bergland, *Maria Mitchell and the Sexing of Science: An Astronomer Among the American Romantics* (Boston: Beacon Press, 2008), as described in "Maria Mitchell and the Sexing of Science," *Beacon Press*, accessed October 17, 2019, http://www.beacon.org/Maria-Mitchell-and-the-Sexing-of-Science-P643.aspx.
5. "About Maria Mitchell," *Maria Mitchell Association*.
6. "Maria Mitchell Discovers a Comet," *APS Physics*, October 2006, https://www.aps.org/publications/apsnews/200610/history.cfm.
7. Elizabeth Howell, "Maria Mitchell: Astronomer & Feminist," *Space.com*, November 12, 2016, https://www.space.com/34709-maria-mitchell-astronomer-feminist.html.
8. "Maria Mitchell, Astronomer," *National Park Service*, updated April 11, 2019, https://www.nps.gov/people/maria-mitchell.htm.
9. Howell, "Maria Mitchell: Astronomer & Feminist."
10. Bergland, *Maria Mitchell and the Sexing of Science*.
11. "Maria Mitchell, Astronomer," *National Park Service*.

12. Ibid.
13. "Maria Mitchell Discovers a Comet," *APS Physics*.
14. "Maria Mitchell," *National Women's History Museum*.
15. "About Maria Mitchell," *Maria Mitchell Association*.
16. Bergland, *Maria Mitchell and the Sexing of Science*.

Eunice Newton Foote

1. Leila McNeill, "This Lady Scientist Defined the Greenhouse Effect But Didn't Get the Credit, Because of Sexism" *Smithsonian.com*, December 5, 2016, https://www.smithsonianmag.com/science-nature/lady-scientist-helped-revolutionize-climate-science-didnt-get-credit–180961291/.
2. Ibid.
3. The symposium was sponsored by UCSB's Orfalea Center for Global and International Studies, the Program in Environmental Studies, the Office of the Dean of the Humanities, and the Environmental Humanities Initiative.
4. "TALK: John Perlin, "Science Knows No Gender? In Search of Eunice Foote, Who, 162 Years Ago Discovered the Principal Cause of Global Warming," *EJ/CJ UCSB*, May 17, 2018, http://ejcj.orfaleacenter.ucsb.edu/2018/05/talk-john-perlin-science-knows-no-gender-in-search-of-eunice-foote-who–162-years-ago-discovered-the-principal-cause-of-global-warming/.
5. McNeill, "This Lady Scientist Defined the Greenhouse."
6. Ibid.

Marianne North

1. Robin Cembalest, "In a Post-Audubon Era, Things Can Take a Nasty Tern," *Art News*, November 19, 2012, http://www.artnews.com/2012/11/19/post-audubon-bird-art/.
2. "About Marianne North (1830–1890)," *Botanical Art & Artists*, accessed October 17, 2019, https://www.botanicalartandartists.com/about-marianne-north.html.
3. Alisa Ross, "The Victorian Gentlewoman Who Documented 900 Plant Species," *Atlas Obscura*, April 22, 2015, https://www.atlasobscura.com/articles/marianne-north-early-female-explorer.
4. Ibid.
5. "About Marianne North (1830–1890)," *Botanical Art & Artists*.
6. Ibid.
7. Ibid.
8. Ibid.
9. Ambra Edwards, "Travels with My Brush," *The Guardian*, December 18, 2009, https://www.theguardian.com/lifeandstyle/2009/dec/19/marianne-north-painter-botanist.
10. Ibid.
11. Robin Powell, "Gardening: Marianne North, the Tale of a Globe Trotteress Who Painted Exotic Plants," *The Sydney Morning Herald*, April 28, 2016, https://www.smh.com.au/entertainment/gardening-marianne-north-the-tale-of-a-globe-trotteress-who-painted-exotic-plants-20160421-goc1zp.html.
12. Zoe Wolstenholme, "Marianne North: Pioneering Botanical Artist," *Artist's Studio Museum Network*, https://www.artiststudiomuseum.org/blog/marianne-north-pioneering-botanical-artist/.
13. Edwards, "Travels with My Brush."
14. Powell, "Gardening: Marianne North."

Savitribai Phule

1. Sanjana Agnihotri, "Who is Savitribai Phule? What Did She do for Women's Rights in India?" *India Today*, New Delhi, updated January 3, 2017, https://www.indiatoday.in/fyi/story/who-is-savitribai-phule-what-did-she-do-for-womens-right-in-india-952499-2016-01-03.
2. "Savitribai Phule," *Google Arts & Culture*, accessed October 17, 2019, https://artsandculture.google.com/exhibit/UwKCW6eHcTWSLg; Bhadru, G. "Contribution of Shatyashodhak Samaj to the Low Caste Protest Movement in 19th Century." *Proceedings of the Indian History Congress* 63 (2002): 845–54.
3. "Savitribai Phule," *Google Arts & Culture*.
4. "Who Was Savitribai Phule? Remembering India's First Woman Teacher," *Financial Express*, January 3, 2018, https://www.financialexpress.com/india-news/who-was-savitribai-phule-remembering-indias-first-woman-teacher/999987/.
5. "Savitribai Phule," *Google Arts & Culture*.
6. Ibid.
7. Mariam Dhawale, "AIDWA Observes Savitribai Phule Birth Anniversary," *People's Democracy*, January 12, 2014, https://peoplesdemocracy.in/content/aidwa-observes-savitribai-phule-birth-anniversary.
8. Annie Zaidi, ed., *Equal Halves: Famous Indian Wives* (New Delhi: Juggernaut Books), excerpted in Ruchika Sharma, "Why We Need to Know the Story of Savitribai Phule, India's First Feminist," *Daily O*, March 13, 2018, www.dailyo.in/arts/savitribai-phule-dalits-maharashtra-jyotiba-phule-education-feminist-untouchability/story/1/22815.html.

9. "Who Was Savitribai Phule?" *Financial Express*.
10. Ibid.
11. Ibid.
12. Agnihotri, "Who is Savitribai Phule?"
13. Ibid.
14. Ibid.
15. Ibid.
16. Zaidi, *Equal Halves: Famous Indian Wives.*

Mary Edwards Walker

1. "State Policies for Women Veterans," *National Conference of State Legislatures*, March 26, 2019, http://www.ncsl.org/research/military-and-veterans-affairs/state-policies-for-women-veterans.aspx.
2. Ibid.
3. "Mary Edwards Walker (1832–1919): Congressional Medal of Honor, Women in Military Service," *AmericanCivilWar.com*, accessed October 17, 2019, https://americancivilwar.com/women/mary_edwards_walker.html.
4. Ibid.
5. Ibid.
6. Debrah A. Wirtzfeld, "The History of Women in Surgery," *Canadian Journal of Surgery* 52, no. 4 (August 2009), 319.
7. Marylou Tousignant, "Trailblazing Surgeon Mary Walker Still One of a Kind," *The Washington Post*, March 8, 2016, https://www.washingtonpost.com/lifestyle/kidspost/2016/03/08/7ad59648-e180-11e5-8d98-4b3d9215ade1_story.html?noredirect=on&utm_term=.b38e4b6bf168.
8. Ibid.
9. "Mary Edwards Walker (1832–1919)," *AmericanCivilWar.com*.
10. Ibid.
11. Tousignant, "Trailblazing Surgeon Mary Walker."

12. Katie Lange, "Meet Dr. Mary Walker: The only female Medal of Honor recipient," *U.S. Army*, March 7, 2017, https://www.army.mil/article/183800/meet_dr_mary_walker_the_only_female_medal_of_honor_recipient; Debrah A. Wirtzfeld, MD, "The History of Women in Surgery."
13. Lange, "Meet Mary Walker."
14. Ibid.
15. Tousignant, "Trailblazing Surgeon Mary Walker"; Lange, "Meet Mary Walker."
16. Cate Lineberry, "I Wear My Own Clothes," *The New York Times*, December 2, 2013, https://opinionator.blogs.nytimes.com/2013/12/02/i-wear-my-own-clothes/.
17. Lange, "Meet Mary Walker."

Margaret E. Knight

1. The Industrial Revolution was the transition from agriculture-based economies to new machine-based manufacturing processes originating in Britain about 1760 and ending in the mid-nineteenth century.
2. Ryan P. Smith, "Meet the Female Inventor Behind Mass-Market Paper Bags," *Smithsonian.com*, March 15, 2018, https://www.smithsonianmag.com/smithsonian-institution/meet-female-inventor-behind-mass-market-paper-bags.
3. Ibid.
4. Ibid.
5. Ibid.
6. Henry Petroski, "The Evolution of the Grocery Bag," *The American Scholar* 72, no. 4 (2003): 101.
7. Smith, "Meet the Female Inventor."
8. Petroski, "The Evolution of the Grocery Bag," 102–103.
9. Smith, "Meet the Female Inventor."

10. Smith, "Meet the Female Inventor"; Katherine Handcock, "Sisters in Innovation: 20 Women Inventors You Should Know," *A Mighty Girl*, September 19, 2018, https://www.amightygirl.com/blog?p=12223; The Editors of Encyclopædia Britannica, "Margaret E. Knight: American Inventor," updated October 8, 2019, *Encyclopædia Britannica*, https://www.britannica.com/biography/Margaret-E-Knight.
11. Petroski, "The Evolution of the Grocery Bag," 103.
12. Ibid., 101.

Bertha von Suttner

1. "Lay Down Your Arms," *Austrian Embassy Washington*, June 24, 2015, https://www.austria.org/austrianinformation/2015/6/24/lay-down-your-arms.
2. Ibid.
3. Laurie Cohen, "Suttner, Bertha von," eds. Ute Daniel, Peter Gatrell, Oliver Janz, Heather Jones, Jennifer Keene, Alan Kramer, and Bill Nasson, *International Encyclopedia of the First World War 1914–1918*, October 8, 2014), https://encyclopedia.1914-1918-online.net/article/suttner_bertha_von.
4. Ibid.
5. Ibid.
6. Ibid.
7. Ibid.
8. Ibid.
9. "Bertha von Suttner," *Women in World History*, accessed October 17, 2019, http://www.womeninworldhistory.com/contemporary-02.html.
10. Cohen, "Suttner, Bertha von."
11. Ibid.
12. Ibid.

13. Ibid.

Augusta Holmès

1. "Augusta Holmès," *The Art Song Project*, July 6, 2011, http://theartsongproject.com/augusta-holmes/.

2. James Bennett II, "Celebrating the Music of Augusta Holmès," WQXR (blog), December 19, 2016, https://www.wqxr.org/story/celebrating-music-augusta-holmes/; Elaine Fine, "Biography of the Day: Augusta Holmès," *Musical Assumptions* (blog), February 24, 2008, https://musicalassumptions.blogspot.com/2008/02/biography-of-day-augusta-holmes.html.

3. John Haag, "Holmès, Augusta (1847–1903)," *Encyclopedia.com*, January 17, 2019, https://www.encyclopedia.com/women/encyclopedias-almanacs-transcripts-and-maps/holmes-augusta-1847-1903.

4. Rollo Myers, "Augusta Holmès: A Meteoric Career." *The Musical Quarterly* 53, no. 3 (1967): 369; Fine, "Biography of the Day."

5. Fine, "Biography of the Day."

6. Fine, "Biography of the Day"; Myers, 369.

7. Fine, "Biography of the Day."

8. Rovi Staff, "César Franck," *AllMusic*, accessed October 17, 2019, https://www.allmusic.com/artist/c%C3%A9sar-franck-mn0000168874/biography.

9. Haag, "Holmès, Augusta (1847–1903)."

10. Ibid.

11. Myers, "Augusta Holmès," 372; James Bennett II, "Celebrating the Music of Augusta Holmes."

12. Fine, "Biography of the Day."

13. Alice Gregory, "A History of Classical Music (The Women-Only Version)," *The New York Times*, December 2, 2016, https://www.nytimes.com/interactive/2016/12/02/arts/music/01womencomposers.html.

14. Karen Henson, "In the House of Disillusion: Augusta Holmès and 'La Montagne Noire,'" *Cambridge Opera Journal* 9, no. 3 (1997): 233.

Sofia Kovalevskaya

1. Sofia Kovalevskaya, *A Russian Childhood*, trans. and ed. Beatrice Stillman (New York: Springer-Verlag, 1978), 35.

2. Mary Ann Rygiel, "Sofya Kovalevskaya's 'A Russian Childhood' As Poetic Autobiography," *Biography* 10, no. 3 (1987): 209.

3. Rygiel, "Sofya Kovalevskaya's 'A Russian Childhood,'" 208.

4. Roger Cooke and Margherita Barile, eds., "Kovalevskaya, Sofia (1850–1891)," *Wolfram Research*, http://scienceworld.wolfram.com/biography/Kovalevskaya.html.

5. "Famous Russian Scientists," *Best of Russia*, https://web.archive.org/web/20110903172506/http://www.tristarmedia.com/bestofrussia/scientists.html.

6. Ibid.

7. Cooke, *The Mathematics of Sonya Kovalevskaya* (New York: Springer-Verlag, 1984), 10.

8. Ibid.

9. Ann Hibner Koblitz, *A Convergence of Lives: Sofia Kovalevskaia—Scientist, Writer, Revolutionary*, (New Brunswick: Rutgers University Press, 1993), 88.

10. Rygiel, "Sofya Kovalevskaya's 'A Russian Childhood,'" 209.

11. Cooke, *The Mathematics of Sonya Kovalevskaya*, 21; Rygiel, "Sofya Kovalevskaya's 'A Russian Childhood,'" 209.

12. "Sofia Kovalevsky," *History of Scientific Women*, accessed October 17, 2019, https://scientificwomen.net/women/kovalevsky-sofia-50.

13. Cooke, and Barile, eds., "Kovalevskaya, Sofia (1850–1891)."

14. Rygiel, "Sofya Kovalevskaya's 'A Russian Childhood,'" 209.

15. Ibid.

Bibi Khanum Astarabadi

1. *The Education of Women and The Vices of Men: Two Qajar Tracts*, trans. Hasan Javadi and Willem Floor (Syracuse: Syracuse University Press, 2010), ix.

2. Ibid., 64–65.

3. Ibid., xiv.

4. Ibid., 64–65.

5. Ibid., 134.

6. Published in the Majles daily newspaper, March 28, 1907.

7. Janet Afary, *The Iranian Constitutional Revolution 1906–1911: Grassroots Democracy, Social Democracy, and the Origins of Feminism* (New York: Columbia University Press, 1996).

8. Shahnaz Zolghadr, "50 Iranian Women you Should Know: Bibi Khanoom Astarabadi," *IranWire*, September 30, 2015, https://iranwire.com/en/features/1374.

Diana Agabeg Apcar

1. Ann Towns and Birgitta Niklasson, "Gender, International Status, and Ambassador Appointments," *Foreign Policy Analysis* 13, no. 3 (July 2017), https://academic.oup.com/fpa/article-abstract/13/3/521/2625550.

2. Sarah Soghomonian, "Lucille Apcar Introduces New Book," *Hye Sharzhoom*, December 1, 2004, https://

hyesharzhoom.com/lucille-apcar-introduces-new-book/.

3. "Historical Summary," *Diana Apcar: The Stateless Diplomat*, accessed September 30, 2019, https://dianaapcar.org/historical-summary.

4. Ibid.

5. Diana Agabeg Apcar, *Peace and No Peace* (Yokohama, Japan: Japan Gazette Press, 1912), https://dianaapcar.org/dianas-writings/quotes/.

6. Ibid.

7. Diana Agabeg Apcar, *From the Book of One Thousand Tales: Stories of Armenia and Its People, 1892–1922* (AuthorHouse, 2004).

8. "Historical Summary," *Diana Apcar: The Stateless Diplomat*.

9. Ibid.

Nettie Maria Stevens

1. Brian Resnick, "Nettie Stevens discovered XY sex chromosomes. She didn't get credit because she had two X's," *Vox*, updated July 7, 2017, https://www.vox.com/2016/7/7/12105830/nettie-stevens-genetics-gender-sex-chromosomes.

2. Marilyn Bailey Ogilvie and Clifford J. Choquette, "Nettie Maria Stevens (1861–1912): Her Life and Contributions to Cytogenetics," *Proceedings of the American Philosophical Society* 125, no. 4 (1981): 294.

3. "Nettie Stevens: A Discoverer of Sex Chromosomes," *Scitable by Nature Education*, accessed November 4, 2019, https://www.nature.com/scitable/topicpage/nettie-stevens-a-discoverer-of-sex-chromosomes-6580266.

4. Ogilvie and Choquette, "Nettie Maria Stevens," 310.

5. "Nettie Stevens," *Scitable by Nature Education*.

6. Ogilvie and Choquette, "Nettie Maria Stevens," 298.

7. "125 Stanford Stories, No. 25: Early Stanford Women," *Stanford 125*, accessed November 4, 2019, https://125.stanford.edu/early-stanford-women/.

8. Ogilvie and Choquette, "Nettie Maria Stevens," 298.

9. The Editors of Encyclopædia Britannica, "Nettie Stevens: American Biologist and Geneticist," *Encyclopædia Britannica*, updated July 3, 2019, https://www.britannica.com/biography/Nettie-Stevens.

10. "Nettie Stevens," *Scitable by Nature Education*.

11. Ogilvie and Choquette, "Nettie Maria Stevens," 292, 298.

12. Ibid., 292.

13. Ibid., 306.

14. Ibid., 302.

15. Ibid., 300.

Clelia Duel Mosher

1. Kara Platoni, "The Sex Scholar," *Stanford Magazine*, March/April 2010, https://stanfordmag.org/contents/the-sex-scholar.

2. Ibid.

3. Ibid.

4. Meredith G. F. Worthen, *Sexual Deviance and Society: A Sociological Examination* (Oxfordshire, UK: Routledge), June 26, 2016, 174.

5. Ibid.

6. Platoni, "The Sex Scholar."

7. Ibid.

8. Ibid.

9. Ibid.

10. Ibid.

11. Worthen, *Sexual Deviance and Society*, 174–175.

12. Gabriella Pastor, Chelsea Mageland, and Sarah Findley, "Clelia Duel Mosher," *History of Human Sexuality in Western Culture* (blog), accessed November 4, 2019, http://historyofsexuality.umwblogs.org/clelia-duel-mosher/.

13. Platoni, "The Sex Scholar."

Zoila Ugarte de Landívar

1. "Zoila Ugarte: Pionera del feminismo ecuatoriano," *El Telégrafo*, November 13, 2013, https://www.eltelegrafo.com.ec/noticias/cultura1/1/zoila-ugarte-pionera-del-feminismo-ecuatoriano.

2. Ibid.

3. Ibid.

4. Ibid.

5. Mary Borowiec, "Women and the Welfare State: Deconstructing Women's Relationship to the State in Ecuador from 1925–1935," (Thesis, Department of History, Georgetown University, 2014): 61.

6. Ibid.

7. "Zoila Ugarte," *El Telégrafo*.

8. Ibid.

9. Ibid.

Alimotu Pelewura

1. Nigeria was a British colony until 1960, when it gained its independence.

2. Cheryl Johnson, "Grass Roots Organizing: Women in Anticolonial Activity in Southwestern Nigeria," *African Studies Review* 25, no. 2/3 (June–September 1982): 138–139.

3. Teslim Opemipo Omipidan, "The Heroic Life of Alimotu Pelewura," *OldNaija.com*, accessed November 4, 2019, https://oldnaija.com/2017/06/30/the-heroic-life-of-alimotu-pelewura/.

4. Gracia Clark, "African Market Women, Market Queens, and Merchant Queens," *Oxford Research Encyclopedias: African History* (July 2018), https://oxfordre.com/africanhistory/view/10.1093/acrefore/9780190277734.001.0001/acrefore-9780190277734-e-268.

5. Johnson, "Grass Roots Organizing," 139–141; Omipidan, "The Heroic Life of Alimotu Pelewura."

6. Johnson, "Grass Roots Organizing," 139.

7. Omipidan, "The Heroic Life of Alimotu Pelewura."

8. Cheryl Johnson, "Grass Roots Organizing," 139.

9. "Alimotu Pelewura," *Litcaf.com*, accessed November 4, 2019, https://litcaf.com/alimotu-pelewura/

10. Johnson, "Grass Roots Organizing," 140.

11. Ibid.

12. Ibid., 142.

13. Ibid., 143.

14. Women's suffrage began in 1950 in southern Nigeria, while women in northern Nigeria received full electoral franchise in 1976. See "The Women Suffrage Timeline," *Women Suffrage and Beyond*, accessed November 4, 2019, http://womensuffrage.org/?page_id=69.

Alice Hamilton

1. Catherine E. Forrest Weber, "Alice Hamilton, M.D.: Crusader Against Death on the Job," *Traces of Indiana and Midwestern History* 7, no. 4 (Fall 1995): 39.

2. "Dr. Alice Hamilton," *Changing the Face of Medicine*, accessed November 4, 2019, https://cfmedicine.nlm.nih.gov/physicians/biography_137.html.

3. "Alice Hamilton and the Development of Occupational Medicine," *American Chemical Society*, accessed November 4, 2019, http://www.acs.org/content/acs/en/education/whatischemistry/landmarks/alicehamilton.html.

4. Weber, "Alice Hamilton, M.D.," 32.

5. Ibid., 33.

6. "Dr. Alice Hamilton," *Changing the Face of Medicine.*

7. Ibid.

8. Kevin Desmond, "Alice Hamilton: A Pioneer for Occupational Health," *Planet Savers: 301 Extraordinary Environmentalists* (Sheffield: Greenleaf Publishing, 2008), 55.

9. Ibid.

10. Ibid., 55–56.

11. Immigration to the United States (online), "Hull-House," http://immigrationtounitedstates.org/559-hull-house.html.

12. "Dr. Alice Hamilton," *Changing the Face of Medicine.*

13. "Alice Hamilton," *American Chemical Society.*

14. "Dr. Alice Hamilton," *Changing the Face of Medicine.*

15. Desmond, "Alice Hamilton," 56; "Alice Hamilton," *American Chemical Society.*

16. "Dr. Alice Hamilton," *Changing the Face of Medicine.*

17. Ibid.

18. Ibid.

19. "Alice Hamilton," *American Chemical Society.*

Marion Mahony Griffin

1. Frank Lloyd Wright was credited with the creation of the first indigenous American architecture, the Prairie Style, which mirrored the flat landscape of the Midwestern United States with buildings that emphasized horizontality and natural materials, usually with broad, flat roofs and wide, overhanging eaves. See "Frank Lloyd Wright: American Architect and Designer," *The Art Story*, July 14, 2017 (https://www.theartstory.org/artist-wright-frank-lloyd.htm.

2. Michael H. Ebner, *Creating Chicago's North Shore: A Suburban History* (Chicago: University of Chicago Press, 1988), 83.

3. Elizabeth Birmingham, "Marion Mahony Griffin," *Pioneering Women in American Architecture*, accessed November 4, 2019, https://pioneeringwomen.bwaf.org/marion-mahony-griffin/.

4. Birmingham, "Marion Mahony Griffin."

5. Ibid.

6. Claire Zulkey, "Meet Marion Mahony Griffin, Frank Lloyd Wright's Best Frenemy," *Curbed*, June 8, 2017, https://www.curbed.com/2017/6/8/15755858/marion-mahony-walter-burley-griffin-wright-drawings.

7. Ibid.

8. Eric Emmett Davis, Karen Indeck, Dwight Heald Perkins, and Gallery 400, *Dwight Heald Perkins: Social Consciousness and Prairie School Architecture: An Exhibition at the University of Illinois at Chicago, April 1989* (Chicago: Gallery 400 of the University of Illinois, Chicago, 1989), 76.

9. Zulkey, "Meet Marion Mahony Griffin."

10. Birmingham, "Marion Mahony Griffin."

11. Fred A. Bernstein, "Rediscovering a Heroine of Chicago Architecture," *The New York Times*, January 1, 2008, https://www.nytimes.com/2008/01/01/arts/design/01maho.html.

12. Birmingham, "Marion Mahony Griffin."

13. Brenna Decker, "Marion Mahony Griffin's Signature Style and Pioneering Influence," *The Institute of Classical Architecture & Art (ICAA)*, March 27, 2018, https://www.classicist.org/articles/marion-mahony-griffin/.

14. Barry Byrne, review of *The Drawings of Frank Lloyd Wright*, by Arthur Drexler, *Journal of the Society of Architectural Historians* 22, no. 2 (May 1963): 109; Birmingham, "Marion Mahony Griffin."

15. Birmingham, "Marion Mahony Griffin."

16. Ibid.

17. Ibid.

18. Ibid.

19. Ibid.

20. Decker, "Marion Mahony Griffin's Signature Style."

21. Bernstein, "Rediscovering a Heroine of Chicago Architecture."

Charlotte Maxeke

1. "A Tribute: Dr. Charlotte Manye Maxeke 7 April 1874–16 October 1939," *South African History Online*, archived December 1, 2017, http://web.archive.org/web/20171201114932/https://www.sahistory.org.za/tribute-dr-charlotte-manye-maxeke-7-april-1874-16-october-1939.

2. "Charlotte (née Manye) Maxeke," *South African History Online*, updated September 3, 2019, https://www.sahistory.org.za/people/charlotte-nee-manye-maxeke.

3. Ibid.

4. Athambile Masola, "Inspirational African Women: Charlotte Mannya Maxeke," *Win Win Solutions 4 Africa*, October 21, 2016, https://www.solutions4africa.com/index.php/news-publisher/730-inspirational-africa-women-charlotte-mannya-maxeke.

5. Zubeida Jaffer, "Heralded Heroine: Why is Charlotte Maxeke's Life Such a Blurry Memory for SA?" *Mail & Guardian*, September 8, 2016, https://mg.co.za/article/2016-09-08-00-heralded-heroine-why-is-charlotte-maxekes-life-such-a-blurry-memory-for-sa.

6. Phumeza Mgxashe and Leila Dougan, "Charlotte Maxeke Written Back into History," *The Journalist*, July 26, 2016, http://www.thejournalist.org.za/spotlight/charlotte-maxeke-written-back-into-history.

7. Ibid.

8. "Bantu Women's League," *South African History Online*, updated August 11, 2017, https://www.sahistory.org.za/topic/bantu-womens-league.

9. Ibid.

10. Jaffer, "Heralded Heroine."

11. Thozama April. "Charlotte Maxeke and the Struggle for Liberation in South Africa," *South African History Online*, 17. http://www.sahistory.org.za/sites/default/files/Thozama_April_paper.pdf.

12. "Charlotte (née Manye) Maxeke," *South African History Online*.

13. Masola, "Inspirational African Women."

Zitkala-Ša

1. The Editors of Encyclopædia Britannica, "Zitkala-Sa: American Writer," *Encyclopædia Britannica*, updated February 18, 2019, https://www.britannica.com/biography/Zitkala-Sa.

2. Susan Bernardin, "The Lessons of a Sentimental Education: Zitkala-Ša's Autobiographical Narratives," *Western American Literature* 32, no. 3 (1997): 223.

3. "Zitkala-Sa," *Encyclopædia Britannica*.

4. Ibid.

5. P. Jane Hafen, "A Cultural Duet Zitkala Ša and *The Sun Dance Opera*," *Great Plains Quarterly* 18, no. 2 (Spring 1998): 104.

6. Zitkala-Sa, "Why I Am a Pagan," *Atlantic Monthly* 90 (1902): 801–803.

7. "Heyoka" is a Native American term meaning "sacred clown" or "fool."

8. Hafen, "A Cultural Duet," 103.

9. Ibid., 105.

10. Ibid.

11. "Zitkala-Sa," *Encyclopædia Britannica*.

12. Zitkala-Sa, "Why I Am a Pagan."

Lise Meitner

1. Ruth Lewin Sime, *Lise Meitner: A Life in Physics* (Berkeley: University of California Press, 1996), 4.

2. Ibid., 5.

3. Ibid., 8.

4. Founded in 1553, the Akademisches Gymnasium is the oldest secondary school in Vienna. During Lise Meitner's time, education focused on languages, history, mathematics, and the natural sciences.

5. Otto Robert Frisch, "Lise Meitner, 1878–1968," *Biographical Memoirs of Fellows of the Royal Society* 16 (November 30, 1970): 405–426.

6. Sime, *Lise Meitner: A Life in Physics*, 18.

7. Ibid., 19–22.

8. Ibid., 22–24.

9. Ibid., 24–25.

10. Ibid., 26.

11. Ibid., 28.

12. Mike Sutton, "Hahn, Meitner, and the Discovery of Nuclear Fission," *Chemistry World*, November 5, 2018, https://www.chemistryworld.com/features/hahn-meitner-and-the-discovery-of-nuclear-fission/3009604.article.

13. "Lise Meitner: A Battle for Ultimate Truth," *San Diego Supercomputer Center UCSD*, accessed September 30, 2019, https://www.sdsc.edu/ScienceWomen/meitner.html.

14. Stanley Goldberg, "With Friends Like These…," review of *Lise Meitner: A Life in Physics*, in the *Bulletin of the Atomic Scientists* (July/August 1996): 56.

15. Nuclear fission is a nuclear reaction in which a heavy nucleus splits spontaneously or on impact with another particle, with the release of energy.

16. Goldberg, "With Friends Like These…," 56.

17. "Women in STEM: Lise Meitner," *SmarterU*, accessed September 30, 2019, https://www.smarteru.com/women-in-stem/lise-meitner.

18. Ibid.

19. Ibid.

20. Ibid.

21. Sime, *Lise Meitner: A Life in Physics*, 375.

Lillian Gilbreth

1. "Industrial and Organizational Psychology," *American Psychological Association*, accessed November 4, 2019, https://www.apa.org/ed/graduate/specialize/industrial.

2. Lisa Held, "Profile of Lillian Gilbreth," in A. Rutherford, ed., *Psychology's Feminist Voices Multimedia Internet Archive*, 2010, retrieved from http://www.feministvoices.com/lillian-gilbreth/.

3. "'A Genius in the Art of Living': Industrial Psychology Pioneer Lillian Gilbreth," *Association for Psychological Science*, September 22, 2017, https://www.psychologicalscience.org/publications/observer/obsonline/a-genius-in-the-art-of-living-lillian-moller-gilbreth-industrial-psychology-pioneer.html.

4. Held, "Profile of Lillian Gilbreth."

5. Ibid.

6. Ibid.

7. Ibid.

8. Ibid.

9. Ibid.

10. Ibid.

11. "'A Genius in the Art of Living,'" *Association for Psychological Science*.

12. Held, "Profile of Lillian Gilbreth."

13. "'A Genius in the Art of Living,'" *Association for Psychological Science*.

14. "'A Genius in the Art of Living,'" *Association for Psychological Science*.

15. Held, "Profile of Lillian Gilbreth."

16. Ibid.

17. "'A Genius in the Art of Living,'" *Association for Psychological Science*.

18. Held, "Profile of Lillian Gilbreth."

19. Ibid.

20. "'A Genius in the Art of Living,'" *Association for Psychological Science*.

Lois Weber

1. "Facts to Know About Women in Hollywood, 2018," *Women and Hollywood*, accessed November 4, 2019, https://womenandhollywood.com/resources/statistics/.

2. Howie Movshovitz, "Lois Weber, Hollywood's Forgotten Early Pioneer, Has 2 Films Restored," *NPR*, January 5, 2019, https://www.npr.org/2019/01/05/682372051/lois-weber-hollywoods-forgotten-early-pioneer-has-2-films-restored.

3. First presented in 1902 in France by Léon Gaumont, the phonoscène was an early version of a music video and is considered a forerunner of sound film.

4. Shelley Stamp, *Lois Weber in Early Hollywood* (Oakland: University of California Press, 2015), 14–15; Alison McMahan, *Alice Guy Blaché: Lost Visionary of the Cinema* (London: Bloomsbury Publishing, 2002), xxvi.

5. Shelley Stamp, "Lois Weber," in Jane Gaines, Radha Vatsal, and Monica Dall'Asta, eds. *Women Film Pioneers Project*, New York, NY: Columbia University Libraries, 2013, https://wfpp.columbia.edu/pioneer/ccp-lois-weber/.

6. Ibid.

7. Ibid.

8. Ibid.

9. "Shoes (by Lois Weber)," *Milestone Films*, accessed November 4, 2019, https://www.milestonefilms.com/collections/blu-ray/products/shoes-by-lois-weber?variant=5845379088411.

10. "Bluebird Photo Plays," *The Saturday Evening Post* 188 (June 24, 1916): 28; Rob Byrne, "Shoes," *San Francisco Silent Film Festival*, accessed November 4, 2019, http://silentfilm.org/archive/shoes.

11. Byrne, "Shoes."

12. Byrne, "Shoes"; Stamp, "Lois Weber."

13. Stamp, "Lois Weber."

14. Ibid.

15. Ibid.

Huda Sha'arawi

1. "Harem: Orgin," *Lexico*, accessed November 4, 2019, https://en.oxforddictionaries.com/definition/harem.

2. Hana Khaled, "Revolutionary Egyptian Feminist, Huda Shaarawy," *Sada Elbalad English*, July 19, 2018, http://see.news/revolutionary-egyptian-feminist-huda-shaarawy/; Melissa Spatz, "Shaarawi, Huda," *Postcolonial Studies at Emory*, updated May 2017, https://scholarblogs.emory.edu/

postcolonialstudies/2014/06/12/
shaarawi-huda/.

3. Huda Sha'arawi, *Harem Years: The Memoirs of an Egyptian Feminist (1879–1924)* (New York: The Feminist Press, 1987), 41.

4. Ibid., 42.

5. Jennifer Jaffer, "Huda Sharawi: Egyptian Feminist and Nationalist," *Encyclopædia Britannica*, accessed November 4, 2019, https://www.britannica.com/biography/Huda-Sharawi.

6. Keri Engel, "Huda Shaarawi, Egyptian Feminist & Activist," *Amazing Women in History*, November 12, 2012, https://amazingwomeninhistory.com/huda-shaarawi-egyptian-feminist/.

7. Jaffer, "Huda Sharawi."

8. Ibid.

9. Ibid.

10. "Badass Ladies of History: Huda Shaarawi," *Persephone Magazine*, accessed November 4, 2019, http://persephonemagazine.com/2011/07/badass-ladies-of-history-huda-shaarawi/.

11. Maureen Moynagh and Nancy Forestell, eds., *Documenting First Wave Feminisms: Volume 1: Transnational Collaborations and Crosscurrents*, (Toronto: University of Toronto Press, 2012), 268–269.

María Blanchard

1. Sabine Rewald, "Cubism," in *Heilbrunn Timeline of Art History* (New York: The Metropolitan Museum of Art, October 2004), https://www.metmuseum.org/toah/hd/cube/hd_cube.htm.

2. Ibid.

3. María Jose Salazar, "María Blanchard, The Great Unknown," *Museo Nacional Centro de Arte Reina Sofia*, accessed November 4, 2019, https://virtual.
fundacionbotin.org/visita_blanchard/page.php?lang=en.

4. "Cubism: María Blanchard," *Spanish Arts*, accessed November 4, 2019, https://www.spanish-art.org/spanish-painting-blanchard.html.

5. "Maria Banchard (1881–1932)," *Art Experts*, accessed November 4, 2019, https://www.artexpertswebsite.com/pages/artists/blanchard.php.

6. Ibid.

7. "Cubism: María Blanchard," *Spanish Arts*.

8. "Cubism: María Blanchard," *Spanish Arts*.

9. "María Blanchard," *Museo Nacional Centro de Arte Reina Sofia*, accessed November 4, 2019, https://www.museoreinasofia.es/en/exhibitions/maria-blanchard.

10. Salazar, "María Blanchard."

11. Ibid.

12. Ibid.

13. Ibid.

Bessie Coleman

1. Amelia Earhart earned her pilot's license from the Fédération Aéronautique Internationale on May 15, 1923, two years after Bessie Coleman became the first American woman to do so. See "Amelia Earhart Biography," *Biography*, updated September 6, 2019, https://www.biography.com/explorer/amelia-earhart.

2. "Coleman, Bessie," *The National Aviation Hall of Fame*, accessed November 4, 2019, https://www.nationalaviation.org/our-enshrinees/coleman-bessie/.

3. Doris L. Rich, *Queen Bess: Daredevil Aviator* (Washington: Smithsonian Institution Press, 1993), 12.

4. "Coleman, Bessie," *The National Aviation Hall of Fame*.

5. "Fly Girls: Bessie Coleman," *American Experience (PBS)*, accessed November
4, 2019, https://www.pbs.org/wgbh/americanexperience/features/flygirls-bessie-coleman/.

6. Ibid.

7. Maria Lynn Toth, "Daredevil of the Sky: The Bessie Coleman Story," *The Los Angeles Times*, February 10, 2001.

8. "Fly Girls: Bessie Coleman," *American Experience (PBS)*; The Editors of Encyclopædia Britannica, "Bessie Coleman: American Aviator," *Encyclopædia Britannica*, updated April 26, 2019, https://www.britannica.com/biography/Bessie-Coleman/.

9. "Bessie Coleman," *Encyclopaedia Britannica*; Historically, *The Chicago Defender* is considered the "most important" paper of what was then known as the colored or Negro press. Abbott's newspaper reported and campaigned against Jim Crow era violence and urged blacks in the American South to come north in what became the Great Migration. Under his nephew and chosen successor, John H. Sengstacke, the paper took on segregation, especially in the U.S. military, during World War II. See Brent Staples, "'The Defender,' by Ethan Michaeli," *The New York Times*, January 9, 2016, https://www.nytimes.com/2016/01/10/books/review/the-defender-by-ethan-michaeli.html.

10. "Fly Girls: Bessie Coleman," *American Experience (PBS)*.

11. Ibid.

12. Ibid.

13. Rich, *Queen Bess*, 38.

14. Maria Lynn Toth, "Daredevil of the Sky: The Bessie Coleman Story," *The Los Angeles Times*, February 10, 2001.

15. "Fly Girls: Bessie Coleman," *American Experience (PBS)*.

16. D. Cochrane and P. Ramirez, "Women in Aviation and Space History: Bessie Coleman," *Smithsonian National Air and Space Museum*, accessed November 4, 2019, https://airandspace.si.edu/explore-and-learn/topics/women-in-aviation/coleman.cfm.

17. Roman Mikhail, "Bessie Coleman, the First Female African American Pilot, *Medium*, December 9, 2017, https://medium.com/a-moment-in-history/bessie-coleman-the-first-female-african-american-pilot-in-the-world-f45e57c1ebcd.

18. Cochrane and Ramirez, "Bessie Coleman."

19. "Coleman, Bessie," *The National Aviation Hall of Fame.*

20. Ibid.

21. Cochrane and Ramirez, "Bessie Coleman."

Alice Ball

1. "History of Leprosy," *Stanford University*, accessed September 30, 2019, https://web.stanford.edu/class/humbio103/ParaSites2005/Leprosy/history.htm.

2. Ibid.

3. Carisa D. Brewster, "How the Woman Who Found a Leprosy Treatment Was Almost Lost to History," *National Geographic*, February 28, 2018, https://news.nationalgeographic.com/2018/02/alice-ball-leprosy-hansens-disease-hawaii-womens-history-science/.

4. Employing a complex chemical process, daguerreotype was the first successful form of photography. The process of making a daguerreotype starts with a silver-plated copper plate. That plate is first buffed and polished until it looks like a mirror. Then the plate is sensitized to light over iodine and bromine in specialized, light-proof boxes.

5. Miles Jackson, *Alice Augusta Ball (1892–1916)*, *BlackPast*, September 20, 2007, https://www.blackpast.org/aaw/vignette_aahw/ball-alice-augusta–1892–1916.

6. Brewster, "How the Woman Who Found a Leprosy Treatment Was Almost Lost to History."

7. Ibid.

8. Ibid.

9. Paul Wermager and Carl Heltzel, "Alice A. Augusta Ball: Young Chemist Gave Hope to Millions," *ChemMatters* 25, no. 1 (February 2007): 16–19.

10. Erika Cederlind, "A Tribute to Alice Bell: A Scientist Whose Work with Leprosy Was Overshadowed by a White Successor," *The Daily of the University of Washington*, February 29, 2008, http://www.dailyuw.com/features/article_b749ad5a-9e0b-575e-9e61-59ea5f8cc07f.html.

11. Brewster, "How the Woman Who Found a Leprosy Treatment Was Almost Lost to History."

12. E. A. Johansen, "Current Data on Promin Therapy," *The Star* 62, no. 4 (October-December 2003): 8–10.

13. Beverly Mendheim, "Lost and Found: Alice Augusta Ball, an Extraordinary Woman of Hawai'i Nei," *Northwest Hawaii Times*, September 2007, http://www.northwesthawaiitimes.com/hnsept07.htm.

14. Jeannette Brown, *African American Women Chemists* (New York: Oxford University Press, 2012), 19–24.

BEYOND ANONYMITY

1. Elena Marcu, "A Letter to Virginia Woolf, On Translating *A Room of One's Own* into Romanian," *Literary Hub*, March 6, 2019, https://lithub.com/a-letter-to-virginia-woolfon-translating-a-room-of-ones-own-into-romanian/.

2. Woolf, *A Room of One's Own*, 49.

3. "Anonymous is a Woman Theatre Company," *Anonymous Is a Woman Theatre Company*, accessed September 27, 2019, https://www.aiawtc.com.

4. Alex Greenberger, "Long-Running 'Anonymous Was a Woman' Grants Awarded for 2018, With Betty Tompkins and Deborah Roberts Among 10 Winners," *ArtNews*, December 11, 2018, http://www.artnews.com/2018/12/11/anonymous-woman-names-winners–2018-grants/.

5. Fred Shapiro, "Anonymous Was a Woman," *Yale Alumni Magazine* LXXIV, no. 3 (January/February 2011): 2, https://yalealumnimagazine.com/articles/3064-anonymous-was-a-woman?page=2.

6. Ibid.

Index

Book titles are in italics. Articles are in quotes.

⸺ ABOUT THE ARTISTS ⸺

THE BOOK COVER ARTIST: LEYLI RASHIDI RAUF

The book cover painting is by Iranian artist Leyli Rashidi Rauf.

Born in Tehran in 1986, Rashidi Rauf received her BFA in painting from Shahed University's College of Art in 2010. A member of the Association of Iranian Painters (AIP), she is the recipient of many awards, including the Moscow Art Fair International Painting Symposium and the London Young Artists Competition. Rashidi Rauf has participated in many group exhibits in Tehran as well as solo shows in Shiraz.

Her subjects are usually women, often self-portraits or people in her life. She is interested in highlighting issues of identity and gender, and oppressed desires in a traditional society.

Leyli Rashidi Rauf is married to the artist Morteza Pourhossieni.

INTERIOR ILLUSTRATION ARTIST: PETRA DUFKOVA

Petra Dufkova is a freelance illustrator and designer. Born in Czech Republic, Petra is a graduate of the international fashion school ESMOD in Munich, Germany. Her illustration style is a combination of traditional methods and modern looks with a focus on fashion, beauty and lifestyle.

Petra was featured as one of twenty-eight masters of fashion illustration from across the word by Tony Glenville in his book *New Icons of Fashion Illustration* (Laurence King Publishing, 2013). She has completed projects for a range of iconic publications such as *ELLE*, *Vanity Fair Italy*, *Vogue Japan*, and brands such as Cartier, Harry Winston NY, Hermès, and Swarovski.

About the Author

DR. NINA ANSARY is an internationally recognized Iranian-American scholar, award-winning author, and women's rights advocate. As a UN Women Global Champion for Innovation and a Visiting Fellow at The London School of Economics Centre for Women, Peace & Security, she regularly presents her work on women's rights and the impact of institutionalized gender discrimination at major universities and conferences in the US and UK, including Columbia, Oxford, Cambridge, and Harvard, as well as the Carnegie Endowment for International Peace in Washington D.C., the US Senate Human Rights Caucus, and the World Affairs Councils of America.

Dr. Ansary's previous book, *Jewels of Allah: The Untold Story of Women in Iran*, garnered multiple awards—including the 2016 International Book Award in "Women's Issues."

She is the recipient of the 2019 Ellis Island Medal of Honor, the 2019 Iranian American Women Foundation (IAWF) Women of Influence Award, and the 2018 Trailblazer Award from Barnard College, Columbia University. Ansary has also been recognized as one of "14 Privileged Women to Change the World" by *Marie Claire*, featured in *Angeleno* Magazine's "Living Legacies of 2016" and selected as one of "Five Iranian Visionaries You Need to Know" and "6 Women Who Build Bridges Not Walls" by *The New York Times*. Dr. Ansary has appeared on Fox News, Larry King, and the BBC, as well as a variety of top publications, including CNN.com, *Newsweek*, the *Los Angeles Times*, The *UK*

Daily Telegraph, Glamour, Elle, Teen Vogue, and the *Yale Journal of International Affairs.*

Dr. Ansary holds an MA in Middle Eastern Studies and a PhD in History from Columbia University. She serves on the Board of Directors of the New York-based organization The Center for Human Rights in Iran (CHRI), the Board of Trustees at Barnard College, Columbia University, the International Advisory Board at University of Cambridge Middle East and North Africa Forum (MENAF), the Iranian American Women Foundation (IAWF), and Persia Educational Foundation.

Connect with Nina on
Twitter (@drninaansary) | Instagram (@ninaansary) | Facebook (facebook.com/ninaansary)